Essays on Russian and East European Music

Essays on
Russian and East European
Music

GERALD ABRAHAM

CLARENDON PRESS · OXFORD
1985

Oxford University Press, Walton Street, Oxford OX2 6DP

London New York Toronto
Delhi Bombay Calcutta Madras Karachi
Kuala Lumpur Singapore Hong Kong Tokyo
Nairobi Dar es Salaam Cape Town
Melbourne Auckland
and associated companies in
Beirut Berlin Ibadan Mexico City Nicosia

Oxford is a trade mark of Oxford University Press

Published in the United States
by Oxford University Press, New York

British Library Cataloguing in Publication Data
Abraham, Gerald
Essays on Russian and East European Music
1. Music, Russian
I. Title
781.7'47   ML300
ISBN 0-19-311208-6

Library of Congress Cataloging in Publication Data
Abraham, Gerald, 1904–
Essays on Russian and East European Music.
Contents: Foreword / by Denis Arnold — Russian song
— Czechoslovakian song — Polish song — [etc.]
1. Abraham, Gerald, 1904–   — Addresses, essays,
lectures.   2. Music — Addresses, essays, lectures.
3. Music — Soviet Union — Addresses, essays, lectures.
I. Title.
ML60.A2 1983   780'.947   83-24995
ISBN 0-19-311208-6

Set by Hope Services, Abingdon
Printed in Great Britain by
Billing & Sons Limited, Worcester

Acknowledgements

The publishers would like to thank the following for permission to reprint the essays in this volume:

Arno-Volk Verlag, for 'Heine, Queuille, and "William Ratcliff"', from *Musicae Scientiae Collectanea: Festschrift Karl Gustav Fellerer* (1973).

Allen & Unwin (Publishers) Ltd., and Da Capo Press, for 'Some Eighteenth-Century Polish Symphonies', from *Studies in Eighteenth-Century Music: A Tribute to Karl Geiringer* (1970).

Basil Blackwell Publisher, for 'The Early Development of Opera in Poland', from *Essays on Opera and English Music in Honour of Sir Jack Westrup* (1975).

Hutchinson Publishing Group Ltd., for 'Russia', 'Czechoslovakia' and 'Poland' from *A History of Song* (edited by Denis Stevens, 1960), and for 'V. V. Stasov: Man and Critic' from *Vladimir Vasilevich Stasov: Selected Essays on Music* (Cresset Press, 1968).

Oxford University Press, for 'Satire and Symbolism in *The Golden Cockerel*', and 'Arab Melodies in Rimsky-Korsakov and Borodin' from *Music and Letters*, lii (1971) and lvi (1975); and for 'The Operas of Serov' from *Essays Presented to Egon Wellesz* (edited Westrup, 1966).

G. Schirmer Inc., For '*Pskovityanka*: the Original Version of Rimsky-Korsakov's First Opera', from *Musical Quarterly*, liv (1968). Copyright © 1968 by G. Schirmer Inc.

Foreword

Gerald Abraham became a great musicologist in a typically English way: he was, at least from the point of view of his future profession, self-taught. He did not study at one of our ancient universities – though, considering their attitudes to musical education in the 1920s, it is doubtful whether he would have found it very profitable – nor did he spend a period in Germany sitting at the feet of a renowned scholar such as Riemann or Adler. Instead, he read books and developed a technique of writing by studying the masters of the past.

It was probably no coincidence that among his earlier works were books on Nietzsche, Tolstoy, and Dostoevsky; for literary studies (in whatever language) have always been more highly developed than musicology in this country. The essays in the present volume show the advantage of this approach on every page. Music, for Gerald Abraham, has never been merely an artefact to be measured and described. Rather it must be considered in its cultural context – an attitude rapidly disappearing nowadays, alas, under the inexorable advance of specialization. It is remarkable that he can enliven our view of the Russian scene without his actually having lived there for a prolonged period. Neither is he afraid of stating preferences and judgements. He has thereby avoided much of the dross which musicologists today feel impelled to discuss.

This is perhaps unexpected, since he has been untypical (for an English scholar) in not being a critic on a newspaper (his brief essay in this profession came too late to make any difference to his musicological approach). So he has been able to take the long perspectives, has made the judgements from the distance of history. It was altogether appropriate that, although no doctor or even *magister*, he was made a professor, albeit for only half each year and, as it turned out, for a shorter period than many of us hoped. And he further frustrated our hopes by spending the years correcting other men's mistakes in the *New Oxford History of Music* rather than giving us his own writings. Where, some of us asked, was the necessary, sensible study of Wagner the musician (as distinct from all the other books on Wagner, theatre, influence and the rest) that we learned of in conversation with him?

The end result turned out to be *The Concise Oxford History of Music*, not at all an English-style account, rather the successor of Ambros, Riemann, and Adler. The cries (or rather murmurs) of 'Foul! Impossible! Too much for one man!' came largely from those who have never thought about their debt to these German scholars, the writers of synthesis as opposed to analysis. Without them we should still be waiting to know where to begin the mammoth task. No doubt any one-volume, one-man history is restricted in completeness and perhaps even in accuracy (though the COHM is remarkable both in the amount of its material and the fewness of mistakes). But the point must be the wisdom of the approach and the sense of historical flow: and that book shows both in goodly measure. Indeed, probably because his studies began with Russia rather than Central Europe, there is a breath of the wider world which other histories cannot match.

The essays in this present volume are all mature works and deserve their rescue from their relatively transient first estate. That they are mainly concerned with throwing light on dusty corners of music history does not mean that they are only for the specialist or expert: they are as interesting for anyone interested in the recorded culture of our world. Writing this introduction a few days after Gerald Abraham's eightieth birthday of necessity makes me reflect that he has no successor in breadth of knowledge or attitude. But he, least pompous of learned men, would be the first to urge the rest of us to carry on. *Avanti, ragazzi!*

Farrò di Follina   Denis Arnold
March, 1984

Contents

1. Russian Song   1
2. The Operas of Serov   40
3. Heine, Cui, and 'William Ratcliff'   56
4. *Pskovityanka*: The Original Version of Rimsky–Korsakov's First Opera   68
5. Satire and Symbolism in *The Golden Cockerel*   83
6. Arab Melodies in Rimsky-Korsakov and Borodin   93
7. Vladimir Stasov: Man and Critic   99
8. Some Eighteenth-Century Polish Symphonies   113
9. The Early Development of Opera in Poland   122
10. Polish Song   141
11. The Operas of Stanisław Moniuszko   156
12. Czechoslovakian Song   172

Index   185

1. *Russian Song*

When César Cui published 'an outline of the development of the Russian art-song'[1] in 1896, he began with Glinka. Nine years later, Findeisen declared that 'the Russian art-song came into being at the same time as the first attempts in the field of Russian opera – in the epoch of Catherine the Great'.[2] But in 1916 Bulich revealed the existence of a 'great-grandfather' of Russian song,[3] to wit the courtier and writer Grigory Nikolaevich Teplov (1711–79), tutor of Kirill Razumovsky (the father of Beethoven's Razumovsky), and so far Teplov's claim has not been disputed. Not that he made any claim himself. When he published his volume *Mezhdu delom bezdel'e ili Sobranie pesen s prilozhennïmi tonami na tri golosa* (Idleness amid work, or A collection of songs with music added in three parts),[4] he modestly appended only the initials 'G. T.' *Mezhdu delom bezdel'e* consists of seventeen songs, settings of feeble lyrics by Sumarokov and others, laid out on three staves with no indication of the manner of performance; but the lowest part is an obviously instrumental bass and the two upper parts, proceeding mostly in parallel thirds or sixths, with the words printed between, were doubtless to be played too, with voice or voices doubling one or both. One song has only one upper part; No. 13 is undoubtedly a duet. The three-part layout follows the Russian tradition of the *kantï* (three-part vocal pieces) popular during the first half of the eighteenth century, but there is nothing else particularly Russian about them. They have reminded more than one critic of the weaker songs in Sperontes' *Singende Muse* by their artlessness, their simple sentiment, and the occasional suggestion of instrumental melodic origin. Four are marked 'Menuet', two 'Siciliana'; all but one of the others bear a slow tempo-marking, but the opening of the one exception, No. 10, is worth quoting since it is perhaps the most attractive of all. It may be of interest to give it in the original orthography.

Ex. 1

'Why am I captivated by you so that, ardently loving,
I lament hourly?'

The second part of each stanza is an *andantino* in 3/4 time.

Individual songs from Teplov's volume crop up in various Russian song-collections all through the rest of the century. They were evidently popular; indeed they are primitive examples of a type of song that persisted right up to Glinka's day: the sentimental products of cultured dilettanti whose limited musical technique restricted them to the simplest types of texture and structure. But the development of Russian song soon came under two influences less widely separated than one might suppose: folk-song and opera. Folk-song arrangements had figured among the earlier *kantï* but it was the introduction of 'Russian songs' in the operas of Catherine II's reign – in the Russian operas of the visiting foreigners, Paisiello, Cimarosa, Sarti, and the rest, to say nothing of the native operas – that made the native idiom really fashionable. These 'Russian songs', both genuine folk-songs forced into Western European dress and imitations of folk-song, some even Western compositions with Russian words, were arranged for domestic performance and are preserved in almanacks and journals, in various manuscript collections, and in such printed ones as the *Sobranie nailuchskikh rossiyskikh pesen* (Collection of the best Russian songs) issued by the bookseller Meyer at Petersburg in 1781, in five parts each containing six songs, all anonymous. Such songs were always printed on two staves, sometimes tune and figured or unfigured bass only, sometimes with

meagre harmonic filling-in. In 1776, 1778, and 1779, V. F. Trutovsky
had brought out the first three parts of his *Sobranie prostïkh russkikh
pesen s notami* (Collection of simple Russian songs with music)[5] in
which he attempted to set down genuine folk-tunes accurately, and
provided them with basses; when he published his fourth part in 1795
and the third edition of Part I the following year, he went further
and printed full harmonies in small type. But by that time he had to
compete with the much more famous *Sobranie narodnïkh russkikh
pesen* (Collection of Russian folk-songs—here for the first time actually
called *narodnïe*: folk, popular, national) published by Ivan Prach in
1790. Prach—he was really a Czech, Johann Gottfried Pratsch or Prač
—printed the voice-part on a separate stave and composed genuine
keyboard accompaniments, sometimes surprisingly sympathetic, usually
conventionally Western in harmony and figuration; these are Russian
parallels to Haydn's almost exactly contemporary harmonizations of
Scottish songs. But Prach included, beside his genuine *narodnïe* songs,
others—such as the once very popular setting of Sumarokov's 'Chem
tebya ya ogorchila?' (How have I grieved you?) printed in the second
edition (1806)—which are evidently attempts by dilettanti to affect a
national accent.

Most of these *romances* and pseudo-folk-songs are anonymous, often
signed with initials, but in the case of the six anonymous 'Russian songs'
in the *Karmannaya kniga dlya lyubiteley muzïki na 1795 god* (Pocket
book for music-lovers, for 1795), published by the Petersburg bookseller
Gerstenberg, the composer has been identified as Fedor Mikhaylovich
Dubyansky (1760-96), a Petersburg banker and amateur violinist
who usually took refuge behind the pseudonyms 'Brigadier D.' and
'F. M. D∗∗∗.' The opening of his best-known song 'Golubok' (The
Little Dove) may be quoted:[6]

Ex. 2

'The grey dove moans, moans day and night.'

both because the vein is characteristic and because the three-part layout
belatedly continues the *kantï* tradition. But Dubyansky usually wrote

an independent right-hand part for the accompanist. The poem, by his friend I. I. Dmitriev, one of the 'sentimental' poets, was a great favourite for many years and was set by several composers;[7] Dubyansky repeats each of its seven stanzas to the same ten bars of music.

Gerstenberg's *Karmannaya kniga* for 1796 contains four songs by Józef Kozłowski (1757–1831), a Pole in the Russian service who is credited with the introduction of the polonaise into Russia. (His polonaises include not only piano and orchestral but also vocal polonaises, sometimes based on Italian opera arias.) French songs and French titles were becoming more fashionable in the 1790s and we find Kozłowski publishing *Six romances de Florian avec l'accompagnement de forte-piano*. He set French, Italian, and Russian texts. Kozłowski styled himself 'amateur', but his compositions include an opera and a quantity of Catholic church music and, although most of his songs are modest enough, he sometimes shows real dramatic ability. For instance, his 'Prezhestokaya sud'bina' (Most cruel destiny)[8] has considerable, though conventional, expressive power; each of the two strophes is framed by a 12-bar prelude and 12-bar postlude in which the piano writing, unremarkable in itself, is strikingly superior to that of Kozłowski's dilettante contemporaries. Moreover he has a wider range; he can write the simple 'Russian song' ('Vïydu l' v temnïy ya lesochek'), a *Lied* such as Zumsteeg might have composed ('Ya tebya moy svet teryayu'), and the pathetic or dramatic monologue ('Prezhestokaya sud'bina') in which he is at his most characteristic.

The same dramatic note is sounded with much less technical competence in 'K ravnodushnoy' (1819)[9] by a naval officer, A. S. Kozlyaninov (1777–1831), while a fresh one—that of satire, later very important in Russian song—was struck by A. Shaposhnikov in a setting of Derzhavin's 'Filosofi p'yanïy i trezvïy' (The intoxicated and sober philosophers) published in a set of 'Anacreontic songs' in 1816. Shaposhnikov also set Derzhavin's elegy 'Potoplenie' (Drowning)[10] on Dubyansky who was drowned in the Neva. But the two most notable contemporaries of Dubyansky and Kozłowski were the blind composer Aleksey Dmitrievich Zhilin (*c.* 1767–*c.* 1848) and the Muscovite Daniil Nikitich Kashin (1769–1841), serf for most of his life, pupil of Sarti, all-round professional musician, and notable composer of patriotic songs of the 1812 period.[11] Zhilin won considerable contemporary popularity with his 'Malyutka' (A little boy)—or, to give it its correct title, 'Belizariy' (1806);[12] he commands both grace (e.g. the setting of Neledinsky's 'Tï velish' mne ravnodushnïm', also composed by Kozłowski) and gloomy power (e.g. 'Udaril chas', The hour has struck, one of those songs of parting always popular in time of war). There is nothing particularly Russian in many of his songs, which lean rather to the style of the contemporary *romances* of Boieldieu, Isouard, and Paër; on the other hand, Kashin's numerous songs – he left more than 250, as well as a collection of folk-songs with piano accompaniment (1833-4) – are decidedly Russian in flavour though technically feeble.[13]

These two strains – the sentimental *romance* (Russian: *romans* – the word was at first applied in Russia only to songs with French words, e.g. in Bortnyansky's French operas, with simple, strophic structure) and the *russkaya pesnya* (the 'Russian song' imitating folk-song, often with varied repetitions) – are clearly distinguishable throughout the second and third decades of the nineteenth century, though mutual influence often softens the distinction between the two styles; *romances* were sometimes based on genuine, if re-styled, folk-tunes, and conversely some passed into the popular repertory of the cities. The composers of this generation, the older contemporaries of Glinka, were almost all essentially amateurs though their amateurishness was of varying degrees, from the pure dilettantism of the Titovs and A. P. Esaulov to the near-professionalism of Alyabyev.[14] They were luckier than their predecessors in that they had better lyrics to set; instead of the stiff pseudo-classicism of Sumarokov and Derzhavin, and the feeble pastorals and love-poems of the 'sentimentalists' (I. I. Dmitriev, Neledinsky-Meletsky, Kapníst, Merzlyakov and the rest), they had Zhukovsky – whose narrative ballads, first set by his friend, the dilettante A. A. Pleshcheyev (1775-1827),[15] inspired a new genre of Russian song – they had Delvig and above all they had Pushkin. Poets and composers alike were Byronic romantics; the typical romantic themes of loneliness, dissatisfaction with oneself and the world, longing for some far-off land (Italy or some ideal country), were all too easy to cultivate under the autocracy of Nicholas I; but the composers for the most part lacked the ability to express all this fully. Even in his school-days Pushkin's juvenilia were composed by his friend Yakovlev (1798-1868), one of the dilettanti,[16] but his fertilizing and stimulating influence was not fully felt until later; yet from the first the composers recognized the challenge of fresh rhythms and metres.

Yakovlev is typical of the aristocratic, widely cultured dilettanti who copiously wrote *romances* at this period. Another was Count Mikhail Vielgorsky (1788-1856), who played an important part in Russian musical life generally and appears in every biography of Liszt, Berlioz, and the Schumanns. But the technical weakness of these composers has left their songs with more social than musical interest. The best of them was undoubtedly Nikolay Alekseyevich Titov (1800-75)—not to be confused with his brother Mikhail (1804-53) or his cousin Nikolay Sergeyevich Titov (1798-1843), both of whom composed songs occasionally reprinted under his name.[17] Nikolay Alekseyevich was actually christened 'the grandfather of Russian song'[18] —so that when Teplov was rediscovered he had to be the 'great-grandfather'. Titov, on his own confession, began by modelling his *romances* on 'those of Boieldieu, Lafont, and others'; his first composition was on a French text, 'Rendez-la moi, cette femme chérie'. His first published song, 'Sosna' (The pine-tree),[19] appeared in 1820, and Bulich lists about sixty. They are simple and the keynote is gentle melancholy, for which reasons they enjoyed vast popularity throughout Russia, not merely (like those of his predecessors) in St Petersburg and Moscow. Bulich says that 'old men . . . will tell you that in the 1840s there was no musical young lady who would not sing Titov's *romance*, "Kovarnïy drug, no serdtsu milïy" '. It is worth while to quote the opening of this song,[20] not only because it is characteristic but because the melodic line is a foretaste of a typically Tchaikovskian cast of melody.

Ex. 3

'Insidious friend, but dear to my heart, I vowed I
would forget thy wiles.'

Bars 1-3 curiously echo an aria in an opera by the composer's father (produced 1805).[21]

Modern Russian critics sometimes speak of the 'Triad' of song-composers, Alyabyev—Varlamov—Gurilev, a judgement perhaps coloured

by over-valuation of the folk element in Varlamov and Gurilev. They
were contemporaries of the Titovs but more accomplished technically.
This is particularly marked in the case of Alyabyev (1787–1851). Like
the Titovs, he was an aristocratic amateur but, unlike them, a semi-
professional amateur who worked seriously at music particularly during
and after his years of imprisonment (on a trumped-up charge of murder)
and Siberian exile (1825–32). It was in his hands that the Russian art-
song began to rise toward the artistic level of the contemporary German
Lied. His wider range of harmony, his musicianly and imaginative
accompaniments, his varied and extended forms, his greatly extended
choice of subjects, place him above all his predecessors. It is unfortunate
that he is best known by his setting of Delvig's 'Solovey' (The Nightingale), which Liszt transcribed for piano and on which Glinka wrote
piano variations (as well as orchestrating the accompaniment); 'Solovey'
is a beautiful example of a *romance* influenced by 'Russian song', but
it is a relatively early work (composed about 1826–8 and published in
1831) and far from characteristic of Alyabyev at his best. (He quoted
it himself in a much later song, 'Chto poesh', krasa devitsa', where he
contrasts the nightingale's song with a barcarolle-like 'song of golden
Italy'; he also wrote two 'farewells to the nightingale'.)

Alyabyev was a romantic in that his art is one of personal expression
and experience. Both temperament and experience combined to make
him a Byronist and it is not surprising to find that some of his best
songs, particularly his lyrical ones, were inspired by Pushkin: 'Dva
vorona' (The two crows), 'Zimnyaya doroga' (The winter road),
'Probuzhdenie' (Awakening – Dreams, dreams, where is your sweetness?),
an extended *durchkomponiert* song in three sections contrasted in key
and tempo, 'Sasha' (in which 'Russian song' seems to be crossed with
Schubert, who was just beginning to be known in Russia), 'Ya perezhil
svoi zhelan'ya' (I have outlived my desires), and a dozen others. The
first two of these alone would suffice to show Alyabyev's ability to set
a scene or mood with the piano's opening bars – the harsh dissonances
suggesting the cries of the evil birds, the tinkle of sleighbells on the
winter road – though perhaps his most striking piano-part is that of his
setting of Kozlov's 'Vecherniy zvon' – based on Moore's 'Those evening
bells', where the leaden sounds at once create the mood of the poem,
which is gloomier than Moore's original. (Ex. 4).

Ex. 4

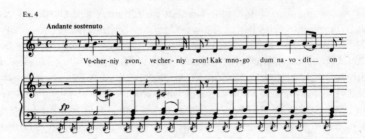

'The evening bell! How many a thought it calls to mind!'

'Pedals' like this are a favourite device of Alyabyev's.

Another Kozlov setting—of the famous 'Lyubovnik rozï, solovey' (Lover of the rose, the nightingale—a free rendering of Byron's 'This rose to calm my brother's cares', *The Bride of Abydos*, *I*, X)—now sounds rather conventionally pseudo-oriental, with its chromatic neighbour-notes, though it must have been charming in the early 1830s. But much of Alyabyev's oriental, or at least Caucasian, music is copied 'from life'; after his Siberian exile he lived for a time in the Caucasus and at Orenburg, and noted down and arranged Bashkir and Kirgiz (as well as Ukrainian) songs. His two 'Circassian songs'—to Pushkin's 'V reke bezhit gremuchiy val' and Lermontov's 'Mnogo dev u nas v gorakh'—particularly the latter with the augmented seconds in the melody, his 'Georgian song', 'Plachet deva gor' (which might have suggested the third movement of *Sheherazade*), and the fine 'Kabardinian song' 'Na Kazbek' (from Bestuzhev-Marlinsky's *Ammalet-Bek*, on which Alyabyev based an opera): these, with Glinka's *Ruslan*, are the foundations of the Russian oriental convention in music. Another outstanding song, the dramatic 'Irtïsh' with its tone-painting and its sharp distinction between narrative and direct speech, though not oriental, has an Asiatic setting.

In the 1840s Alyabyev opened yet another new vein—the realistic song of peasant life, anticipating Dargomïzhsky and Musorgsky—with settings of three poems by Ogarev: 'Kabak', 'Derevenskiy storozh', and 'Izba'. Related to these and from the same period is the powerful 'Nishchaya', a setting of Dmitry Lensky's translation of Béranger's 'La pauvre femme', the effect of which depends largely on an *ostinato* figure in the left-hand of the accompaniment. And in very different mood Alyabyev could throw off such light-hearted things as 'Sovet' (Advice – to a hussar about to marry).[22]

Neither Varlamov (1801–48) nor Gurilev (1803–58) possessed anything like Alyabyev's range or ability, yet they too contributed notably to the store of Russian song at this period when, as Professor Pekelis has put it,[23] it was 'a laboratory in which the elements of the Russian national musical style crystallized'. Love of minor keys, appearance of certain characteristic melodic cadences, fertilization from folk music, gradual elimination of Italianisms and Gallicisms: all these traits and developments were 'crystallizing' not only in opera but, perhaps even more effectively, in song.

Varlamov's most striking quality is his rich fund of melody, a melody saturated in the folk-style, so that his best-known song, 'Krasnïy sarafan' (The Red Sarafan),[24] has often been taken for a genuine folk-song. His favourite poets were Koltsov, like himself a 'man of the people' who cultivated the popular vein with great skill, and Tsïganov, the author of 'The Red Sarafan', an actor and poetaster probably of gypsy origin. Varlamov himself was influenced by the gypsy musicians of the Moscow restaurants; his more impassioned songs often suggest something of their manner of performance. He was not entirely free from Western influences; he sometimes writes in the measure of the waltz ('Tyazhelo, ne stalo silï'), the barcarolle ('Paduchaya zvezda'), or the bolero or polonaise ('Molodaya ptashechka', 'Grustno zhit'' and the setting of Lermontov's 'Beleyet parus odinokiy'). (Alyabyev wrote vocal mazurkas.) And these foreign rhythms are not always introduced as local colour, as the bolero rhythm is in Esaulov's 'Ispanskaya pesnya'. He also essayed the ballad with success in 'Pesnya razboynika' (Brigand's Song), 'Pesnya starika' (Old Man's Song – 'I saddle my horse'), 'Mechta ob Italii' (Dream of Italy), and other pieces. But when all is said, it is by his long-drawn and melancholy melodies that one remembers Varlamov, melodies such as that of 'Akh tï, vremya, vremyachko' (Ah, dear time, golden time), so near to the folk-melodies which he also arranged with sympathy and skill. But his poverty-stricken, conventional accompaniments – that of 'Akh tï, vremya', though better than most, doubles the voice much of the time – are unworthy settings for his gems.[25]

Conventional accompaniments also mar the work of Gurilev, who may be not unfairly described as a minor Varlamov; they fall into the idioms of guitar-strumming even more often than Varlamov's. Like Varlamov, to whose memory he dedicated a song entitled 'Vospominanie' (Remembrance), he was attracted to Koltsov who provided him with the text of what is probably his best song, 'Razluka' (Parting) – which ends with a dozen bars of dramatic recitative. Like Varlamov, he was attracted by the music of the gypsies and his 'Matushka-golubushka' (1845) within five years achieved the distinction of re-publication as a genuine gypsy song in the album *Tsiganskiy tabor* (St Petersburg, 1850). Yet, given a lyric such as Lermontov's 'I skuchno, i grustno' (It's boring and sad), Gurilev would turn out a *romance* that sounds like an anticipation of Tchaikovsky.

Alyabyev, Varlamov, and Gurilev were all essentially, though not exclusively, song-writers. Their contemporary Verstovsky (1799–1862) was essentially an opera-composer who also wrote *romances* (such as the setting of Zhukovsky's 'Dubrava shumit' (The oak-trees rustle) (1827) which he used again, with different words, in Nadezhda's aria in Act III of *Askold's Grave*)[26] and 'Russian songs' and gypsy songs (such as his setting of Pushkin's 'Stariy muzh, grozniy muzh' (Old husband, cruel husband)). But Verstovsky's speciality was the ballad. Even Alyabyev wrote little in this genre; Verstovsky, with his dramatic gift, excelled in it. It is true that his 'Nochnoy smotr' (Midnight Review) –Zhukovsky's translation of Zedlitz's 'Die nächtliche Heerschau'[27]– has been completely eclipsed by Glinka's, but he was the real founder of the Russian ballad (which he sometimes at first called 'cantata'). Two of his finest ballads, also Zhukovsky settings, the heroic 'Tre pesni skal'da' (after Uhland's 'Die drei Lieder')[28] and 'Bedniy pevets' (The Poor Singer), date from as early as 1823. In the same year his setting of Pushkin's 'Moldavian' song 'Chernaya shal' (The Black Shawl), one of his most popular songs, was performed in Moscow in costume and with scenery.

'Chernaya shal' was also sung with orchestral accompaniment – as indeed had been A.A. Pleshcheyev's 'Svetlana', as early as 1814–but one of the most important contributions of the ballad in general to Russian song was that its dramatic and picturesque features encouraged composers to write more adventurous piano parts, with descriptive or at least suggestive figuration and more expressive harmony. The form also offered them the challenge of a bigger canvas; the technique of the opera monologue was applied to the song with piano accompaniment and it is probable that the emancipation of the *romance* after the 1820s was largely due to the example of the ballad.

Glinka and Dargomïzhsky are regarded by almost all Russians as their first 'classic' song-composers.[29] Much of their work was, of course, contemporary with that of the musicians whose songs we have just been considering, but their best songs came a little later; whereas Alyabyev reached maturity in the 1830s, Glinka's most characteristic songs were written only at the end of that decade and in the 1840s, Dargomïzhsky's later still. Both belonged to the same milieu and we can measure their achievement best by seeing them in relation to it. One at once recognizes Glinka's superiority and Dargomïzhsky's innovations.

One might almost say that Glinka (1804–57) contributed little to the *evolution* of Russian song; he was not, for instance, more many-sided than Alyabyev; he was simply a very much better composer. His earliest songs, those written before he went to Italy in 1830, hardly show him as that. The earliest of all, 'Moya arfa' (My harp), composed in 1824, is preserved only in the form in which Glinka wrote it down from memory thirty years later, and the second, 'Ne iskushay' (Do not tempt me needlessly), was revised in 1851; it is a typical sentimental *romance* of the period with a typically conventional accompaniment. It has a number of similar companions; indeed Glinka went on writing this kind of song all his life, though a late example, such as 'Lyublyu tebya, milaya roza' (I love thee, dear rose), composed in 1843, is likely to be given distinction by touches of characteristic Russian harmony (here, the free use of sharpened fifth/flattened sixth). The early songs also include 'Russian songs' (e.g. 'Akh, tï dushechka' (Ah, you darling) and the Delvig 'Akh, tï noch' li' (Ah, night)), a couple of *romances* with French words by Prince S. G. Golitsïn which were republished with Russian texts for Stellovsky's edition in 1854, and seven or eight arias and *canzonette* to Italian words, which were also published posthumously with Russian words. More interesting is the 'Georgian' song 'Ne poy krasavitsa' (Do not sing thy songs of Georgia) in which Glinka used not only Pushkin's words but the genuine Georgian melody, perhaps a little modified, to which he wrote them.

Glinka spent the years 1830–3 in Italy, and the winter of 1833–4 in Berlin studying composition with Siegfried Dehn. In Italy he wrote one or two more Italian songs of which the best – published posthumously with Russian words as 'Zhelanie' – is a beautifully Bellinian setting of Felice Romani's 'Il desiderio' ('Ah se tu fossi'). But his composition of Zhukovsky's 'Pobeditel'' (The Conqueror – 'A hundred bright-eyed beauties') is also Italianate, in the style of an opera polonaise, and the setting of Kozlov's 'Venetsianskaya noch'' (Venetian Night) – actually conceived in Milan – is appropriately a barcarolle. As we have seen, the siciliana and barcarolle were nothing new in Russian music, but Glinka's barcarolles sound a little more authentic; he returned to the barcarolle in one of the *Farewell to Petersburg* songs of 1840, 'Usnuli golubïya' (The pigeons have gone to rest), and in one of his last songs, 'Palermo' (published as 'Finskiy zaliv'— The Gulf of Finland). On the other hand, the Zhukovsky song 'Dubrava shumit' was composed in Berlin (rewritten in 1843), which clearly accounts for its Schubertian flavour. And the words of Pushkin's 'Ya zdes', Inezil'ya' (Barry Cornwall's 'Inesilla! I am here') demanded a Spanish idiom, though they received only the conventional 'Spanish' treatment of the time; indeed, it is rather ironical that all but one of Glinka's Spanish songs— and they include the beautiful Pushkin 'Nochnoy zefir' (Nocturnal Zephyr)[30] and two in the *Farewell to Petersburg*—were written before he visited Spain; the exception is 'Milochka' (Darling), based in 1847 on a genuine *jota* melody.

With his newly strengthened technique and his new resolution to 'write music in Russian', Glinka was now poised for higher flights. At first he was occupied with the search for an opera-subject and then with the composition of *Life for the Tsar*, but most of his best songs date from the years 1837-40, that is, from the period between the production of the first opera and the composition of *Ruslan*: the famous 'Nochnoy smotr' (Midnight Review), the 'wedding song' 'Severnaya zvezda' (North Star—introducing the slow folk-melody later used in *Kamarinskaya*), four outstanding Pushkin songs—'Nochmoy zefir', 'Gde nasha roza?' (Where is our rose?), 'V krovi gorit' (Fire of longing in my blood'—but originally written to different words), and 'Ya pomnyu chudnoe mgnoven'e' (I remember the wonderful moment), and the twelve songs published by Gurskalin under the title *Proshchaniya s Peterburgom* (Farewell to Petersburg). The entirely declamatory *fantaziya* or ballad 'Nochnoy smotr' is tremendously effective but, as with most songs of this kind, the effect depends largely on the words and the manner of performance; the song occupies a curiously isolated place in Glinka's output. Utterly different, though also consisting of music that simply carries the words, is 'Gde nasha roza', a tiny gem which was to have enormous influence on the next generation of Russian musicians, suggesting the technique of Musorgsky's 'Savishna' and 'Ozornik' (Ragamuffin) and the manner of Borodin's epigrammatic songs. The whole piece is only seventeen bars long, ten in 5/4 time, seven in 3/4, and almost the only note-value used in the voice-part is the crotchet (see Ex. 5).

Ex. 5

'Where is our rose, my friends? Has it wilted, that child
of the dawn? Do not say: "Thus youth fades".'

More conventionally beautiful, an idealized *romance*, is 'Ya pomnyu
chudnoe mgnoven'e'. The poem is one of the most perfect love-lyrics in
the Russian language and has tempted a number of composers, from
N. S. Titov and Alyabyev onward, yet Russian critics seem to agree that
no other setting matches it as perfectly as Glinka's. It is not one of
those compositions that overwhelm the poem with superb music; as
Serov put it, it 'follows the poet's every thought'—and not only the
shades of his thought but the subtleties of his rhythms. It is in the
ternary form common in the *romance* of this period but the form is
transfigured in accordance with the sense of the poem, the six stanzas
of which also fall into three parts: the enchanted recollection of the
first sight of beauty, the passing of years and forgetfulness, and now the
fresh meeting and the renewal of passion—so that the music of the
third part is first harmonically, then melodically, changed, grows and
rises to a climax, and—with a sigh—sinks to rest.

In the songs of *Farewell to Petersburg* there was no question of
matching immortal verse. The poet, Glinka's friend Kukolnik, was no
master—and Glinka knew it. In at least two cases, 'K Molli' (To Molly)
and 'Poputnaya pesnya' (Song of Travel), the words were written to
pre-existent music. (The 'Poputnaya pesnya' must be one of the earliest
of *railway* songs.) The best that can be said for Kukolnik is that he
knew how to provide a wide range of ideas and verses suited to music.
The best known song of the set is 'Zhavoronok' (The Lark), an idealized
'Russian song'. Others are almost operatic. The variety is obviously

deliberate; there are theatrical pieces—David Rizzio's song from
Kukolnik's *Mary Stuart*, a 'Hebrew song' afterwards orchestrated for
his *Prince Kholmsky*,[31] the Crusader's 'Virtus antiqua'—and there are a
bolero, a cavatina, a cradle song, a barcarolle, and a fine *fantaziya*
(ballad), 'Stoy, moy verniy burniy kon' (Stand, my trusty, fiery steed)
of which the subject—but not the music—is Spanish. The set ends with
a 'Proshchal'naya pesnya' (Song of Farewell), an idealization of the
zastol'naya pesnya (drinking song with chorus). The idea of parting, of
travel, is suggested in other of the songs but there is no real connecting
thread; the set is not a cycle; the title refers only to Glinka's intention
of leaving St Petersburg at that time.

Dargomïzhsky (1813-69)[32] began song-composing, in the early
1830s, in the familiar contemporary styles: *romances* with French
words ('Au bal' in waltz rhythm, Hugo's 'O ma charmante', and others)
or Russian ones, 'Russian songs', a pseudo-oriental song or two. A little
later he was attracted by Spanish subjects. He often chooses poems set
by Glinka, by whom he was influenced for a time, only to show his
marked inferiority as a lyrical composer; the melodies of his *romances*
tend to be rather colourless and sentimental even in his more mature
work, the accompaniments to be conventional. One or two of the early
songs, however—notably 'Baba staraya' (The Old Woman)—hint at the
directions in which his real strength lay: the comic, the dramatic (or, at
least, the assumption of a character), the 'realistic' approach to peasant
life. But at first his technique was too weak to do justice to his ideas. In
the setting of Delvig's 'Shestnadtsat let' (Sixteen years old), for instance,
the girl's calf-love is charmingly sketched in a mazurka melody but the
harmony and the accompaniment are naïve without suggesting naïveté.

The later *romances* are naturally more imaginative, harmonically
more adventurous. There is real passion in the setting of Pushkin's 'V
krovi gorit'. But the best of Dargomïzhsky's straightforward *romances*
are two Lermontov songs dating from 1847-8: 'I skuchno, i grustno'
(It's boring and sad) and 'Mne grustno' (I'm sad because I love you).
Here the melodic utterance becomes more laconic, more fragmentary,
closer to the intonation of the words; the lyricism is modified by
character, as in opera. Yet in both, and in the later, rather similar
setting of Kurochkin's 'Rasstalis' gordo mï' (We parted proudly, without
a word or tear), the piano figuration is very conventional. Later still, in
the late 1850s, Dargomïzhsky achieved a little masterpiece in this genre
of lyrical monologue: 'Mne vse ravno'. Here the Byronic hero, speaking
through the lips of a poet far inferior to Lermontov, has outlived all

passion. The vocal line, more laconic than ever, is perfectly in character and perfect in its verbal intonation, and the piano merely supports it without distracting the listener by inept arpeggio-figuration.

Ex. 6

'It's all the same to me—come pain or pleasure. To suffering I'm long accustomed.'

It might be the very voice of Evgeny Onegin.

Dargomïzhsky's 'Russian songs' show a similar development, though his interest in the genre was later in growing: they became numerous only in the 1850s. One of the most beautiful—a typical crossing of *romance* with 'Russian song', with a great deal of gypsy bravura in both slow and fast sections—is the setting of Lermontov's 'Tuchki nebesnïya' (Heavenly Clouds). And Dargomïzhsky could throw off a straightforward racy piece such as the Koltsov 'Okh, tikh, tikh, tikh, ti!' But in this field, too, he is at his best when he makes himself the mouthpiece of a dramatic character: for instance, the drunken miller coming home late at night and his scolding wife in Pushkin's 'Mel'nik' (The Miller). That is straightforward comedy, but 'Likhoradushka'—a folk poem on the theme of the old and unloved husband—is bitter and subtle, despite its simple strophic form, and perhaps suggested Musorgsky's 'Gathering Mushrooms'.

Dargomïzhsky's more and more deliberate striving toward 'realism' and dramatic truth—in which he was completely in tune with contemporary tendencies in Russian thought and literature[33]— naturally found its fullest scope in the ballad or *fantaziya*. Even his earliest essay, the Delvig 'Moy suzhenïy, moy ryazhenïy', is more interesting than most of his songs of the same period, weak as it is. And his 'Svad'ba' (The Marriage), a glorification of free love ('It was not in church we married, with crowns and candles . . . but at midnight in the dark forest') published as early as 1843, justly maintained its popularity for half a century; the piano writing in the very Russian *andante* section, which alternates with more commonplace quick ones, again anticipates Musorgsky. The later 'Paladin' (Zhukovsky) is a worthy companion-piece to Glinka's 'Virtus antiqua'. But the most famous of all Dargomïzhsky's ballads—he calls it 'dramatic song'—is 'Stary kapral', Kurochkin's translation of Béranger's 'Le vieux caporal', the ballad of the old soldier, condemned to death for insulting a young officer, who encourages the reluctant execution squad as they march him along: 'In step, lads . . . one, two!' (At the end, after the fatal shot, Dargomïzhsky oddly writes four bars of two-part chorus echoing the old man's refrain.)

'Stary kapral' was written in the early 1860s (perhaps prompted by Moniuszko's setting of a Polish version), after the composer had made his often quoted assertion, 'I want the sound directly to express the word. I want truth' (letter to Lyubov Karmalina, 9 December 1857). Two other songs from the same late period of his life are usually considered his masterpieces of satirical comedy: 'Chervyak' (The Worm), another of Kurochkin's translations of Béranger ('Le Sénateur'), and 'Titulyarny sovetnik' (The Titular Councillor).[34] They are very amusing, and no doubt stimulated Musorgsky's satirical pieces, but the music of 'Titulyarny sovetnik', at any rate, is feeble; the fun lies less in it than in the words. Similarly, 'Stary kapral'—like Glinka's 'Nochnoy smotr', to which it stands in very close relationship—is essentially a vehicle for the words and for a dramatic performer. In 'Chervyak' Dargomïzhsky even gives 'stage' directions: 'very humbly', 'with profound respect', 'smiling and hesitating', 'screwing up the eyes'. But in this song, a self-portrait of a humble gentleman who is 'a mere worm' by comparison with the Count for whose friendship he is indebted to his own dear wife, the music itself is comic; here indeed are novelty and dramatic truth, for the vocal line—a sort of arioso mostly in even quavers—crawls and cringes with the inflexion of each sentence.

Finally two other declamatory songs must be mentioned, if only because of their influence on the next generation: 'Ti" vsya polna ocharovan'ya' (Thou art all full of charm) and 'Vostochnïy romans' (Oriental Song). Unlike 'Paladin' and 'Stary kapral', they are not dramatic in content. The setting of Yazïkov's address to a ballerina is actually styled 'recitative' though some phrases are melodious enough: the conception is orchestral, the pianist's right hand keeping up an almost uninterrupted demisemiquaver tremolo while the bass—suggesting pizzicato strings—interjects motives in the rhythm ⁷ ♫♫ |♩ . A bass

Ex. 7

motive (*x* in Ex. 7) plays an even more important part in the 'Vostochnïy romans' (a setting of Pushkin's 'Tï rozhdena vosplamenyat') where the augmented-triad harmony and the fragment of whole-tone scale in the bars quoted, which open and close the song, are derived from Glinka's *Ruslan*, although the falling semitones of the voice-part – which never spreads melodious wings – and the diminished-seventh harmonies are nearer to the orientalism of Spohr's *Jessonda*. All the same, the 'Vostochnïy romans' and 'Paladin' were at first the only songs of Dargomïzhsky's that were thought anything of by the group of young musicians who gathered around Glinka's protégé Balakirev in the 1860s. At least, that is what Rimsky-Korsakov tells us in his memoirs.

The outstanding event in the history of Russian song in the 1860s was, of course, the advent of a strikingly original genius: Modest Musorgsky. Yet, even apart from Musorgsky, Russian song underwent notable changes in the hands of his friends, the group known as the 'mighty handful': Balakirev, Cui, Borodin, Rimsky-Korsakov – and an almost unknown composer, one of the last and most technically gifted of the dilettanti, Nikolay Nikolaevich Lodïzhensky (1843-1916), a diplomat who as a young man produced a handful of beautiful and sensitive songs, six of which were published by Bessel in 1873. During the period 1855-65, Balakirev (1837-1910) produced a couple of dozen songs. Cui (1835-1918) composed about the same number between 1856 and 1870, mostly grouped in his Opp. 3, 5, and 7, with a few in Opp. 9 and 10. Beginning with a pseudo-Italian barcarolle in 1861, Rimsky-Korsakov (1844-1908) turned to song-writing more seriously in 1865 and in five years produced more than a score of pieces (his Opp. 2, 3, 4, 7, 8, and Op. 25, No. 1). Borodin (1833-87) also made a 'false start' with some early *romances* with cello obbligato, but composed the first of his tiny group of masterpieces, 'Spyashchaya knyazhna' (The Sleeping Princess – written, like most of his songs, to his own words) in 1867. In this considerable corpus of song one can detect a good many common tendencies.

Perhaps the most striking novelty is the treatment of the piano parts.

Not, of course, that even conventional arpeggio figuration or repeated chords completely disappear. We find them whenever the composer— for instance, Cui in 'Ya uvidel tebya' (I saw thee) or 'Prosti' (Forgive), Op. 5, Nos. 1 and 5—falls into the old *romance* style in the voice part. But the piano parts are not only well wrought or mood-enhancing as in the best songs of Alyabyev, Glinka, and Dargomïzhsky; they are more important, sometimes even seeming to outweigh the voice part, often to equal it in interest (e.g. Balakirev's 'Pesnya zolotoy rïbki' (Song of the Golden Fish) and Rimsky-Korsakov's 'Plenivshis rozoy, solovey' (Enslaving the rose, the nightingale)[35] Op. 2, No. 2, and 'V temnoy roshche' (In the dark grove) Op. 4, No. 3. And the voice parts are apt to be correspondingly less vocal. For this there are two explanations. The Balakirev circle was very much under the influence of Schumann and Liszt, both exponents of the 'pianistic' *Lied*. And whereas Alyabyev, Varlamov, Glinka, and Dargomïzhsky had all been more than competent singers, even teachers of singing, and had composed songs primarily for themselves (like all the dilettanti) or for women-friends,[36] Musorgsky was the only member of the 'mighty handful' with any vocal ability. Consequently, even the finest of their songs—Borodin's 'Sleeping Princess', for instance—are apt to have somewhat instrumental melodies.

Another consequence of this tendency is that voice-part and piano-part often seem to alternate: the picturesque or figurative piano-part changes to mere chordal accompaniment, or even stops altogether, when the voice enters (Balakirev's 'Pesnya Selima' (Selim's Song), Rimsky-Korsakov's 'Plenivshis rozoy' and 'Tikho vecher' (Quietly the Evening) Op. 4, No. 4), or voice and piano seem to proceed simultaneously on different planes (as in Balakirev's 'Golden Fish'). The young Rimsky-Korsakov, in particular, is all too ready to take refuge in recitative or quasi-recitative over a striking piano part: hardly the best solution of the problem of 'making the sound directly express the word'. Some of these piano parts are finely wrought and beautifully congruous—for instance, Balakirev's 'Gruzinskaya pesnya' (Georgian Song: another setting of Pushkin's 'Ne poy, krasavitsa')—but it is comparatively rare to find really close musical integration of voice and accompaniment, as in Lodïzhensky's 'Da ya vnov' s toboy' (Yes, I am with you again—a setting of his own words).

Ex. 8

'Yes, I am with you again; in my breast my heart
beats so quietly; in my spirit all is light.'

Balakirev generally developed familiar genres, breathing new life into
them: the 'Russian song' (e.g. the Koltsov 'Pesnya razboynika'—Brigand's
Song), a barcarolle (with a translated Heine text), *romances* (sometimes
in waltz or mazurka rhythm), and above all the 'oriental song', a vein in
which he early produced three masterpieces: the already mentioned
'Georgian Song' (not using the original melody, like Glinka, but with an
even more authentic-sounding one—Balakirev had visited the Caucasus
—and an accompaniment, afterwards orchestrated, brilliantly suggesting
an ensemble of native instruments), the virile setting of Lermontov's
'Selim's Song', and the fantastic one of his 'Golden Fish' (so very
different from Dargomïzhsky's). While Balakirev continues the Glinka
tradition, even in the straightforward *romance* (e.g. 'Pridi ko mnc',
Come to me, by Koltsov), Cui tends to follow Dargomïzhsky. His
'Lyubov mertvetsa' (A dead man's love), Op. 5, No. 2, is modelled on
'Paladin', 'Nedavno obol'shchen' (Lately beguiled), No. 3 of the same

set, on the older man's 'Ti vsya polna ocharovan'ya'. Both in his critical writings and in his compositions, Cui laid stress on 'truth to the words' and he makes extensive use of arioso, though his declamation is by no means always faultless. His detailed treatment of poems is heard at its best in such songs as the Maykov song 'Lyublyu, esli tikho' (I love, though quietly) Op. 7, No. 6, and in the Heine settings. It was at this period that Heine made his full impact on Russian song, partly of course because of the Schumann settings but even more as a result of the publication of Mikhaylov's volume of translations in 1858; all the members of the 'handful', as well as Tchaikovsky, composed Heine poems during the 1860s, most of them in Mikhaylov's versions though Borodin preferred to make his own. The musical influence of Schumann is also apparent sometimes in Cui, for instance in the Maykov song 'Istomlennaya gorem' (Weary with sorrow), Op. 7, No. 5.

Rimsky-Korsakov, being a little younger, often shows the influence of Balakirev or Cui. His beautiful setting of the lullaby from Mey's play *The Maid of Pskov*, Op. 2, No. 3, later incorporated in the opera *Vera Sheloga* (which is based on the first part of the play), is a close companion to Balakirev's 'Kolïbel'naya pesnya' (Cradle Song), and the Lermontov 'Kak nebesa tvoy vzor blistaet' (Thy glance is radiant as the sky), Op. 7, No. 4, is a pale reflection of the 'Georgian Song', while the arioso, half-declamatory element in others sometimes suggests Cui. Yet these early songs of Rimsky-Korsakov's include some beautiful and individual things, notably the Pushkin 'Na kholmakh Gruzii' (On the hills of Georgia), Op. 3, No. 4. Even the best of them, however, are surpassed in power and originality by some of the songs which Borodin began to produce towards the end of the 1860s.[37] First came the already mentioned 'Sleeping Princess', with the famous incessant syncopated seconds in the accompaniment which contribute so much to the fantastic, dreamlike quality of the music, and the tremendous descending whole-tone scale when the 'noisy swarm of wood-spirits flew over the princess'. Next came a companion-piece, 'Morskaya tsarevna' (The Sea King's Daughter) and the tremendous 'Pesnya temnavo lesa' (Song of the Dark Forest) which deserves much more than Cui's 'Menisk' (Op. 7, No. 4) the description 'epic fragment'; the words, again the composer's own, are an imitation of the *bïlini*, the old folk epics; they are set to a repetitive, metrically free melody which is doubled by the piano in bare powerful octaves; the 'harmony' is for the greater part of the song produced only by the sustaining of some notes for two or three beats against the movement of the rest. In strongest contrast are the two highly civilized, finely polished miniatures which followed: 'Fal'shivaya nota' (The false note) and 'Otravoy polnï moi pesni' (a translation of Heine's 'Vergiftet sind meine Lieder'); in these there is a superficial, stylistic affinity with Cui but both are inspired by a creative power far superior to Cui's; they have the gem-like hardness of great epigrams. Then, again, in 'More' (The Sea) Borodin gave Russian song-literature one of its great descriptive ballads, the piece which Stasov acclaimed as 'supreme among all Borodin's songs'—adding with typically Stasovian enthusiasm 'and, in my opinion, the greatest in creative strength and depth of all songs that have been written up to this time'. Without endorsing Stasov's judgement, one can agree that 'More' is a very fine piece which, unlike so many things in this genre, does not depend largely on the words to make its effect. Borodin later orchestrated the tempestuous piano part.

In 1873 Borodin wrote another Heine song, setting his own translation of 'Aus meinen Tränen', and in the 1880s another little group of songs, including his only Pushkin piece, 'Dlya beregov otchiznï dal'noy' (For the shores of thy distant fatherland), an 'Arabskaya melodiya' employing a genuine Arab tune (see p. 97), an elaborated 'Russian song' (Nekrasov's 'U lyudey-to v domu', In those people's house) and a companion-piece to Dargomïzhsky's 'Worm' and 'Titular Councillor': on Aleksey Tolstoy's 'Spes' (Pride). These show the extent of Borodin's reach rather than add to his stature.

Musorgsky's range as a song-writer was, of course, wider still, his originality more profound, his output vastly larger. But before considering it, it may be as well to glance at the later songs of the three longer lived members of the group: Balakirev, Rimsky-Korsakov, and Cui. Balakirev had two later bursts of song-writing: in 1895-6 and 1903-4. Like most of his later work, this score or so of later songs shows little stylistic advance on the early ones; one can say only that they include some beautiful things in the old manner, such as 'Zapevka', to words by Mey, in the purest folk-song idiom and treated like his own wonderful folk-song arrangements (of which he published two collections, in 1866 and 1898). 'Videnie' (A Vision), inspired by a poem by the Slavophile Khomyakov, is diffuse and sectional but extremely impressive; the vision is a typical Pan-Slav one, of Orthodox ceremonial and 'Slavonic prayers' resounding in the cathedral on the Petřín at Prague. In the Mey drunkard's song 'Kak naladili, durak' (As they kept on saying, 'You fool'), Balakirev successfully ventures on to Musorgsky's special ground, the comic-pitiful character-study; bitter, tragic words are set ironically to a gay folk-like tune.

Rimsky-Korsakov's later songs were also conceived at two widely separated periods: 1877–83 (Op. 25, No. 2, Op. 26, and Op. 27) and 1897–8 (Opp. 39–43, 45, 46, 49, 50, 51, 55, and 56). Of these, the earlier group are much more technically assured than the songs of the 1860s but mostly follow the same lines. However, in 'V porïve nezhnosti serdechnoy' (Op. 26, No. 1: a translation of Byron's 'In moments to delight devoted') and the Aleksey Tolstoy 'Gornïmi tikho letela dusha nebesami' (Softly the spirit flew up to heaven) Op. 27, No. 1, both in D flat as it happens, we at last find real lyrical warmth and expansive vocal melody in Rimsky-Korsakov's songs; 'V porïve' reminds one a little of Schumann but still more of the 'kiss' scene in *Snowmaiden*, which had been written a year or two before; the A. K. Tolstoy song is weaker but still attractive. And it was this new 'vocal' approach to song that predominated in the nearly fifty songs of 1897–8. The composer was quite conscious of this; he tells us in his memoirs:

> It was long since I had written any songs. Turning to the poems of Aleksey Tolstoy, I wrote four songs and felt that I was composing them differently from before. The melody, following the turns of the text, poured out from me in a purely vocal form, i.e. it was so in its very origin, accompanied only by hints at harmony and key-plan. The accompaniment was devised and worked out after the composition of the melody, whereas formerly – with few exceptions – the melody was conceived as it were instrumentally, i.e. apart from the text and only harmonizing with its general content, or evoked by the harmonic basis which sometimes preceded the melody. Feeling that the new way of composing produced true vocal music, and being satisfied with my first attempts in this direction, I composed one song after another to words by A. Tolstoy, Maykov, Pushkin and others.

The very choice of poets is significant; Aleksey Tolstoy and Maykov – with Tyutchev, Fet and Polonsky – were the later nineteenth-century champions of art for art's sake, not for truth's; they represent the retreat from 'realism'. And Rimsky-Korsakov, like the other composers of this period, now wished to compose essentially lyrical music.

The four Aleksey Tolstoy songs were published as Op. 39 and, although the new style is not fully developed in them, they point to most of its characteristics. No. 1, 'O, eslib tï mogla' (Oh, if thou couldst for one moment), melancholy, with an undercurrent of passion, suggests Tchaikovsky; the shadow of Tchaikovsky – of his moods, sometimes

even of his style—falls from time to time over this last crop of songs.
No. 2, 'Zapad gasnet' (The west dies out in pallid rose), is a beautiful
lyrical piece in the vein of the *romances* of half a century earlier. In
No. 3, 'Na nivï zheltïe' (Silence descends on the golden cornfields), a
shapely melodic phrase is answered by an arioso one, *a piacere*. No. 4,
'Usni, pechal'nïy drug' (Sleep, my poor friend), similarly alternates
arioso with snatches of a lullaby which is the twin sister of the one
from *The Maid of Pskov*. The best of the lyrical songs of this period
—Russian critics seem to agree in giving the palm to Op. 42, No. 3
(Pushkin's 'Redeet oblakov letuchaya gryada', The clouds begin to
scatter)—are beautiful indeed, but too often the lyricism seems a little
facile, the harmony and piano-figuration commonplace. The simple
workmanship is sometimes highly effective, as in Op. 40, No. 1 (Lermontov's 'Kogda volnuetsya zhelteyushchaya niva', When the golden
cornfield waves), where the left-hand piano melody accompanying the
singer's first phrase then passes to the voice, sometimes rather slipshod.
The three cycles, *Vesnoy* (In Spring), Op. 43, *Poetu* (To the Poet),
Op. 45, and *U morya* (By the Sea), Op. 46, are disappointingly uneven,
and the new 'Eastern songs', such as Op. 41, No. 4 (the Maykov
'Posmotri v svoy vertograd', Look in thy garden) and Op. 51, No. 2
(Pushkin's 'Georgian Song' once more), lack the savour of the old.
Op. 50, settings of Maykov's translations of modern Greek poems,
contains two or three of the better songs. Everywhere arioso is liable
to intrude. Op. 55, No. 3 (Pushkin's 'Snoviden'e' (Dream)) even begins
by returning to the lay-out of Dargomïzhsky's 'Tï vsya polna ocharovan'ya'. Several songs are actually styled 'arioso', notably the two bass
pieces, Op. 49, settings of Pushkin's 'Anchar' (The Upas-Tree) (the first
version of which dates from 1882) and 'Prorok' (The Prophet), both
orchestrated later; they can only be described as noble failures; neither
poem needs music or is suitable for music, and the subjects are outside
Rimsky-Korsakov's reach.

Surprisingly, the later Cui has a wider range than either the later
Rimsky-Korsakov or the later Balakirev. He attempted everything from
the tiny six-bar 'Epitafiya' of Op. 57 to the big dramatic ballad on
Richepin's 'Les deux ménétriers', Op. 42, which he afterwards orchestrated. During the late 1870s and the 1880s he set a number of French
poems by Hugo, Musset, Richepin, and others; he composed German
and Polish poems in the original languages and his Mickiewicz songs are
among his best. (He was half Lithuanian and he had studied with
Moniuszko.) He sometimes threw back to the simple *romance* of earlier

days; in the *21 Stikhotvoreniy Nekrasova* (21 Poems by Nekrasov, Op. 62) (1902) he unexpectedly turned toward Musorgsky though tamely conventional harmony replaces Musorgsky's expressive empiricism; and in 'Sozhzhennoe pis'mo' (The Burned Letter) Op. 33, No. 4, produced at least one outstandingly successful dramatic song. But Cui's natural gift was for the lyrical arioso, and the polished miniature, and in the *25 Stikhotvoreniy Pushkina* (25 Poems by Pushkin, Op. 57) (1899) he produced a real masterpiece of this kind, 'Tsarskosel'skaya statuya' (The Statue at Tsarskoe Selo), a perfect synthesis of poem and music, deceptively simple and as subtly delicate as a scent. 'A girl has dropped her jar of water[38] and smashed it'; and there, oh miracle, the water still flows and she sits for ever sadly watching . . . . The temptation to quote must be resisted; one would have to quote the entire song to show how perfect it is.

It would be difficult to find a greater contrast with Cui's polished but generally insipid art than the rough-hewn songs of his comrade Musorgsky (1839–81). He too began as a cultivated amateur, but whereas Cui always belonged in spirit to the tradition of the dilettanti— anaemic, impersonal in style, and conventional—these adjectives are the last one would apply to most of Musorgsky's work. Even his very first song, 'Gde tï, zvezdochka?' (Where art thou, little star?), dated 1857, has a certain tang.[39] A number of his early songs are in the old *romance* vein—one of the feeblest 'Akh, zachem tvoi glazki poroyu' (Why are your eyes sometimes so cold?) dates from as late as 1866—but most of them have some touch—boldly empirical harmony, a striking 'last word' on the piano—which shows that the mind behind them was no ordinary one. Real creative individuality begins to reveal itself in the songs written in 1863-4: the two Koltsov songs, 'Mnogo est' u menya teremov i sadov' (I have many palaces and gardens) and 'Duyut vetrï' (The wild winds blow), 'Tsar' Saul' (adapted from Kozlov's translation of Byron's 'Song of Saul before his Last Battle'), the Nekrasov 'Kalistratushka', and the *fantaziya*, 'Noch'' (Night). The last of these exists in two versions so different that they must almost be considered separate songs: the first, and better, is a beautiful and fairly faithful setting of a Pushkin poem which Rimsky-Korsakov composed a little later as his Op. 7, No. 1, the second a composition of a text largely rewritten by the composer himself;[40] the passage at the words 'vo t'me nochnoy tvoi glaza blistayut predo mnoy' (your eyes shine before me in the dark night), substantially identical in both versions, is in every respect characteristic of the mature Musorgsky. So is practically everything in 'Kalistratushka', the first

version of which is headed 'study in folk-style': Kalistratushka, a
peasant remembering his mother's lullaby (a folk-lullaby heard on the
piano), sings in that flexible, unsymmetrically melodious cantilena which
was later to flow through so many pages of *Boris* and *Khovanshchina*.

Most of Musorgsky's best and best-known songs were written soon
afterwards, during the years 1866–8. The lyrical vein continued in such
songs as 'Na Dnepre' (On the Dnieper, first version), 'Evreyskaya pesnya'
(Hebrew Song), 'Detskaya pesenka' (Child's Song), all by Mey, and the
Koltsov 'Po nad Donom' (Down by the Don), but it is a fresh and
unconventional lyricism no longer owing anything at all to the *romance*
type and far more sophisticated musically, even in the simplest examples,
than any of the old 'Russian songs'. However, it was not the lyrical
songs that created such landmarks in the history of Russian music, but
the realistic, half-comic, half-tragic ones written to the composer's
own words. The first, epoch-making example was 'Svetik Savishna',
inspired in 1866 by an incident Musorgsky had seen in the country,
the previous summer:

an unhappy idiot . . . declaring his love to a young woman who had
attracted him; he was pleading with her, though ashamed of his un-
seemliness and his unhappy condition; he himself understood he could
have nothing in the world—least of all the happiness of love.[41]

He set the idiot's courtship to an uninterrupted, unvaried stream of
even crotchets in 5/4 time; the technique is that of Glinka's 'Gde nasha
roza' (see Ex. 5) but here it is applied to a very different subject. It was
the choice of subjects quite as much as the musical technique that made
such songs so shockingly novel. 'Savishna' was the first of a series: 'Akh
ti, p'yanaya teterya' (Ah, you drunken sot), 'Seminarist', 'Ozornik'
(The Ragamuffin), 'Kozel' (The He-Goat), 'Klassik' (The Classicist),
'Sirotka' (The Orphan). They are a gallery of realistic portraits: comic,
pitiful, satirical, sardonic by turns. The convention of even note-values
is by no means always preserved, but, without being at all like recitative,
the vocal line is always controlled, if not dictated, by the inflexions
of prose speech; the infusion of a lyrical element may be greater or
less according to the subject. Closely related to these are the Mey
'Hopak' (which, like 'Na Dnepre', is a translation from the Ukrainian
Shevchenko's 'Haydamaky'), 'Po gribï' (Gathering Mushrooms—also
by Mey), the Koltsov 'Pirushka' (The Little Feast), and 'Strekotun'ya
beloboka' (Chattering Magpie—based on two unconnected poems by
Pushkin, described as 'a joke', and in fact a delightful piece of nonsense).

Musorgsky's 'realism' culminated, so far as his songs are concerned, in the cycle *Detskaya* (The Nursery). This consisted originally of five songs, composed 1868-70 and published in 1872; two more were composed in 1872 and published posthumously. In this series of musical transcriptions of a child's speech, caught with extraordinary truth and total absence of adult sentiment, all existing musical conventions were thrown overboard; the voice part is often the purest musical prose – 'S nyaney' (With Nurse), the first piece, is an extreme example – and though 'S kukloy' (With the doll) borders on the lyrical, even here the child's crooning never lapses into a near-conventional lullaby. From the same period dates an elaborate musical lampoon, 'Raëk' (The Peepshow), in which Musorgsky mocks a number of his musical enemies or supposed enemies; in the closed circle for which it was written this must have seemed extremely funny, but its musical allusions and parodies are lost on all modern hearers.

After *The Nursery*, Musorgsky changed direction. The cycle *Bez solntsa* (Sunless), to words by his friend Golenishchev-Kutuzov (composed in 1874), abandons the objective image. These are songs of subjective, pessimistic emotion; the musical technique is the same but Musorgsky now speaks in his own person, not as village idiot, sex-tormented theological student, or little boy, and his utterance is touched by almost lyrical melancholy – which becomes quite lyrical in the last song, 'Nad rekoy' (On the River).[42] Another Golenishchev-Kutuzov poem, 'Zabïtïy' (Forgotten–inspired by Vereshchagin's painting of a soldier's abandoned body), was set as a 'ballad' in the Glinka-Dargomïzhsky tradition, the same year, and probably suggested the cycle of *Pesni i plyaski smerti* (Songs and Dances of Death – again to Golenishchev's words) composed in 1875. Each of these songs is a grim dramatic scene – the child dying in its mother's arms, Death serenading the sick girl, Death dancing with the drunken peasant who is lost in the snowstorm at night, Death riding over the moonlit battlefield – and these images evoked from Musorgsky some of his most masterly and subtle music: perfect fusion of verbal sense and musical sense in the vocal line, supported by the most vividly expressive empirical harmony. Last of all, if we except a few unimportant oddments, in 1877 came a group of songs of which one, 'Viden'e' (The Vision) is by Golenishchev-Kutuzov, the remaining five by Aleksey Tolstoy; they show an astonishing falling-off in creative power. Lyrical arioso predominates, but even the equal-crotchet declamation is stiff and insensitive; the piano parts consist largely of common chords *tremolo*, or even in triplet repetition or broken into simple 'harp' arpeggios. Even 'Spes' (Pride), afterwards set by Borodin, failed to produce anything comparable with the earlier comic pieces. In 'Gornimi tikho letela dusha nebesami' (Softly the spirit flew up to heaven) Musorgsky placed himself in the – for him – very unusual position of inferiority to both Rimsky-Korsakov (Op. 27, No. 1) and Tchaikovsky (Op. 47, No. 2).

Musorgsky and his friends were, through Glinka and Dargomïzhsky, the musical descendants of the dilettanti. In the 1860s a new force began to make itself felt, that of the 'sound professional education' offered by the newly founded conservatoires of Petersburg and Moscow; yet even the best representatives of the 'conservatoire movement' – Anton Rubinstein (1829-94), its head, and Tchaikovsky (1840-93), its first distinguished product – were notably inferior to the heirs of the dilettanti as song-writers. All too many of Rubinstein's 200 songs show him as merely a highly competent imitator of Mendelssohn or Schumann, with little personality; he set German words with at least as much facility as Russian; indeed his best-known song, 'Der Asra', comes from a collection of Heine pieces, Op. 32. But one set is outstanding in each language: the so-called *Persian Songs – Zwölf Lieder des Mirza Schaffy aus dem persischen von F. Bodenstedt*,[43] Op. 34, surprisingly successful essays in the field of *Ruslan*-like orientalism – and the six *Basni Krïlova* (Fables by Krïlov), an early work, dating from 1851, showing unexpected, if rather heavy-handed, humour.

Tchaikovsky – whose name it would be both sensible and logical to spell Chaykovsky – cuts a much more important figure, yet only a small proportion of his songs shows him at his best. He possessed a gift invaluable to a song-writer – natural lyricism – but was defective in an essential one: the sense of the miniature. He tends to be heavy-handed and to inflate; for instance, far too many of his songs are marred by over-long piano preludes and postludes which make no particular point and are often rather clumsily written. (A classic instance is the Apukhtin song, 'Den' li tsarit' (Does the day reign?), Op. 47, No. 6, which must be much better in its orchestral version of 1888.) He was more sensitive to the general mood of a poem than to its details; a key phrase in the words would give him a melodic idea and this would dominate the whole or the greater part of the song (e.g. the Apukhtin 'Zabït' tak skoro' (To forget so soon), an inflated companion-piece to Dargomïzhsky's 'Mne vse ravno', the Mey 'Zachem zhe tï prisnilasya' (Why did I dream of you?), Op. 28, No. 3, or the Khomyakov 'Vcherashnyaya noch' (Last night), Op. 60, No. 1). Most of his songs are essentially *romances*.

He wrote straightforward, melodious *romances* all his life, from the Heine–Mey 'Otchego' (Warum sind dann die Rosen so blass?), Op. 6, No. 5, of 1869, to 'V etu lunnuyu noch'' (On this moonlit night), No. 3 of the six D. M. Rathaus songs, Op. 73 (1893); but, as with the later Dargomïzhsky, declamation keeps breaking in, in one form or another, and the majority of Tchaikovsky's songs might be described as arioso-*romances*. There are several examples of these in the very first published set, Op. 6, notably No. 6, the familiar 'Net, tolko tot, kto znal' (Mey's version of 'Nur wer die Sehnsucht kennt'). 'Zabït' tak skoro' is another early example. The Grekov 'Ne dolgo nam gulyat'' (We have not far to walk) (1875), with its curious anticipation of Tatyana's letter song, is a finer one. (Relationships with this central scene of *Onegin* may be detected in several songs of that period, e.g. Op. 38, Nos. 2 and 4 (1878), the D flat passage in the middle of Op. 47, No. 3 (1880).) The well-known 'Blagoslovlyayu vas, lesa' (I bless you, forests), Op. 47, No. 5, from Aleksey Tolstoy's poem 'John of Damascus', again belongs to this class. In some of the last songs, the Rathaus group, Op. 73, the balance is tipped more than ever on the declamatory side; in No. 6, Tchaikovsky's last song, the principle of the verbally inspired motto is also carried to an extreme. On the lighter side, the more melodious songs seem to throw back to the serenades and waltz-songs of the 1840s: 'Serenada Don Zhuana', Op. 38, No. 1, 'Prostïe slova' (Simple words), Op. 60, No. 5, 'O, ditya, pod tvoim oknom' (O child, beneath thy window), Op. 63, No. 6.

Yet, however much Tchaikovsky's corpus of song is dominated by the *romance* tradition—and naturally it is nowhere more marked than in the six French songs, op. 65 (written as late as 1888)—there are many exceptions. The specifically Russian note is sounded in 'Kak naladili durak' (As they kept on saying, 'You fool'), Op. 25, No. 6; but while Tchaikovsky anticipates Balakirev in setting Mey's poem *giocoso*, he fails to convey a sense of irony as Balakirev does; it is as if he had read the poem as a straightforward drinking-song. In another Mey song, 'Vecher' (Evening), Op. 27, No. 4—one of his translations from the Ukrainian of Shevchenko—the piano part is 'Russian' and pictorial (it is a picture of peasant life) while the voice part is declamatory; the separated planes remind one of the earlier Rimsky-Korsakov. A later Shevchenko poem, this time translated by Surikov, 'Ya li v pole da ne travushka' (Was I not a little blade of grass in the field?), Op. 47, No. 7, moved Tchaikovsky as far as he was capable of being moved in the direction of Musorgsky. Yet, when all is said, his most beautiful song in purely Russian vein is the exquisitely simple 'Legenda', Op. 54, No. 5 (The Christ-child had a garden).[44]

'Legenda' is one of a set of *16 Pesen dlya detey* (Songs for Children), nearly all composed in 1883 and nearly all with words—original or translated—by A. N. Pleshcheyev. Unlike Musorgsky's *Nursery*, they are intended to be sung to children, some of them by children; as with Schumann's similar pieces, the degree of childishness varies considerably. The Russian note is sounded in several other of the songs: No. 8, 'Kukushka' (The Cuckoo—one of the best), No. 10, 'Kolïbel'naya v buryu' (Lullaby in a Storm), No. 16, 'Moy Lizochek' (My Lizzie).

Tchaikovsky seldom shows interest in non-Russian themes; the Mey 'Kanareyka' (The Canary), Op. 25, No. 4, is one of his few oriental compositions, but 'Pimpinella', Op. 38, No. 6, is a charming Italian song based on one that he had heard sung by an urchin in the streets of Florence.[45] Another unusual type of song is 'V temnom ade' (In dark Hell), Op. 16, No. 6, one of Maykov's translations from the modern Greek, which is based from beginning to end on the *Dies irae* in either voice or accompaniment. Another powerfully gloomy song, though of quite a different kind, is 'Korol'ki' (The Corals), Op. 28, No. 2, Mey's translation of a dramatic Polish poem by Syrokomla, the story of a Cossack who brings back from the wars a string of corals for his sweetheart, only to find her dead. It is curious that Tchaikovsky was so little attracted to the dramatic ballad—though some of his songs, for instance 'Blagoslovlyayu vas, lesa', have the feeling of opera numbers—but in 'Korol'ki' he produced one of the finest of all Russian specimens of the genre.

During the thirty years or so before the Revolution of 1917 a great number of songs were produced by the pupils of Rimsky-Korsakov and Tchaikovsky, and in turn by their pupils. Confronted by this vast corpus of work by Taneyev, Arensky, Lyadov, Glazunov, N. N. Cherepnin,[46] Myaskovsky, Rebikov, Vasilenko, Grechaninov, Rakhmaninov, Metner and others, one is struck by a certain sameness. Consider the six songs of Glazunov's Op. 59, Taneyev's Op. 17, Nos. 8 and 9, Grechaninov's 'Na nivï zheltïe' (Over the yellow cornfields) and 'Krinitsa' (The Well) Op. 73, No. 2, Rakhmaninov's popular 'Siren' (Lilac), Op. 21, No. 5, or his 'Son' (Dream), Op. 38, No. 5, Metner's 'Den' i noch'' (Day and Night), Op. 24, No. 1: they might all be late Rimsky-Korsakov. Despite occasional influences from the contemporary *Lied*, the central place in Russian song was still held by the passionate or elegiac *romance*, the direct descendant through Glinka and Dargomïzhsky, Rimsky-Korsakov and Tchaikovsky, of the *romances* of the dilettanti—though the arioso variety was by this time predominant. Nor did the other favourite genres lose their popularity: there are still successful lullabies (Cherepnin's Op. 7, No. 6, and Op. 33, No. 9; Grechaninov's Op. 1, No. 5, which laid the foundation of his popularity—like Cherepnin's earlier effort, a setting of the favourite Lermontov words), barcarolles (Glazunov's Op. 60, No. 6; Taneyev's Op. 9, No. 1), dance-*romances* (Arensky's 'Davno-li pod volshebnïe zvuki' (Magic sounds), Glazunov's Op. 60, No. 1, Taneyev's Op. 34, No. 3, Metner's Op. 32, No. 5), oriental songs (Glazunov's 'V krovi gorit', Op. 27, No. 2—a languorous setting instead of the usual passionate treatment—Cherepnin's Hafiz-Fet songs, Op. 25, Rakhmaninov's 'Ne poy, krasavitsa', Op. 4, No. 4), and of couse many deliberately 'Russian-flavoured songs' even by such composers as Rakhmaninov (Op. 26, Nos. 4 and 14) and Metner (Op. 24, No. 3; Op. 29. No. 2), whom one does not commonly associate with national tendencies. The ballad or ballad-like song survives in Arensky's 'Volki' (Wolves), Op. 58, and 'Kubok' (Goblet), Op. 61, Cherepnin's 'Trubnïy glas' (Merezhkovsky's Last Trumpet), Taneyev's 'Zimniy put' ', Op. 32, No. 4, Metner's 'Vor Gericht' and 'Der untreue Knabe' (both settings of Goethe in the original), Op. 15, Nos. 6 and 10, and his fine music for Pushkin's 'Kon' (The Horse), Op. 29, No. 4. Among the later writers of children's songs—Arensky, Cherepnin, and the rest—Lyadov and Grechaninov are outstanding. And at the other end of the scale we have Grechaninov's cultivation of the concert aria with orchestra, beginning with his 'musical picture' 'Na rasputi'i' (a bass setting of Bunin's At the Cross-Roads), Op. 21 (1901). However, one also notes occasional experiments such as Rebikov's 'vocal scenes' for voice and piano, intended to be performed with simple scenery (a study with writing-table, a Chinese room, a snow-covered meadow in the moonlight) usually with another actor who remains mute, or (as in Op. 20, No. 5) speaks, or wordless song in Rakhmaninov's familiar 'Vokaliz', Op. 34, No. 14, Metner's 'Sonata-Vokaliz' and 'Suite-Vokaliz', Op. 41, and Grechaninov's 'Polka-Vokaliz' (though the last three are later in date—1921 and 1933—than the period we are considering).

The technical level of most of these songs—especially of those specifically mentioned—is generally very high. The highly polished workmanship of the musicians matches that of their favourite poets: at first Pushkin and the 'Parnassians' (Fet, Tyutchev, Aleksey Tolstoy, Polonsky), later the 'Decadents' and Symbolists, Merezhkovsky, his wife Zinaida Hippius, Sollogub, Bryusov, Balmont (particularly his

—very free—translations from Shelley), and Vyacheslav Ivanov, later still Bely and Blok. The workmanship may take the form of greater elaboration of detail, as with Metner and Rakhmaninov, or refinement to bare essentials, as in Lyadov's children's songs and Grechaninov's *Musulmanskiya pesni*, Op. 25 (settings of Tatar and Bashkir melodies): the harmony may be luscious or reduced to a limpid sketch. There is considerable variety and much beautiful music within the framework of inherited conventions, but little genuine freshness and no really strong creative personality. The essential conservatism of the harmonic idiom is remarkable. Rebikov's experiments with mildly 'impressionistic' harmony at the beginning of the century do not conceal the poverty of his invention. It is only in the decade immediately preceding the Revolution that we find Myaskovsky employing impressionistic harmonies in his Hippius songs, Op. 4, or Grechaninov turning to the idiom of Skryabin in his cycle *Ad astra*, Op. 54 (1911), only to drop it again soon afterwards.

The 'real song-writers' who stand out from the crowd of those who 'also wrote songs' are Grechaninov (1864-1956), Rakhmaninov (1873-1943), and Metner (1880-1951). (Perhaps one should add Taneyev.) Grechaninov's songs were undoubtedly the most important part of his work and they cover a wide range: the already mentioned children's songs (from Op. 31 in 1903 to Op. 122 in 1929) and concert arias, settings of four Krïlov fables, Op. 33 (done with delightful humour) and five of Baudelaire's *Fleurs du mal*, Op. 48, arrangements of Scottish songs, Belo-Russian songs, Tatar and Bashkir songs. But the majority are *romances*.

The *romance* completely predominates in the work of Rakhmaninov and Metner. Both were first and foremost piano-composers; like Tchaikovsky—from whom they derive, through Taneyev—they usually write heavily overloaded piano parts, with protracted epilogues, though their piano writing is far more beautifully polished (and far more difficult) than Tchaikovsky's and their epilogues are better justified. Metner's most overpowering piano parts occur in his earlier German songs of 1907-10; he set Goethe, Heine, and Nietzsche in the original and his treatment of Heine's 'Ein Fichtenbaum steht einsam', Op. 12, No. 2, and Goethe's 'Bei dem Glanze der Abendröte', Op. 18, No. 2, provides two classic examples of what one can only call 'over-composition'. But Metner, though often accused of being a German at heart, was really happier with Russian poems and it is interesting to observe how at the same period, confronted with Bely's 'Epitafiya',

Op. 13, No. 2, he writes not a Russian *Lied* but a *romance*; indeed he
even sets Goethe's 'Nähe des Geliebten' in a *romance*-like vein (Op. 15,
No. 9), though with a close integration of voice and accompaniment
rather rare in Russian song. And when he turns in Opp. 24 and 28 to
his beloved Fet and Tyutchev and in Opp. 29 and 32 to Pushkin, he
is in perfect sympathy with his poets; there is much more restraint,
much less overloading of the piano part; these four sets of 1912-14
contain some of his best work. Such Fet songs as 'Shopot, robkoe
dïkhan'e' (A whisper, a timid breathing), Op. 24, No. 7, 'Ne mogu ya
slïshat' etoy ptichki' (I cannot listen to this bird), Op. 28, No. 2, and
'Babochka' (The Butterfly), Op. 28, No. 3, are the perfect counterparts
of the 'Parnassian' poems. And the opening of the Pushkin 'Roza',[47]
Op. 29, No. 6, must be quoted to show how beautiful, and how Russian,
Metner can be in extreme simplicity.

Ex. 9

Rakhmaninov, with all his lyrical *élan*, never achieved anything as
exquisite as the best of Metner's songs, though his last set, the six songs
by Symbolist poets, Op. 38 (1916), shows him breaking away from his
over-rich euphony; the first song, in particular, the Blok 'Noch'yu v
sadu u menya' (At night in my garden), is almost Skryabinesque in its
harmony and its compression—but Skryabinesque like early Skryabin,
and Skryabin was already dead.

It is only when one measures them against this beautiful, belated
Parnassianism and this belated modernism, that one realizes how shocking
the early songs of Stravinsky (1882-1971) and Prokofiev (1891-1953)
must have sounded. They are not very important, these Gorodetsky,
Verlaine, and Balmont songs of Stravinsky's nonage (1907-11). (He

also anticipated Rakhmaninov and Metner in his wordless 'Pastoral' of 1908). Even the still earlier Pushkin *Favn i Pastushka* (Faun and Shepherdess) songs with orchestra show talent[48], and Opp. 6 and 9, with all their obvious debts to Rimsky-Korsakov and Debussy and Musorgsky, sound far fresher and more individual when set against the background of the contemporary Russian song than when considered simply on their merits. As for the *Tri stikhotvoreniya iz yaponskoy liriki* (Three Japanese Lyrics) or the *Tri pesenki (iz vospominaniy yunosheskikh godov)* (Three Little Songs, from memories of my childhood), sophisticated and naïve respectively (1912-13), they could have been written at that date by no one but Stravinsky. The *Japanese Lyrics* were originally accompanied by an instrumental ensemble (though there is an alternative version with piano), and Stravinsky followed this track further in the *Pribautki* (Facetiae) of 1914 and *Koshach'i kolïbel'nïe pesni* (Cat's Lullabies) of 1915-16. With these, and the *Tri istorii dlya detey* (Three Stories for Children), with piano, he disappears from the history of Russian song.

The early songs of Prokofiev—of which the most important is 'Gadkiy utenok', Op. 18—a setting of a cut version of Hans Andersen's *Ugly Duckling* in prose, made in 1914—are more straightforward, more diatonic, and more euphonious than Stravinsky's. Ex. 10, a typical passage of early Prokofiev from *The Ugly Duckling*, is a long way indeed from the Parnassian *romance* but not really so very far from Musorgsky.

Ex. 10

'It would be too heartrending to tell of the hardships
he had to put up with that winter,'

After the Revolution, some Russian composers settled abroad, others accepted the new régime. The émigrés continued in their chosen paths and most of them found nothing new on them; the one who continued to develop – Stravinsky – ceased to write songs. But Prokofiev returned to the USSR, first as a visitor and then permanently, and a glance at his choice of poets before and after his return will be illuminating. Of his early songs, Opp. 9, 18, 23, and 27 (composed 1910-16) and the two sets written in exile, Opp. 35[49] and 36 (composed 1920-1), the majority are settings of Balmont and Anna Akhmatova (one of the 'Perfectionists' who reacted against Symbolism). Those written after his return, Opp. 66, 68, 73, 79, and 121 (1935-50), are (with three exceptions) settings of Soviet poets or popular texts glorifying partisans or Voroshilov or Stakhanov, or on similar themes. Op. 68 are children's songs. The three exceptions are the three Pushkin settings, Op. 73, published in 1937 in a Pushkin centennial volume.[50] A similar change occurs in the songs of Prokofiev's older friend Myaskovsky (1881-1950), who never emigrated; Opp. 1, 4, 7, 8 and 16 (1907-14) consist mostly of settings of Hippius, Balmont and Vyacheslav Ivanov; after the Revolution, during 1921-5, came Opp. 20, 21 and 22[51] on Blok, Tyutchev, and Delvig; then after a ten-year gap in Myaskovsky's song-writing, the twelve Lermontov songs of Op. 40 (composed 1935-6), two sets, Opp. 45 and 52 (1938 and 1940), mostly to words by the Soviet poet Stepan Shchipachev, and various songs without opus-number addressed to Stalin, Romain Rolland, the Soviet Polar explorers, and 'a young warrior'.

The critical change in Soviet music generally, particularly marked in the field of solo song, occurred during the period 1930-4; the firm dividing line was drawn by the pronouncement of the Central Committee of the Communist Party on literature and all the arts in April 1932. Until then, beside the work of such minor conservative talents as Glier and Ippolitov-Ivanov, a good deal of mild modernism – mostly watered-down Skryabin (as in the songs of Alexander Krein) – had flourished under the aegis of ASM (Association for Contemporary Music) (1924-31). The Symbolist poets were still in favour, with lyrics from the Japanese and translations of Sappho. Myaskovsky's Opp. 20-2 belong to this phase. The more pronounced modernist Mosolov even composed in 1926 a cycle of *Gazetnïe obyavleniya* (Newspaper Advertisements – including one 'How to get rid of corns'). It is true that there was bitter opposition from RAPM (Association of Proletarian Musicians) which was against both modernism and the classics, indeed all manifestations of lyricism, and wished composers to abandon the *romance* altogether for the 'mass song' (unison with piano). But both these points of view were swept aside by the pronouncement of 1932. The classics were to be revered, but modernism and all forms of 'subjectivism' or abstract 'formalism' were taboo; 'Socialist realism' was demanded and — despite the very varied definitions officially accepted at different periods — has been demanded ever since. 'Modernism' was not difficult to get rid of; it had never struck very deep roots in Russia; but 'subjectivism' was a different matter, particularly in the field of solo song. Such composers as Myaskovsky found great difficulty in re-orientating themselves and writing simply and 'naturally' enough, some took refuge in the making of folk-song arrangements, an art in which every generation of Russian composers from that of Balakirev and Rimsky-Korsakov onward has excelled, turning not only to Russian songs but to those of the Eastern peoples of the Soviet Union and to those of Western Europe, English and Scottish ones always being favourites. Some important composers of the younger generation — Shostakovich, Khachaturyan, Kabalevsky, Shebalin, Dzerzhinsky, Khrennikov—wrote comparatively few songs, though most of them paid dutiful tribute to Pushkin (e.g. Shostakovich's Op. 46 and Khrennikov's Op. 6) just before the centenary of his death.

On the other hand, the former RAPM composer Koval (1907-71) now found it possible to publish a *Pervaya tetrad' liriki* (First Book of Lyrics) in 1934 and actually composed Pushkin (*Pushkiniana*, 1932-4) as well as Nekrasov. It is true that Koval avoided the familiar lyrics and chose poems that reflect Pushkin's conflict with his environment — 'Tak, polden' moy nastal' (So, my noonday hour has struck), 'V Sibir'' (In Siberia), and others — and he set them in a rather dry declamatory style that reminds one of Dargomïzhsky; moreover, the ten songs are linked by excerpts from Pushkin's diaries and letters which are intended to be read as a part of the performance.

Much more conventional, but musically much finer, are the Pushkin songs of Shaporin (1887-1966), a natural conservative. In his Op. 10 (published in 1937, though some of the songs were written much earlier) Shaporin was not afraid to turn to such a favourite poem as 'Zaklinanie' (Evocation), already composed by Rimsky-Korsakov, Cui, and Metner, set it to such music as they might have written — though his melody is actually rather Tchaikovskian — and (as it happens) surpass all three. So with his cycle of ten Blok songs, *Dalekaya yunost* (Far-off Youth); they are old-fashioned *romances*, two of them waltz-*romances*, the music of an epigone but sensitive, beautifully fashioned music. The same may be said of the Blok and Essenin songs of Nechayev (1895-1956), who put the best of himself into his songs. In other cases, striving for simplicity and 'objectivity' led to unfortunate results. Boris Asafyev, known as historian and critic under the pseudonym 'Igor Glebov', published a cycle entitled *Liricheskie Stranitsi (na temu 'Odinochestvo Lermontova'* (Lyrical Pages, on the theme of Lermontov's solitude), in which he took nine of the most popular of Lermontov's lyrics—'Nochevala tuchka zolotaya', 'Tuchki nebesnïe', and the rest—and set them to music of incredible feebleness. The first song, 'Solntse' (Sunshine), is given the sort of arpeggio accompaniment that nearly died with Glinka; one might imagine that one of the early nineteenth-century dilettanti had come to life again or that the musicologist 'Glebov' was trying his hand at pastiche or parody or leg-pull. But Asafyev was never a very strong creative talent; Myaskovsky, on the other hand, was one of the best of the older composers of the USSR, a master of his craft, yet his simple and 'objective' treatment of the same poem (Op. 40, No. 5) is, if anything, still more banal.

Ex. 11

'How beautiful is the winter sunshine when, breaking through grey clouds, it vainly throws a pale ray on the white snow!'

To try to bridge the gap that separates the modern composer from the modern listener is praiseworthy, but such art as this is not a bridge but a *cul-de-sac*, unworthy of the great tradition of Russian song.

NOTES

1. *Russkiy romans: ocherk evo razvitiya* (St Petersburg, 1896).
2. *Russkaya khudozhestvennaya pesnya* (Moscow, 1905), p. 7.
3. S. K. Bulich, ' "Pradedushka" russkavo romansa', *Muzïkal'nïy Sovremennik*, ii (1916), 1, p. 11.
4. Published by the Academy of Sciences, St Petersburg, during the 1750s; second edition 1759, third edition (of 45 copies!), 1776; detailed discussion by A. N. Rimsky-Korsakov in *Muzïka i muzïkal'nïy bït Staroy Rossii* (Leningrad, 1927), p. 30; complete reprint in T. Livanova, *Russkaya muzïkal'naya kultura XVIII veka*, i (Leningrad and Moscow, 1952), pp. 189–245. The reprints in the volume *Nachalo russkovo romansa* (ed. Trofimova and Drozdov, Moscow 1936) are too heavily edited to be acceptable.
5. A modern edition, ed. M. V. Belyaev, was published by Muzgiz in 1953.
6. Reprinted by Findeisen, op. cit. p. 13, where it is misattributed to the Austrian, Ferdinand Titz; by Ginsburg, *Istoriya russkoy muzïki v notnïkh obraztsakh*, i (Leningrad and Moscow, 1940), p. 360, with two other songs by Dubyansky; and elsewhere.
7. See, for example, the anonymous setting in the musical appendix to Findeisen, *Ocherki po istorii muzïki v Rossii*, ii (Moscow, 1929), No. 115.
8. Reprinted, with one other song, by Findeisen, *Russkaya khudozhestvennaya pesnya*, p. 16; in the *Istoriya russkoy muzïki* ed. M. S. Pekelis, i (Leningrad and Moscow, 1940), p. 181; and in Ginsburg, op. cit. ii (Leningrad and Moscow, 1949), p. 15, with three other 'Russian songs'. On Kozłowski's life and work generally, see in particular the chapter by P. V. Grachev in the volume *Ocherki po istorii russkoy muzïki: 1790–1825*, ed. Druskin and Keldïsh (Leningrad, 1956).
9. Reprinted in Ginsburg, op. cit. ii, p. 344.
10. The two songs by Shaposhnikov are reprinted in Ginsburg, op. cit. ii, pp. 340 and 337 respectively.
11. On Zhilin and Kashin see particularly the chapter by O. E. Levasheva in *Ocherki po istorii russkoy muzïki: 1790–1825*.
12. Reprinted in the Pekelis *Istoriya russkoy muzïki*, i, p. 235, and in Y. Keldïsh, *Istoriya russkoy muzïki*, i (Moscow and Leningrad, 1948), p. 288; a different, obviously later, version is given by Ginsburg, op. cit. ii, p. 330. The words of *Malyutka* are a translation of a song by Lemercier: 'Un jeune enfant, un casque en main'.
13. One *romance* and six folk-song arrangements in Ginsburg, op. cit. ii, pp. 218 ff.
14. Russian scholars will observe that in transliteration, I have allowed myself more latitude with proper names than with titles and texts.
15. One of them was composed at least as early as 1814, though they were not published until 1832.

16. Yakovlev's setting of '*Zimniy vecher*' (Winter evening) is printed in Keldïsh, op. cit. i, p. 286.

17. e.g. N. S. Titov's '*Talisman*', reprinted – correctly – in Ginsburg, op. cit. ii, p. 394.

18. S. K. Bulich, *Dedushka russkavo romansa: N. A. Titov* (St Petersburg, 1900).

19. Ginsburg, op. cit. ii, p. 381.

20. Reprinted in Ginsburg, op. cit. ii, p. 383, and Keldïsh, op. cit. i, p. 282.

21. Printed in Ginsburg, op. cit. ii, p. 85.

22. A complete edition of Alyabyev's songs was published in four volumes by Jurgenson in 1898. There is a chronological list in Grigory Timofeyev's *A. A. Alyabyev* (Moscow, 1912).

23. Op. cit. I, p. 232.

24. Published with eight other songs in *Muzïkal'ny al'bom na 1833 god*, Varlamov's first opus (Moscow, 1833).

25. On Varlamov, see S. K. Bulich, *A. K. Varlamov* (St Petersburg, 1902); a 12-volume edition of his songs was published by Gutheil.

26. Nadezhda's very first song in the opera, 'Gde tï, zhenikh moy', was also adapted from an earlier *romance*. Glinka followed suit in *Life for the Tsar*, borrowing the music for Antonida's song in Act III from his setting of Delvig's '*Ne osenniy chastïy dozhdichek*' (1829).

27. Loewe's fine composition of the original poem, his Op. 23, was composed in 1832 and published the following year. Schubert had declined to tackle it: cf. O. E. Deutsch, *Schubert: die Erinnerungen seiner Freunde* (Leipzig, 1957), p. 87.

28. Loewe also set this (Op. 3, No. 3) but his version was not published until 1825.

29. On the 'classical' Russian song, see, in addition to general histories and works on individual composers, particularly B. V. Asafiev (ed.), *Russkiy romans* (Moscow, 1930) and V. A. Vasina-Grossman, *Russkiy klassicheskiy romans XIX veka* (Moscow, 1956).

30. Also set in Pushkin's lifetime by Verstovsky, N. S. Titov and Esaulov.

31. In 1855 Glinka orchestrated the accompaniments of '*Nochnoy smotr*' and one or two other songs.

32. The best edition of his songs is the *Polnoe sobranie romansov i pesen*, ed. Pekelis (Moscow, 1947).

33. Chernïshevsky's *Aesthetic Relationship of Art and Reality*, the 'bible' of the truth-in-art movement, was published in 1855.

34. A rank in the Tsarist civil service. The words are by Peter Weinberg, who was first and foremost a translator, so there may again be some Western original by Béranger or Heine?

35. By Koltsov. Not to be confused with the Byron–Kozlov *Lyubovnik rozï*, *solovey*, which Rimsky-Korsakov set sixteen years later (Op. 26, No. 4).

36. Dargomïzhsky gave lessons gratis to ladies but would take no male pupils. He often said, 'But for the existence of women-singers, I should never have been a composer. They have inspired me all my life'.

37. They are all published, together with Borodin's juvenilia (of which the most striking feature is the use of cello obbligato), in a volume edited by Lamm (Moscow, 1947).

38. The statue, by P. I. Sokolov, really depicts La Fontaine's *La laitière et le pot au lait*.

39. Like other of Musorgsky's early songs, it exists in two versions; in this case, the second is orchestral. Both versions are printed in the complete edition of Musorgsky's works, edited by Pavel Lamm, v, 1–2 (Moscow, 1931), which should always be used where possible. The original editions of many of Musorgsky's songs were more or less drastically 'revised' by Rimsky-Korsakov, who also published what he called a 'free musical rendering' of the first of the *Nursery* songs. There is a separate monograph on Musorgsky's songs by Keldïsh: *Romansovaya lirika Musorgskovo* (Moscow, 1933).

40. Both versions were later orchestrated: the first by the composer in 1868, the second by Rimsky-Korsakov in 1908.

41. Stasov, 'M. P. Musorgsky', *Vestnik Evropi*, iii (1881), p. 506.

42. A poem which Balakirev set twenty years later as '*Nad ozerom*' (On the Lake).

43. The later Russian translation was made by Tchaikovsky.

44. This was the original form of the piece; the popular *a cappella* version was made six years later, in 1889. Tchaikovsky also orchestrated the accompaniment of the original version.

45. *Perepiska s N. F. von Mekk*, i (Moscow and Leningrad, 1934), p. 222, where the original tune is given.

46. Whose son, A. N. Cherepnin, was also a song-composer.

47. Cf. Glinka's setting, quoted as Ex. 5.

48. Most remarkable of all is the still unpublished 'Kak gribï nad voinu sobirilis'' of 1904.

49. The five songs of Op. 35 are wordless. The Russian interest in wordless song reached its climax in Glière's two-movement Concerto for coloratura soprano and orchestra, Op. 82 (comp. 1943).

50. *A. S. Pushkin v romansakh i pesnyakh sovetskikh kompozitorov.*

51. The opus number 22 was originally given to another Hippius set which the composer later suppressed as too modern in idiom.

2. The Operas of Serov

That Aleksandr Nikolayevich Serov occupies an oddly ambiguous position in the history of Russian opera is not altogether surprising; he occupied an oddly ambiguous position in the Russian musical world in the middle of the nineteenth century. As a critic he had been Wagner's earliest champion in Russia, thereby endearing himself neither to Rubinstein and the 'westernizing' academics on the one hand nor to the nationalist 'young Russian school' on the other; yet in 1863 he made his serious début as a composer with an opera, *Judith*, which seemed to be a total denial of his critical principles and of almost everything Wagner stood for. The two works which followed it, *Rogneda* (1865) and *Hostile Power* (*Vrazhya sila*) (1871), were equally un-Wagnerian. All three remained popular in Russia for many years—Shalyapin sang Eremka in *Hostile Power* in 1916—but none has ever made the slightest impression abroad. The three performances of Act IV of *Judith*, with Shalyapin as Holofernes, which Dyagilev included in his Paris season of June 1909, are the only productions of Serov in the West that I have been able to trace. The operas remain unknown to almost all Western musicians, even to those most interested in Russian music. If *Judith* is known to them at all, it is likely to be by the long, sneering account (with numerous musical examples) which Musorgsky sent to Balakirev some weeks after the first performance rather than by the score itself; but as Andrey Rimsky-Korsakov pointed out in his edition of Musorgsky letters and documents,[1] Musorgsky was very conscious of the violently anti-Serovian views of his older friends Stasov and Balakirev; even in this letter Musorgsky says that *Judith* is the first opera on the Russian stage since Dargomïzhsky's *Rusalka* that one has to take seriously.

Hardly anyone in Petersburg had expected *Judith* to be a success; as Tchaikovsky put it years later, 'we expected a boring, uninspired, pretentious opera'; Serov was forty-three and had so far given no real evidence of creative ability. In 1842, at the age of twenty-two and with no technical training at all, he had set out to rival Verstovsky with an *Askold's Grave*, a project which collapsed when he tried to write his own libretto. Other subjects had appealed to him from time to time — *The Merry Wives of Windsor*, Lazhechnikov's novel *The Pagan* (*Basurman*) — and in 1845 he had actually achieved a little operetta based on a French vaudeville, *La Meunière de Marly*, of which a surviving fragment, some *valse-couplets*,[2] is equally pitiful in both invention and technique. In 1849 he embarked on a *May Night*, with a libretto by Praskovya Mikhaylovna Bakunin (a cousin of the anarchist) based on Gogol's short story, and worked on it until 1853, completing or nearly completing two versions in three acts and a third in two acts. From Serov's correspondence with the Stasov brothers, who were at that time still his closest friends, and with Alexey Bakunin (the anarchist's brother)[3] we know quite a lot about the various numbers. Hanna's prayer from Act III was actually sung, with orchestra, at a charity concert in Petersburg on 29 April/11 May 1851, when Anton Rubinstein remarked to Dmitry Stasov: 'Je ne m'attendais pas à ça du tout. C'est noblement et aristocratiquement musical.' But Hanna's prayer has not come down to us. The score of one version of *May Night* was burned by the composer: and all that survives of the opera in any form is a 20-bar fragment — probably Levko's serenade, which was the opening number of the third version — which Serov transcribed for piano solo in Lyudmila Shestakova's album in May 1855.[4] It was at the time of the third version of *May Night* that Serov discovered Wagner: not his music but *Oper und Drama* and *Das Kunstwerk der Zukunft*. It was Wagner's views that attracted him; a year or two before in one of his own earliest critical essays[5] he had proclaimed that 'in *musical* drama what matters first and foremost is *drama*'. When at last, in 1856, he heard some Wagner — it was the *Tannhäuser* overture — he found it 'only curious, interesting, even striking, but in no-wise beautiful, capable of giving pleasure from a "musical point of view"'. It was only in 1858 when he saw *Tannhäuser* on the Dresden stage and *Lohengrin* at Weimar that he became a fanatical admirer of Wagner's music; he heard the *Tristan* prelude at the Leipzig Tonkünstlerfest in 1859; but when he embarked on *Judith* in 1861, after eight years of almost complete silence so far as composition was concerned, Wagner was to him essentially the Wagner of *Tannhäuser* and *Lohengrin*. And *Judith* was originally conceived not as a Wagnerian but, literally, as an Italian opera.

In 1860, after throwing off a *Christmas Song* for female choir, flute, oboe, and clarinet, and a Latin *Pater noster* for chorus and orchestra,

Serov again began to dream of operas, and took fire at K. I. Zvantsev's suggestion to base one on Zhukovsky's translation of *Undine*. He got as far as casting it for the artists of the Maryinsky Theatre – as he had done with *May Night* – and then abandoned it for a *Poltava*. But during the winter of 1860-1 Adelaide Ristori was appearing at the Maryinsky as guest-artist in spoken drama – Schiller's *Maria Stuart*, Paolo Giacometti's *Giuditta*, and other tragedies – and, to quote Zvantsov:[6] 'On one occasion, actually 20 December, 1860, during the interval after Holo-fernes' orgy in the tragedy *Giuditta* ... I said to Serov: "Well, what about that for an opera finale?" Enraptured by this orgy, he cried out: "Of course! And I will certainly write an opera *Judith*, the more gladly because I've always been attracted by the stories and characters of the Old Testament!" ' (Serov was proud of the fact that his maternal grandfather was a Jew; it would be a quibble to object that the Book of Judith is not a canonical book of the Old Testament.) He did not at first contemplate a Russian *Judith* but enlisted the help of an *improvisatore*, a certain Ivan Antonovich Giustiniani, then living in Petersburg, to prepare an Italian libretto, and set about the composition of the last scene (Judith with the severed head and her hymn of triumph), which he proposed to offer to the soprano La Grua, a famous Norma of the day, for her benefit. The 'hymn' was finished in full score by March 1861, but La Grua turned it down and before long Serov decided to turn his work into a Russian opera. In any case, Serov wrote or roughed out a great deal of the music before he had a text. As a Wagnerian, and a skilled man of letters, Serov might have been expected to produce his own Russian libretto; but he doubted his powers and called in Zvantsev, who was at the same time struggling with the translation of *Tannhäuser*,[7] a young friend, D. I. Lobanov, and even a real poet, Maykov. Towards the end of 1861 Serov submitted the full score of his first act to Balakirev, not directly but through Musorgsky, and received a crushing reply. Balakirev had only glanced at it and, in any case, it was impossible to judge an opera from a single act: 'I can only say that in the orchestra there is a great deal of artistic pretension, but a great deal of it won't come off. The composer handles his masses badly; he is better with light orchestration. Yet one thing I can say: the end is very pretty, beginning with the bar where the basses sing middle C, to which the other voices add chords of *la mineur* (with suspended fifth, G, of a C major chord), and finally to all this the basses – D and A. This is very *pretty*'.[8] It is highly significant that it is this passage at the end of Act I which Musorgsky allows himself to praise with real enthusiasm in the already mentioned letter to Balakirev after the first performance. 'The very end of the first act is beautiful', he says. As for the D and A of the basses, 'the fifths in the basses have a peculiar *mystical* sound;—there is a sort of *solemn calm* which *doesn't come to an end*, and this is beautiful; the impression is true and good—this is the best passage in the opera.' As a matter of fact, Serov was very fond of ending a number like this, dying away almost imperceptibly.

The prelude to Act IV, depicting Holofernes' orgy, had a concert performance in February 1862, and in the summer Johann Strauss's orchestra played Holofernes' march and the dance of the odalisques at Pavlovsk. And when the complete opera was duly performed at the Maryinsky, on 16/28 May 1863, it scored an astounding success— not only with the general public but with the *cognoscenti*, even the Conservatoire staff and the opera personnel. Theophil Tolstoy, who had heralded it with the most malicious advance publicity, was completely conquered and openly recanted. The young Tchaikovsky was 'enraptured' by it and, according to Laroche, he never lost his admiration; he certainly wrote warmly of it in a well-known letter to Nadezhda von Meck (17/29 March 1878). The one important dissentient voice was that of the composer's former friend, now bitter enemy, V. V. Stasov. Stasov attended the performance and the next day wrote a very long, almost hysterical letter to Balakirev,[9] who was far away at Pyatigorsk, demanding to be told why such a work, rubbish which was at the same time, 'serious, unsentimental, without love . . . without roulades', should be at once and unanimously hailed as a masterpiece. Musorgsky had been with him in the theatre 'and seemed to think as I did, but I didn't hear from him one idea, one word of deep understanding . . . He seems to me a perfect idiot.' Seen in this light, Musorgsky's own later letter to Balakirev appears as a weak attempt at exculpation. His true reaction to *Judith* was to begin his own *Salammbô* five months later.

Serov lost little time in following up the success of *Judith*. He at once embarked on the composition of an opera named after the favourite wife of Vladimir the Great, Rogneda, and based to some extent on the ballad by Pushkin's friend Rïleyev. The historical Vladimir was a monarch whose religious enthusiasm must have been a sore trial to his subjects; he first forced them into idolatry on a massive scale and later obliged them, again *en masse*, to adopt Christianity. In Serov's only slightly historical opera the still pagan Vladimir has abducted Olava (a character who never appears), the bride of a young Christian warrior Ruald, and Rogneda's jealous rage provides the pretext for a close

parallel with *Judith*: she determines to murder Vladimir in his sleep.
But Vladimir wakes in time. He had already been struck by Ruald's
magnanimity in rescuing him from a bear while hunting and now, after
sentencing Rogneda to death, he is easily persuaded by a chorus of
Christian pilgrims to pardon her. The action of *Judith* has an epic
simplicity; it only slightly embroiders the story in the Apocrypha—
Holofernes has ambitious dreams of overthrowing his royal master and
tempts Judith with the prospect of becoming queen of Babylon. But
that of *Rogneda* is a preposterous hotchpotch of spectacular or otherwise theatrically effective scenes. (As Dargomïzhsky remarked, Serov
had hunting dogs from the Imperial Kennels on the stage in *Rogneda*,
as he had had camels in *Judith*: 'Why shouldn't his operas succeed?')
Serov himself confessed in his autobiographical notes[10] that he began
with these scenes: 'The music, like that of *Judith*, was composed not to
the words of the text, which did not yet exist, but to situations clearly
defined in the author's imagination', and the task of providing words to
the 'already prepared or half-prepared music' was entrusted to a minor
dramatist, D. V. Averkiev.

The parts of Rogneda and Prince Vladimir were conceived for
Valentina Bianchi and Sariotti, the original Judith and Holofernes, but
Bianchi was now singing Judith in Moscow and the part had to be given
to an inexperienced soprano, Yashchenskaya (Broni), who actually sang
it at the first performance on 27 October/9 November 1865. But shortly
afterwards Serov rewrote the part for a contralto, Darya Leonova, once
a pupil of Glinka, many years later the friend of Musorgsky, though it
is described in the published score as for mezzo-soprano. Vladimir was
actually sung by the greatest Russian bass of the nineteenth century,
Petrov—the original Susanin, Ruslan, Miller (in *Rusalka*), and Varlaam
—while Sariotti was the high priest of Perun.

The popular success of *Rogneda* was even greater than that of *Judith*;
it enjoyed some seventy performances at the Maryinsky in the first five
years—more than any previous Russian opera except *Askold's Grave*
(which is also concerned with Vladimir the Great); and it continued to
be the most popular of Serov's operas at least until the beginning of the
present century. Even Rimsky-Korsakov confessed many years later, in
his autobiography, that at the time '*Rogneda* strongly interested me
and a great deal in it pleased me, e.g. the witch, the idol-worshipping
chorus, the chorus in the audience-hall, the dance of the buffoons, the
hunt prelude, the 7/4 chorus and much else—in snatches. I was also
pleased by the coarse but colourful and effective orchestration . . . I did

not dare to confess all this in the Balakirev circle and even, as one sincerely devoted to their ideas, abused this opera among my acquaintances ... I remembered a great deal, having heard the opera two or three times, and enjoyed playing excerpts from it from memory.' A year or two later his memory was treacherously to offer him the music of the witch scene when he came to write his 'musical picture' *Sadko*,[11] and the triplet figuration of the Act V finale (as he afterwards recognized himself) for the third movement of *Antar*.

After *Rogneda* Serov wanted another Russian subject. He became fascinated by the Ukraine, its Cossack people and its language—as early as 1861 he had become interested in its folk music—and contemplated a ballet or 'symphonic pantomime' on Gogol's *Christmas Eve*, but nothing came of this except two Ukrainian dances for orchestra, *Grechaniki* (= buckwheat cakes) and a *hopak*, though it is true he returned to it as an opera subject in the last months of his life. Another Gogol subject, 'a musical illustration to the second chapter of *Taras Bulba*', got no further than an orchestral *Dance of Zaporozhtsy Cossaks*, which was later published by Bessel; it has a characteristic *pp* ending. What he wanted, he told Zvantsov,[12] was 'something, quick-bloody—with slaughter and shooting (in the right place)', but when his final choice in the spring of 1867 fell on Ostrovsky's *Don't live as you'd like to, but live as God commands* (*Ne tak zhivi, kak khochetsya, a tak zhivi, kak Bog velit*), it at first lacked this element of slaughter. It is a typical Ostrovsky play of contemporary life, a thoroughly Russian subject quite in keeping with the 'naturalism', the 'truth to life', fashionable in Russia in the 1860s. A young merchant (Peter), bored by his wife (Dasha) and life in general, is wildly in love with an innkeeper's daughter (Grunya), to whom he represents that he is a bachelor. Grunya discovers the truth, through an overheard conversation, and will have nothing more to do with him. She goes off with another admirer to the *maslyanitsa*, the Shrovetide fair. Eremka, the evil smith of the inn, persuades Peter to go to the fair, too, and when he is drunk suggests that he should murder his wife so as to be able to marry Grunya. Instead Peter decides to drown himself. But as he is standing by an ice-hole in the Moskva river, the church bells sound for Lent; he pulls himself together and decides to go home and 'not live as he wants to'.

Serov turned to Ostrovsky himself with a request that he would convert his play into a libretto: 'I am convinced that the inner dramatic power calls for warm, truly Russian sounds, quite in character with the matchless *songs* of the Great-Russian people. You yourself—a

connoisseur of the songs, know *what* is in them! Remember that even
in your play all the characters sing from time to time—at every opportunity they take to song.' Ostrovsky complied and all went well so far
as the first three acts were concerned. With the fourth he ran into
trouble, for he wished to introduce in the *maslyanitsa* devilish figures,
horned and tailed, so that Eremka was made 'a sort of *Freischütz*
Caspar: a semi-devil in a peasant's coat'. Serov flatly rejected this idea—
though a phrase in the fourth act libretto at least gave him a suitable
title for his opera: 'hostile power'—but he was being tempted in another
direction. Already Zvantsev had suggested: 'Let your Peter go home
and kill his wife like a chicken, and at once over his head booms out the
first heavy stroke of the Lenten bells', but Serov had sensibly rejected
the idea: 'My hero is no Othello! Peter will go back to drinking as before
for some years yet.' Nevertheless, when the first three acts were finished,
he changed his mind and decided to end with the murder, 'only not at
home behind a screen, but in a tumbledown hut outside the town. Far
off, across the snow, one sees the church and hears the bells.' So, for
the third time, murder (or attempted murder) provided the climax of a
Serov opera.[13] However, Ostrovsky would no more accept this idea for
the fifth act than Serov would his devils in the fourth, and in the end
the libretto for the last two acts had to be supplied by P. I. Kalashnikov,
a well-known hack who had translated *Les Huguenots, Le Prophète,
Traviata,* and Gounod's *Faust.* (The participation of another hand,
A. F. Zhokhov, seems to be apocryphal.) Yet Serov did not live to
finish the music. He died suddenly, on 20 January/1 February 1871,
with Act V only roughed out, and the score had to be completed—
the whole act amounts to only twenty-two pages of vocal score—and
orchestrated by his young friend N. F. Solovyev, who also had to score
the introduction and latter part of Peter's *scena* in Act I. The opera was
produced at the Maryinsky within three months (on 19 April/1 May),
with Sariotti as Eremka and Petrov singing only two minor parts. The
success was very moderate.

Although he had not finished *Hostile Power*, Serov had actually
begun yet another opera. It was on his old favourite subject, Gogol's
Christmas Eve, and no less a poet than Polonsky was to provide the
libretto. He already had two completed dances and some sketches from
the ballet of 1868, and his widow was able to put together and publish
a posthumous suite of four numbers: (1) Oksana, Vakula, and the girls;

(2) The Empress's ball – minuet; (3) mazurka; (4) arietta – Oksana's grief in Vakula's absence. The after-history of Polonsky's libretto, *Vakula the Smith*, and of the competition for settings of it – in which Tchaikovsky won the first prize and N. F. Solovyev the second – is well known.

Serov's operas did not, so far as I have been able to discover, survive the Revolution. One can now contemplate them as historically important museum-pieces and consider their music with more detachment than his contemporaries could command. To begin with, we can dismiss the charges of Wagnerism altogether; whatever Serov has in common with Wagner is due to common factors in their musical ancestry: Spontini, Halévy, and, above all, Meyerbeer. 'Meyerbeer c'est le favori de mon âme', he said in his youth, and, although he came to recognize his favourite's weaknesses, he remained faithful. (Serov makes free use of thematic reminiscence for dramatic purposes, but not more than Weber or Glinka.) *Judith* is a Meyerbeerian grand opera in all but the simplicity of its plot; *Rogneda* lacks that saving condition. *Hostile Power* still retains Meyerbeerian conventions, though the subject and the musical material are totally different; the only opera with which one can compare it is Tchaikovsky's exactly contemporary *Voevoda*, another Ostrovsky subject similarly dressed up in a great deal of folk melody. Indeed the three operas are musically so different that it is hardly possible to consider them synoptically; they need to be looked at separately. Yet they do reveal a few common traits which one can call 'Serov's style'.

The broad plan of *Judith*, its oriental third and fourth acts framed by the Hebrew 'outside' ones, anticipates that of *Prince Igor* and reminds one that – despite its non-Russian subject – it stands in the line from Glinka and Dargomïzhsky to Musorgsky and Rimsky-Korsakov. But Serov's orientalism is much less convincing than Glinka's or Borodin's. It is very much a matter of flattened sixths in the major scale and much of it derives from Glinka; Holofernes' march is clearly the child of Chernomor's in *Ruslan* by the march in *Prince Kholmsky*. But the songs and dances of the odalisques and almahs, languorous with cor anglais and harp, or wild and colourfully scored (almost everyone from Wagner downward admitted the effectiveness of Serov's orchestration in general), compare very favourably with the exotic essays of Meyerbeer or Bizet. And Vagoa ('Bagoas the eunuch', but he is a tenor) has a pretty 'Indian song' (Ex. 1).

Ex. 1

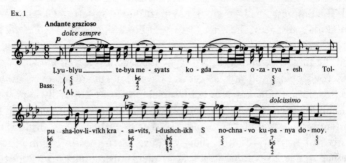

Much more interesting are the points of affinity with Musorgsky. As I have suggested elsewhere,[14] Musorgsky may well have been influenced in his choice of *Salammbô* as an opera subject by the parallel with *Judith*, the heroine's penetration of the besiegers' camp to seduce Mâtho and recover the stolen *Zaïmph*, but I would no longer say 'there is no trace of any musical influence': the scene of Salammbô before the image of Tanit would hardly have been written as it is, if Musorgsky had not had Serov's odalisques in mind. Again: was not the scene of Boris's hallucination probably suggested—dramatically, not musically—by Holofernes'? But the general affinities are also striking. Consider, for instance, Serov's occasional use of curiously angular themes, such as that which accompanies the slow pacing of the elders at the very beginning of Act I (Ex. 2) or Avra's melodic line when, near the end of

Ex. 2

Act II, she pleads with her mistress to give up her plan. A little earlier in the same Act, both Judith's calm (Ex. 3) and the harmony of Avra's

Ex. 3

outburst of horror (Ex. 4) are not far removed from Musorgsky's

musical world. When Judith, near the end of her prayer, sings of 'the wings of angels' protecting her (Ex. 5) this music too must have planted

a general idea in Musorgsky's mind from which was to come Boris's farewell to his son; indeed the accompaniment figure of Boris's blessing (first flute and violas—or harp harmonics and *muted* violas in Rimsky-Korsakov's score)—which we must remember was originally Salammbô's prayer—reflects the figure *X* in Ex. 3. As for bold, empirical, but expressive harmony, while there are examples in *Judith*, Serov was to go further in later operas, notably in *Hostile Power*, when Peter learns that Grunya has discovered he already has a wife, and when the murder is done.

Serov's harmony in general has a good deal in common with Dargomïzhsky's: it is either conventional, in which case it is often clumsy
and amateurish, or experimental, in which case the experiment may or
may not come off. He does not mind ending a scene with a dissonance:
Holofernes' march on its second appearance, where the tonic D is to the
end clouded by an unresolved second, followed by a *ppp* A in the bass.
This last is typical of the quiet endings already mentioned. They are
numerous: the end of Act I (which Musorgsky, as we have seen, praised
even in the letter to Balakirev); the equally quiet end of Act II, where
the muttering quaver-figure of the Judith–Avra duet dies away just as
the semiquavers of Pimen's cell or the quavers of the idiot scene were
to die away in *Boris*; the chorus of worshippers of Perun in Act I of
Rogneda; the penultimate scene of the fourth act of *Hostile Power*,
where as Peter and Eremka leave the stage the overlapping echoes of
the folk-songish theme die away in a manner later made familiar by
Borodin.

Ex. 7

Yet one more point in *Judith* evidently impressed Musorgsky: the
handling of the chorus. In his own day Serov was accused of treating
the chorus, particularly the Jewish choruses, as if the work were an
oratorio; there is indeed some rather clumsy, square-cut fugal writing.
But he must be given full credit for not using the chorus simply as a
musical mass; it is a protagonist even when it is employed monumentally.
But it is not always used monumentally; Serov again and again asks for
'not all' the tenors and basses, for only 'two voices' from the contraltos
(while the sopranos sing *sotto voce* before also being reduced to two
voices), for 'not all' tenors and then 'others'. The waiting crowd in the
last finale of *Rogneda* is handled naturalistically in the same way: 'one
tenor', 'one bass', 'another bass', 'some altos', 'two or three sopranos',
and so on, just like the crowd in *Boris*. The crowd jeering at the
Pecheneg prisoners in the first act finale of *Rogneda* is quite as natural-
istic as the chorus jeering at Khrushchov in Musorgsky's opera.

When *Judith* was first produced in Moscow, a critic complained rather unreasonably of its lack of Russianness. That cannot be said of *Rogneda*. It abounds in Russianness of one sort or another: genuine popular melody (the fool's song in Act III and probably the women's chorus); imitated folk melody (Rogneda's son's little song in Act IV); the *bilina*-type melody at the end of the opera, begun by the old leader of the Christian pilgrims and gradually taken up by the other

Ex. 8

characters, and finally by the chorus, in a really splendid climax which left its mark on more than one fine passage in Rimsky-Korsakov and perhaps on the end of *Igor*; and things like the girls' dance in Act II, with its final effective combination of the two themes which

Ex. 9

(Originally: G major, *Giocoso scherzando*)

might have come straight out of *Life for the Tsar*.[15] Serov's techniques for the treatment of 'Russian' material are also derived from Glinka, though he seems at first to have found it hard not to harmonize modal melodies as major or minor. *Hostile Power* is, of course, full of folk or folk-like melodies which here compensate handsomely for Serov's normal weakness of melodic invention; it is hardly possible to distinguish the genuine from the imitation, and some of the most beautiful, as yet unidentified, must be—incredulously—attributed to Serov himself. Dasha's song at the very beginning of Act I sets the standard—and it will be seen that Serov had at last realized that the best thing to do with a folk-tune may be to leave it almost alone (Ex. 10).

Her innocent admirer Vasya's song at the end of the act is even more beautiful (Ex. 11).

Serov had by now also hit on the idea of using snatches of these melodies to cover the caesuras in the vocal line and fill the gaps in recitative, so that a great deal of the score, like that of Tchaikovsky's *Voevoda*, sounds very 'kuchkist'—at a date when the only *kuchkist* opera so far produced had been Cui's uncharacteristic *William Ratcliff*. (On the other hand, Peter's very Musorgskian 'V polnoch, vo temnom lesu' (At midnight, in the dark forest) was composed *after* the publication of 'Savishna'.) The fair-scene, not so much the *maslyanitsa* procession itself as the bagpipers, the cries of the sellers of bread, cakes, and drinks, and so on, is in the direct line between such late eighteenth-century works as the Pashkevich *Sanktpeterburgsky gostiny dvor* and Musorgsky's *Sorochintsy Fair*, a line which leads on to *Petrushka*.

# The Operas of Serov

In *Hostile Power* Serov also developed the device of sharp musical contrast which he had employed in the two earlier works. A purely musical combination has already been mentioned (cf. Ex. 9); there is a similar example, which it is tempting to call 'pre-Polovtsian', in the oriental dances of *Judith*. A striking passage of dramatic contrast occurs when Judith continues imperturbably singing of her intention to go to the Assyrian camp, against her maid's agitated recitative of protest. This effect is repeated and exaggerated in the Act I finale of *Rogneda*, when Ruald goes on imperturbably praying while the high priest of Perun and the people cry 'Death to him!' But the climax of melodrama is reached in the scene of the attempted murder of the sleeping Vladimir, where a solo violin plays an extended cadenza-like passage, recalling the scène in the witch's cave (x in Ex. 12), over the solemn chords of the pilgrims' chorus from the previous act.

Ex. 12

But in *Hostile Power* contrasts of gay music with sinister action are used with fine irony: for instance, the distant music of the *maslyanitsa* and the drunken revellers in the pothouse as Eremka tightens his hold on Peter. Again, the light-hearted chorus of girls, first heard behind the scenes at the beginning of Act III, sounds again from the distance when Peter has been thrown over by Grunya, and the evil Eremka approaches him for the first time, and is heard in the orchestra in the last Act, when Peter, lurking in the ravine, hears his victim approaching ('Hark, here she is!') (Ex. 13). Coming here suddenly, as it does, after the *ppp*

Ex. 13

storm of whistling wind, suggested by an incessant chromatic semiquaver
figure, with the occasional bark of a dog, it comes like a flash of ironic
lightning.

Even in the Preface to *Rogneda* Serov claimed to be striving for
'*dramatic truth* in sounds, although for the sake of this truth, for the
characteristic nature of the music, "conventional" beauty, the "jewelled"
elegance of musical forms had to be sacrificed'. He was far from achieving
that in most of *Rogneda*, but he came near to it in *Hostile Power*.
Asafiev contended[16] that, after all, *Judith* was Serov's best opera: 'Its
stern, serious language and massively rough rudimentary construction,
have a flavour of archaism ... The score looks like the irregular but
enduring and powerful stonework of the walls and towers of ancient
cities'. That is partly true, yet there is also a good deal of rubble-work
and grouting. But it is something to have fashioned two such totally
different works as *Judith* and *Hostile Power*, as well as the best pages
of *Rogneda*, and to have breathed some real musical life into such
puppets as the Jewish heroine and the evil Russian smith. These are
surprising achievements for a brilliant, cantankerous, critical rather than
creative, mind.

NOTES

1. *M. P. Musorgsky: Pisma i dokumentï* (Moscow, 1932), p. 85. Musorgsky's musical quotations are interesting in that they show the changes made by Serov before his opera was printed, e.g. the Assyrian chorus about 'the coming of the Hebrew beauty' in Act III, where there can be no question of a lapse of memory on Musorgsky's part.

2. Printed in N. Findeisen, *A. N. Serov: evo zhizn i muzïkalnaya deyatelnost*, 2nd edn. (St Petersburg, 1904), p. 41. According to V. S. Baskin, *A. N. Serov* (Moscow, 1890), p. 110, the overture was published by Jurgenson but I have not been able to see it.

3. Findeisen, 'Novïe materialï dlya biografii A. N. Serova. Pisma evo k A. A. Bakuninu (1850–3)', *Ezhegodnik Imperatorskikh Teatrov*, iv (1895), supplement 3, p. 110.

4. Findeisen, 'Otrïvok iz yunosheskoy operï A. N. Serova "Mayskaya noch"', *Russkaya muzïkalnaya gazeta*, iii (1896), col. 29. Findeisen prints the whole fragment.

5. 'Spontini i evo muzïka', *Panteon*, i (1852), p. 1.

6. Reminiscences of Serov in *Russkaya Starina* (August 1888), reprinted in Findeisen, *A. N. Serov*, p. 88.

7. He afterwards translated *Lohengrin*.

8. This letter—with Serov's furious reply, also to Musorgsky, saying he had expected something better from Balakirev than the pedantry of a *musicus ex professo*—was printed by Theophil Tolstoy in *Russkaya Starina*, ix (February 1874), pp. 351–2.

9. *Perepiska M. A. Balakireva s V. V. Stasovïm* (Moscow, 1935), pp. 179–87.

10. Quoted by Findeisen, *A. N. Serov*, p. 113.

11. See Abraham, *Slavonic and Romantic Music* (London, 1968) pp. 196–7. There is an excellent chapter on *Rogneda* in Richard Taruskin, *Opera and Drama in Russia* (Ann Arbor, 1981) with numerous musical examples, pp. 86–120, and four complete numbers, pp. 458–9, 463–8, 481–2, and 489–90.

12. Reminiscences, quoted by Findeisen, *A. N. Serov*, pp. 12 ff.

13. Incredibly, Rosa Newmarch completes the parallel with *Judith* and *Rogneda* by making the woman the murderer: 'The neglected wife discovers her husband's infidelity, and murders him in a jealous frenzy', *The Russian Opera* (London, 1914), p. 158. Since Mrs Newmarch evidently did not know the score in 1914, we need not take too much notice of her critical remarks in the 1908 edition of *Grove*, which still stood in the fifth edition.

14. In my edition of Calvocoressi's *Mussorgsky* (London, 1946), p. 98, n. 1.

15. However, Karatigin, who had seen the sketches for *Rogneda*, tells us that Serov himself had marked this dance 'imitation of Dargomïzhsky'; similarly Rogneda's monologue in Act IV was inscribed 'imitation of Gounod', and the opening chorus of the act 'in Villebois's style' (i.e. of the popular choruses in Villebois's *Natasha* of 1861); see *Ezhegodnik Imperatorskikh Teatrov*, 1910, part iv, p. 108. Another effective combination, like Ex. 9, of contrasted themes previously heard separately, occurs in the odalisques' dances in Act III of *Judith*.

16. *Izbrannïe trudï*, ii (Moscow, 1954), p. 336.

3. *Heine, Cui, and 'William Ratcliff'*

During the period 1869-1914 at least six composers of different nation-alities produced operas based on Heine's youthful tragedy *William Ratcliff*: the Franco-Lithuanian César Cui (1869), the Italians Emilio Pizzi (1889) and Pietro Mascagni (1895), the Frenchman Xavier Leroux (1906), the Dutchman Cornelius Dopper (1909), and the Swiss Volkmar Andreae (1914). In addition, the Hungarian Mór Vavrinecz (1858-1913) is said to have composed a Ratcliff opera but I have not been able to trace its production. Why the subject had to wait nearly fifty years before it attracted a composer, why (so far as I know) it has not attracted one since 1914, and why (to the best of my knowledge) it has never attracted a German musician, are questions I shall not attempt to answer. *Ratcliff* has obvious operatic possibilities, yet the earliest composition remains the most interesting. This, too, is curious: that a play on a Scottish subject by a German Jew should have found its best composer in a man who passed as a Russian but whose father was a French prisoner of war of 1812, Antoine Cui, who married a Lithuanian lady, Julia Gucewicz.

Cui preferred to conceal his origin behind a mask of bellicose musical patriotism and the world has accepted him at his own valuation as a Russian nationalist, as not merely a friend (which he was) but as a co-equal of Balakirev, Borodin, Musorgsky, and Rimsky-Korsakov. But he stated his position correctly and frankly in a letter of 22 June 1897 to Felipe Pedrell:[1]

Un sujet russe d'opéra ne m'irait pas du tout. Bien que russe, je suis d'origine mi-française, mi-lithuanienne et je n'ai pas le sens de la musique russe dans mes veines. J'aurais fait de contrefaçons plus ou moins réussies comme pour exemple Rubinstein, mais j'aurais manqué de sincérité. C'est pourquoi à l'exception de mon premier opéra *Le Prisonnier du Caucase*, tous les sujets de mes opéras sont et seront étrangers.

This first opera, *Kavkazky plennik*, was certainly based on a Russian subject—a narrative poem by Pushkin—and the hero's aria in Act I has a faintly Russian flavour; but the predominant musical colouring of the opera is not Russian but Circassian. Cui had succumbed to the charm of the oriental element in Glinka's *Ruslan i Lyudmila*. *The Prisoner* was never given in its original two-act form of 1857, but in 1881 Cui added a third act between the two original ones, which he also revised and reorchestrated, and this version was produced at the Maryinsky Theatre, St Petersburg, in 1883.

In 1857 Cui was twenty-two years old and had only recently graduated from the Academy of Engineering. (It should be remembered that he was by profession a military engineer, in later years a very distinguished one and recognized as the greatest Russian authority on fortification.) For the libretto of his Pushkin opera he had turned to a younger fellow-student at the Academy, Viktor Aleksandrovich Krïlov,[2] who later became a successful dramatist under the pseudonym 'Viktor Aleksandrov'. In 1858 Krïlov also supplied the text for a little one-act skit, *Sïn mandarina* (The Mandarin's Son), written with piano accompaniment for a domestic performance in which the part of the heroine was sung by the composer's young wife, the mandarin was sung by Musorgsky, and Cui played the piano. Thus it was natural that Cui should turn to Krïlov for help[3] in adapting Pleshcheyev's 'beautiful translation' of *William Ratcliff* when, in 1861, his choice fell on it for his next opera:

I was charmed by its fantastic nature, by the character of the hero himself — vague but passionate, subjected to the influences of fate — by Heine's talent and Pleshcheyev's beautiful translation. (Beautiful verse has always fascinated me and had an undoubted influence on my music.) Heine's text remained almost unchanged, though with some cuts and additions made by Krïlov for the sake of greater development of the choruses.[4]

However, a difficulty arose with the German version of the libretto when the opera was published, as Cui explained in his preface (dated 'Leipzig, den 1. Juli 1869') to the vocal score.[5]

Als ich den Entschluß gefaßt die Heinesche Tragödie *William Ratcliff* als Sujet zu meiner Opera zu benutzen, war mein eifrigstes Bestreben, womöglichst nicht nur das Sujet, sondern auch den Text dieses erhabenen Poeten beizubehalten. In der russischen Sprache (die Musik ist im Original zum ins russische übersetzten Text geschrieben) gelang es mir in einem solchen Grade, daß die Mitte des ersten Actes, die Hälfte des zweiten und der ganzen dritte Act, völlig und ganz ohne Veränderung dem Heineschen Texte, in der ausgezeichneten Uebersetzung des Herrn

Plestchejeff entsprechen; doch da ich mein Werk auch mit deutschem
Text herausgeben wollte, und der Originaltext der Heineschen Tragödie
in vielen Stellen nicht paßte, so war man genöthigt, eine prosaische
Uebersetzung ins deutsche zu unternehmen, die um so schwieriger war,
da sie nicht nur dem russischen Text, sondern auch der regelmäßigen
Declamation der musikalischen Rede entsprechen sollte. Die Liebe zu
den Heineschen Dichtungen, die sich dadurch geoffenbart, daß ich eine
von seinen Tragödien zum Sujet meiner Oper erwählt, wird gewiß
einigermaßen mir zur Rechtfertigung dienen für die obenerwähnte ganz
wider meinen Willen vorgegangene, unumgängliche Verstümmelung.

Incidentally, serious *Verstümmelungen* in Cui's own setting of the
Russian text – the incorrect stressing of Scottish names, even the hero's,
Wil-*liam* Rat-*cliff*, Les-*ley*, and others – are corrected in the German
libretto; but even Heine seems to have thought that Mac*don*ald was
stressed on the last syllable. The nature of the German adaptation may
be seen from MacGregor's opening words:

Heine

Ihr seid jetzt Mann und Weib. Wie eure Hände
Vereinigt sind, so sollen auch die Herzen,
In Leid und Freud, vereinigt sein auf immer.
Zwei mächt'ge Sakramente, das der Kirche
Und das der Liebe, haben euch verbunden;
Ein Doppelsegen ruht auf euren Häuptern,
Und auch den Vatersegen leg ich drauf.

Libretto

Ihr seid nun Mann und Weib, geliebte Kinder, wie eure Hände jetzt
vereint auf ewig, so mögen denn von nun an eure Herzen in Leid und
Freud' vereint auf immer werden. Zwei Sacramente haben euch verbunden, das der Kirche, und das der Liebe, ein Doppelsegen ruht auf
euren Häuptern, Kinder und füg' ich den Vatersegen noch bei.

Elsewhere – e.g. in Ratcliff's narrative (Act II scene 4) at 'Als Knabe
schon sah ich' and throughout the whole of Maria's *Romanze* (Act III
scene 1), 'Ach nein! Im Anfang'– the German libretto is still more
faithful to Heine.

The cuts and insertions are more serious. Whereas Heine plunges
straight into the action with MacGregor's blessing, Cui preceded it with
an extended but undistinguished wedding chorus in mazurka and
polonaise rhythms, which is partly repeated before Douglas's narrative;

the narrative itself is naturally drastically cut, and after Maria's swoon
the chorus re-enters, commenting on everything in conventional operatic
style to the end of the scene. After the conversation between Douglas
and MacGregor there is a completely new scene: a brilliantly lighted
hall in MacGregor's castle with the guests singing a greeting chorus to a
genuine Scottish melody, 'Tibbie Fowler', which has already been heard
in the orchestra at the end of scene 1; it is against this background that
Lesley has to enter unobtrusively, find Douglas and give him Ratcliff's
note. The first three scenes of Act II have no connection with Heine,
except that they are laid in an inn and introduce two characters, besides
Lesley, with the same names: Robin and Tom. Instead of Heine's
wonderfully atmospheric passage, with the little boy's prayer, there is a
scene of drunken revelry with song and dance; Lesley eggs on the girls
to tease the hopelessly intoxicated Robin and then contributes a
drinking-song—which predictably has a choral refrain. It is only with
Ratcliff's appearance—his first in the opera—in scene 4 that we get
back to Heine and Ratcliff's account to Lesley of the phantoms that
have haunted him all his life and of his love-hate for Maria. One textual
cut must be mentioned here, the removal of nine lines which clearly
suggested the basic idea of Pushkin's *Queen of Spades* and hence of a
much more famous Russian opera:

> Sogar beim Pharo fand ich keine Ruh.
> Marias Aug schwamm auf dem grünen Tische;
> Marias Hand bog mir die Parolis;
> Und in dem Bild der eckigen Coeur-Dame
> Sah ich Marias himmelschöne Züge!
> Maria war's, kein dünnes Kartenblatt;
> Maria war's, ich fühlte ihren Atem;
> Sie winkte: ja! sie nickte: ja!—va banque!—
> Zum Teufel war mein Geld . . .

In Pushkin and Tchaikovsky it is the same game, pharo, but the Queen
of Hearts, a beautiful young woman, becomes the Queen of Spades, an
ugly old one.

The scene at the Black Rock compresses Ratcliff's long soliloquy but
otherwise follows Heine closely, as does the whole of Act III: Maria's
Romanze, Margarethe's account of the parallel tragic story of Ratcliff's
father and Maria's mother, Ratcliff's appearance, the love-duet, and the
bloody denouement.

The composition of this libretto took Cui seven years, 1861–8.

Owing to the insufficiency of his salary, he and his wife opened a preparatory boarding-school for youths wishing to enter the Engineering Academy, and he took upon himself the teaching of all subjects except languages.

Even the summer with its holidays was not free; on the contrary this was the busiest pre-examination time. Besides, one had not only to instruct the boarders but to educate them. Thus we were together the whole time like one big family, eating together, living in the country, walking, boating, and so on. It will be understood that in such conditions I could write only at odd moments and I did not write in order from the first scene to the last but separate scenes from different acts which most interested me at the given moment.[6]

If Rimsky-Korsakov's not very reliable memory can be trusted, the scene at the Black Rock and Maria's *Romanze* 'already existed' by 1866.[7] When in 1868 the production date was drawing near and the full score was still unfinished, friends gave a helping hand; Rimsky-Korsakov orchestrated the first scene of Act I, the wedding chorus and blessing, and Balakirev Maria's *Romanze* in Act III.[8] The opera was given its first performance on 14/26 February 1869 at the Maryinsky Theatre, St Petersburg, under Nápravník. Despite the excellent cast, which included Platonova as Maria, Leonova as Margarethe, and Melnikov as Ratcliff, it had only seven performances.

Forty years later, in the autobiographical article already quoted from, Cui explained his non-success in the first place by the hostility he had aroused by his activity as a critic, in the second by 'the novelty of its form':

In it I tried to carry into practice our operatic ideals; it was the first to appear in the battle for them (*The Stone Guest, The Maid of Pskov, Boris Godunov* appeared later). In it the listeners heard, instead of the usual arias consisting of the obligatory *andante* and *allegro*, narratives written in completely free form; they found choruses with a certain symphonic development; they found the *Leitmotiv* of Ratcliff himself, developing and changing in relation to the stage situation and mood, although we had at that time almost no understanding of Wagner's tendencies.

This demands a great deal of commentary. By 'our' operatic ideals, Cui means the ideals of dramatic truth rather than melodic beauty, of 'the note as the direct expression of the word', propounded by Dargomïzhsky and enthusiastically accepted by the Balakirev circle; *The Stone Guest* in which Dargomïzhsky embodied them most drastically, was almost complete when he died on 5/17 January, a few weeks before the production of *Ratcliff*. (The only significant Russian operas since the death of Glinka had been Serov's *Judith* (1863) and *Rogneda* (1865); Tchaikovsky's *Voevoda* was produced in Moscow a fortnight before *Ratcliff*.) But in *Ratcliff*, as in *Boris* and Rimsky-Korsakov's *Maid of Pskov*, dramatic truth is strongly diluted by lyrical melody; the recitative frequently becomes arioso. As to the freer forms, they had become common enough in every form of serious opera by the middle of the century and one wonders how 'new' they were even to the fashionable Petersburg public. *Ratcliff* seldom reminds one of Dargomïzhsky, still less of Schumann whose influence was detected both by a friendly critic – Rimsky-Korsakov, who had to play the delicate role of substitute for Cui in the columns of the *St Peterburgskiya Vedomosti* – and by hostile ones such as Serov and Laroche.[9] The 6/8 theme first heard near the end of the inn scene (Ratcliff's 'blut'ge Rache schwor ich bis an's Grab' and 'Ich gab den Schwur', which is transformed on the cellos at Lesley's reply, and heard again in the duel) is mildly reminiscent of Schumann's early piano style, but Cui's melodic line at its best, as in the love-duet (Ex. 1), is closer to French lyrical opera – Gounod, for

Ex. 1

instance–than to Schumann, while Lesley's song, indeed most of the earlier part of the inn scene, has reminded almost every critic of Auber.

Nevertheless Cui does exhibit considerable dramatic power in laying bare the schizophrenic nature of this strange Byronic or early-Schillerian anti-hero who has dropped into the Walter Scott country. During the first half of the opera we have only heard about Ratcliff, so that all that follows is gradual revelation of his true self. When he enters, there is a sudden change to 'dramatic truth' in his music; for a while we get 'the note as the direct expression of the word' and the whole texture of the beginning of scene 4 suggests one of the less impressive moments of *Boris*. His narrative to Lesley is in the already mentioned arioso style, not particularly individual but dramatically adequate – and remarkable for the non-appearance of 'the *Leitmotiv* of Ratcliff himself'.

On this point, more than any other, Cui's own statement quoted above needs correction and elucidation. There are no genuine *Leitmotive* in *William Ratcliff*. Cui makes generous and effective and skilful use of *Erinnerungsmotive*, which he transforms plastically as Weber had done long before in *Euryanthe*, but neither of the two themes associated with Ratcliff himself is 'heard during his narration; they appear first (except in the Introduction to the opera, a musical portrait of the hero) in the Black Rock scene ('Ha, mein'thalb kann er sich ganz verhüllen' and 'Doch als Beweis der Freundschaft'). What we do hear during the narrative is a theme associated with the two phantoms who have haunted him since boyhood (Ex. 2). (Its slight motivic relationship to the 6/8 'oath' theme already mentioned was probably unintentional.)

Ex. 2   Moderato assai

At the beginning of the *allegro* of his narrative this theme is developed in a more vigorous form. With very different scoring it opens the scene at the Black Rock, which it pervades with varied harmonic and orchestral colourings and associated with very different emotions; sometimes the segment *x* appears alone or with different continuations; when the male phantom (his father) appears to him he sings it in yet another new form, *ppp andantino* ('Was glotzen deine stieren Augen, du Doppelgänger, den ich hasse'), and a further variant of this is thundered out by the orchestra, *ff più mosso*, at the end of the scene. In the last scene, harmonized with ironic sweetness, it appears before he kills Maria ('O! sträub' dich nicht' mein süßes Lieb, der Tod ist ja so süß') and before he kills himself ('Ich bleib mit dir auf immer, du meine Lieb'). But when, upon this, the two phantoms—exorcized at last—appear, embracing, they do so not to this theme but to the music of their love-duet (Ex. 1) played by cello and clarinet.

Although there are some cross-references in the score—for instance the music of MacGregor's blessing in Act I scene 1 is heard in the same key and the same scoring at the beginning of Act III scene 1 (Maria in her bridal dress), the same music is heard when the father's ghost seems to prompt the killing of Maria and again when it comes after the deed is done—the only recurrent theme equally important to Ex. 2 is that to which Margarethe sings her fateful snatch of the famous old Scottish ballad, 'Quhy dois zour brand sae drap wi' bluid? Edward!', which, usually in Herder's translation, has attracted so many composers. I quote Cui's version in the unaccompanied form sung by Margarethe at the beginning of the last scene, after the love duet and leading immediately to his resolve to kill his own love.

Ex. 3

In *Ratcliff* this song belongs to one of the most primitive types of *Erinnerungsmotiv*, like 'Une fièvre brûlante' in Grétry's *Richard Coeur-de-lion*; its significance—known only to MacGregor and Margarethe herself, until she reveals it in the last act—lies in its association with the tragic, guilty love of Maria's mother for William's father and with MacGregor's jealous murder of Edward Ratcliff. It is first heard in the orchestra early in the first scene of Act I, when Margarethe utters the words only in monotone; conversely, the first time she actually sings the melody it is to different words: 'Thu' auf die theuren Aeuglein, mein Püppchen!' Its motives then supply the basis of the following ensemble of Maria's awakening from her swoon and it turns up again in the final chorus of the scene. In the last act it naturally plays a very notable part and at the very end, when the bloody tragedy is accomplished, it is developed in a passage of extraordinary beauty. Instead of ending, like Heine, with Margarethe's crazy laughter, Cui fills her words with a sense of ineffable peace, 'Auch er fand hier endlich Ruh' von des Lebens Mühen', and the chorus comments, *pp*, 'Des Schicksals Opfer sehen wir hier im Todesschlaf versunken, endlich im Todesschlaf Ruh, Versöhnung und Fried' auf ewig' in music which will bear comparison with almost anything in nineteenth-century Russian opera.

Comparison of this work of great talent with the work of genius composed immediately afterwards by Cui's friend Musorgsky is instructive; for, despite the very different gifts of the composers and the very different subjects of the operas, *William Ratcliff* has quite a lot in common with *Boris Godunov*: the same combination of elements of Meyerbeer with elements of Dargomïzhsky, the same mixture of closed vocal forms with freely expanded ones often in not very dissimilar idioms and orchestrally accompanied in much the same way.

Even the effect of alternating, functionally unrelated chords at the beginning of the coronation scene in *Boris* is paralleled at the point where Ratcliff falls in the duel (recalled twice later in the scene). Indeed it is in such harmonic strokes that Cui most clearly affirms his affinity with his colleagues: the similar pivoting of woodwind chords on the C of the horns and F sharp of the drum at 'Maria . . . Blut . . . wer sprach es aus?' near the end of the Black Rock scene (which gave Rimsky-Korsakov a hint for the assembly-bell in *The Maid of Pskov*) and the parallel passage in the last scene of all; the wholetone bass[10] in MacGregor's narration at the words 'der Bräutigam der holden Braut war nicht zu finden'; the unresolved seconds when Ratcliff is excited to the killing ('ihr Leib is marmorstarr, doch aus der Brust schrillt ihr der heiß're Sang . . .').

Musorgsky thought highly of *Ratcliff*. He wrote to Cui (letter of 15 August 1868)—and there is no reason to doubt his sincerity:

Ratcliff is not only yours but ours. It crept out of your artistic womb under our eyes, grew, became strong, and now it is going out to the people before our eyes and not once has it disappointed our expectation . . . What is strange: Heine's *Ratcliff* goes on stilts—your *Ratcliff* is a figure of demoniac passion and so alive that, thanks to your music, one doesn't see the stilts—one is blinded. That's why *Ratcliff* is more than just a good thing; it's the first such thing in music—perfectly realised.[11]

It is true that Rimsky-Korsakov possessed a score of *Ratcliff* in which Balakirev had scribbled sarcastic comments—'What are these magpie hops?', 'What Asiatic part-writing have we here?', and so on[12]— but on the whole the opera was warmly admired by all his colleagues.

Despite the double embarrassment of personal friendship and of having to criticize Cui's opera in Cui's own newspaper, Rimsky-Korsakov's account of the first performance[13] is frank and admirably balanced, so that his praise cannot be dismissed as partial. He points out the touches of subtle comedy in Lesley's recitative but dismisses his song as 'the weakest number of the opera'. He emphasizes the weakness, from the stage point of view, of introducing no fewer than four extended narratives while at the same time he draws attention to the dramatic and musical power of the narratives in themselves. (He does not, very naturally, disclose one thing that he knew:[14] that the middle part of MacGregor's narrative, 'Zwei Jahre drauf kam Philipp Macdonald', was borrowed from a symphonic Allegro which Cui had written in 1862.) And he justly praises the musical characterization of Maria and her father, as well as Lesley and Margarethe; Douglas, he admits, is characterless — but so he is in Heine. It would have tested greater musical dramatists than Cui to convey the falseness of MacGregor's bonhomie, but Maria is embodied in music of a warmth and tenderness that anticipate Yaroslavna and Konchakovna in Borodin's *Prince Igor*, and perfectly defines her character.

The public stubbornly refused to accept *William Ratcliff*, but the circle to which Cui had once belonged never ceased to regard it as a masterpiece. Stasov wrote in 1883[15] that '*Ratcliff* is one of the most important compositions of our time' and roundly declared that 'the duet in the last Act is, in its profound passion and beauty, the finest love-duet in existence'. And Yastrebtsev[16] in 1892, after a private concert performance in which Ratcliff was sung by Rimsky-Korsakov's son Mikhail, wrote that although 'some pages of Act I and the inn scene in Act II *were* pretty mediocre, to say the least, all the rest, and particularly Act III with the amazing love-duet, and likewise the parts of the poetic Maria, the enigmatic Margarethe and Ratcliff himself are the work of positive genius! Ratcliff — this second Karl Moor . . . is a person as it were "outside time" and in this lies the whole tragedy of this most perfect musical figure'. And he ends by describing the opera as 'of its kind, a Russian *Tristan and Isolde*'.

In view of Balakirev's sarcastic references to 'Asiatic part-writing', one would be inclined to dismiss as no more than a kindly gesture of friendship the letter which he addressed to Cui on 14 February 1894:

Twenty-five years ago today you gave the musical world one of the important compositions of our time. After Glinka and Dargomïzhsky I know no opera music in which there is such power, sincerity and beauty as in your *Ratcliff*.[17]

Yet there is a paragraph in Konstantin Chernov's recollections of Balakirev which does something to reconcile the discrepancy:

Cui enjoyed Balakirev's affection and respect mainly on account of *William Ratcliff*. He placed this opera side by side with *Ruslan*. I remember how one day after playing to me a number of passages from this opera, he said thoughtfully: 'Music—this is a little that God has left us from some former heaven on earth. You and I are poor, but God has given us the ability to understand and enjoy music, which is not given to everyone'. The instrumentation of *Ratcliff* Balakirev considered absolutely dilettantish.[18] In the technique of Cui's writing Balakirev also found 'a lot of mud'. He frequently corrected already printed pieces by Cui, leaving them literally with not 'a spot untouched'.[19]

These paradoxical judgements on Cui's *Ratcliff*—that it is a master-piece ruined by harmonic solecisms and inept orchestration—are remarkably similar to those which the same critics passed on Musorgsky's own score of *Boris*. It is true that *Boris* was given a new lease of life and introduced to Western Europe thanks to Rimsky-Korsakov's version of it and it is possible that a similar operation might have saved *Ratcliff*. But in the perspective of a hundred years we can see that Musorgsky's score did not really need 'correction' and reorchestration, that in fact the untouched *Boris* is finer than the revised *Boris*. Until we can study the full score of *Ratcliff* it will be impossible to judge the full validity of Rimsky-Korsakov's criticisms in the 1890s; in 1869 they had been much less harsh:

Mr Cui's instrumentation is always colourful and tasteful, although one sometimes comes across certain faults, e.g. the frequent use of horns in the medium register, the sometimes clumsy use of trombones or ineffective lay-out of the strings. But these are only details; in general the sound of the orchestra is beautiful and poetic. The most beautifully scored parts of the opera include Ratcliff's narrative, the love-duet, the scene at the Black Rock, both Maria's romances, Margarethe's narrative and Douglas's, and the very end of the opera *pp*.[20]

To sum up: however heavily one discounts the hyperbole of Stasov and Yastrebtsev, the evidence of the vocal score is enough to show that in *William Ratcliff* Cui—whose talent lay generally in the cultivation of the elegant miniature—created one major work of great power and beauty which by no means deserves the oblivion that has overtaken it.

NOTES

1. H. Anglés, 'Relations epistolaires entres César Cui et Philippe Pedrell', *Fontes artis musicae* (1966), i, p. 18.
2. Not to be confused with I. A. Krïlov, author of the famous fables.
3. Cui's letter to Musorgsky of 27 July 1868 shows that he wrote part of the text himself.
4. Cui, 'Pervïe kompozitorskie shagi Ts. A. Kyui', *Ezhegodnik Imperatorskikh Teatrov* (1910), i, p. 17.
5. Printed by C. G. Röder, Leipzig, probably at the composer's expense. A slip with the name of Robert Seitz, who had begun his publishing activity only the year before, was pasted on to the title-page later.
6. 'Pervïe kompozitorskie shagi', p. 18. He forgets to mention that from March 1864 he was also the music critic of the *St Peterburgskiya Vedomosti*.
7. *Letopis moei muzïkalnoy zhizni* (5th edn., Moscow, 1935), p. 66.
8. Ibid., p. 91.
9. See Rimsky-Korsakov in *St Peterburgskiya Vedomosti*, no. 52 (21 February 1869); reprinted in *Muzïkalniya stati i zametki* (St Petersburg, 1911); Serov in *Journal de Saint-Pétersbourg*, no. 233 (1869), reprinted in *Izbrannïe stati*, ii (Moscow, 1957), p. 625; Laroche in *Muzïkalny listok*, nos. 20–4 (1874–5), reprinted in *Muzïkalno-kriticheskiya stati* (St Petersburg, 1894).
10. Cui originally intended to end the Introduction to the opera with a whole-tone transformation of one of the hero's themes ('Ha, meinethalb') on solo trombone in order to indicate his death: see V. V. Yastrebtsev, *Vospominaniya* (Leningrad, 1959–60), i, p. 71.
11. M. P. Musorgsky: *Pisma i dokumentï* (Moscow and Leningrad, 1932), p. 149.
12. Yastrebtsev, op. cit., i, p. 145.
13. See note 9.
14. See his *Letopis*, p. 33.
15. 'Nasha muzïka za posledniya 25 let', *Vestnik Evropï* (October, 1883), p. 600; translated in Vladimir Stasov, *Selected Essays on Music* (London, 1968), p. 98.
16. Op. cit., i, p. 50.
17. The entire letter is printed in *Sovetskaya muzïka* (January 1937), p. 88.
18. A criticism endorsed by Rimsky-Korsakov in later years: 'The best thing Cui could do now is to entrust me with the reorchestration of the whole of *Ratcliff* . . . In its present state the opera is unperformable, thanks to its incredible, clumsy orchestration; one can't orchestrate an opera like that – avoiding double-basses as coarse instruments and replacing them by horns', Yastrebtsev, op. cit. i, pp. 145 and 149.
19. M. A. Balakirev ('Po vospominaniyam i pismam'), *Muzïkalnaya Letopis*, iii (Leningrad, 1925), p. 59.
20. *Muzïkalniya stati*, p. 43.

4. Pskovityanka: *The Original Version of Rimsky-Korsakov's First Opera*

Lev Aleksandrovich Mey (1822–62) is an insignificant figure in the history of Russian drama, yet no fewer than three of his plays— *Pskovityanka* (The Maid of Pskov), *Tsarskaya nevesta* (The Tsar's Bride) and *Serviliya* – provided Rimsky-Korsakov with opera-subjects. His love-affair with one of them, *Pskovityanka*, lasted a quarter of a century and has a history so complicated that it is best shown in a tabular form unusual with love-affairs. It began in March 1866, when he composed for voice and piano the cradle-song which Vera Sheloga sings in Act I to her baby daughter, Olga, who is to be the real heroine of the play; the lullaby was published as Op. 2 No. 3. But it was not till the winter of 1867-8 that the idea of taking the play as the subject of his first essay in opera was put into his head by Balakirev and Musorgsky.[1] He quickly decided to scrap Mey's first act, substituting an account of what we learn from it at some later point in the opera. He began by composing the duet for Olga and her lover, and the nurse Vlasyevna's fantastic 'tale of the Tsarevna Lada', from Act II (his own Act I), then the chorus with which the people of Pskov greet Ivan the Terrible (Act III, scene 3); it was probably these which he played at Cui's flat to Borodin and Musorgsky in late September 1868.[2] He apparently began by using a libretto by Vsevolod Krestovsky, obtained for him by or through Tchaikovsky, judging by a letter to the latter dated 29 January 1869:[3]

I've been occupied the whole time with the first act of *Pskovityanka*, which is finished but not orchestrated. Krestovsky's libretto, for which I thank you again, has been very useful though I'm not keeping to it completely.

Indeed, not only did Rimsky-Korsakov himself alter it but Musorgsky and Stasov both made contributions and suggestions.[4] And, if the first act was not yet orchestrated, the greeting chorus was – for Balakirev performed it first at a Russian Music Society concert (4/16 January

1869) and then at a Free School concert (15/27 January 1870), without marked success on either occasion. The whole opera was completed in full score on 4 October 1871, except the overture, which followed in January 1872. It was published by Bessel in vocal score – unobtainable since the 1890s – in May 1872, though no full score was issued; and it was produced with great success at the Maryinsky Theatre, St Petersburg, on 1/13 January 1873, only to be dropped from the repertory after a couple of years. This is the version we may call A, published for the first time in full score (with a reprint of the vocal score) in the Soviet complete edition of Rimsky-Korsakov's works in 1966. It will be convenient at this point to summarize the action:

A.–Act I. The garden of Prince Tokmakov, *posadnik* and vicegerent of the Tsar in the quasi-republican city of Pskov in 1570. His supposed daughter Olga watches her girls playing *gorelki* (tag). Two old nurses work at a table, discussing the horrors inflicted by the Tsar (Ivan the Terrible) on the sister-republic of Novgorod. Vlasyevna tells her 'tale of the Tsarevna Lada'. *Exeunt omnes.* The patriotic young hero Mikhail Tucha appears; Olga returns and tells him her father will never allow him to marry her; she is promised to the boyar Nikita Matuta. Love duet. As Tokmakov and Matuta appear, Tucha flees and Olga hides. She overhears Tokmakov tell Matuta that she is not his daughter but the child of his sister-in-law Vera Sheloga by an unknown father. The Act ends with the sounding of the alarm-bell, summoning the citizens to the popular assembly, the *veche*.

Act II. A square in the kremlin of Pskov. To the assembled citizens comes a messenger from Novgorod, confirming the news of its fate and telling them that the Tsar is now marching on Pskov. The townspeople are at first defiant but Tokmakov appears and soothes them; since they are innocent of treason, they have nothing to fear from the Tsar; let them submit humbly. Tucha will have none of this; he and his followers will leave the city rather than acquiesce.

Act III. Tableau 1: A great square in Pskov; the populace in alarm. Olga appears on the steps of Tokmakov's palace and laments to Vlasyevna that she has never known either true parent. The crowd returns and builds up a chorus of welcomes to the Tsar. Tableau 2: In Tokmakov's house, where he and other notables receive the Tsar, Ivan speaks sarcastically of Pskov's pretension to autonomy, then demands to be waited on by Tokmakov's daughter. Olga is strangely drawn to the terrible monarch – and he is visibly shaken when he looks at her. Folk-song chorus of waiting-maids. When Ivan is left alone with Tokmakov, he enquires about Olga and learns that she is not the Prince's child but the daughter of Vera

Sheloga. The Tsar's mood changes suddenly and he unaccountably proclaims that 'God preserveth Pskov!'

Act IV. Tableau 1: Road through the forest to the Pechersky Monastery. Folk-song chorus of girls, who disappear. Olga runs in alone, to a rendezvous with Tucha. Love-duet, interrupted by the appearance of Matuta and his men who fell Tucha and carry off Olga. Tableau 2: Camp near a riverside. The Tsar, alone, reveals the depths of his divided nature (very like Boris Godunov's). He is haunted by the thought of Olga — and promptly learns of her abduction by Matuta. He is enraged with him and sends for Olga, whom he addresses as 'Olga *Ivan*ovna'. She begs him for protection against Matuta, and he replies that he will take her to Moscow to marry a man of *his* choice, while Tucha shall not be killed but thrown into a dungeon where she shall feed him with white bread on holidays . . . Olga pleads; she has always prayed for the Tsar since childhood, being fascinated by his image. At this moment Tucha and his men attack the camp; they are beaten off but Olga is shot in attempting to join her lover.[5] Ivan sobs over her body, 'But I . . . I'm your father, my darling!'

In 1877, under the very different impressions of his studies in counterpoint and of Glinka's opera scores (which he had been editing), Rimsky-Korsakov became profoundly dissatisfied with the score of his first opera. (The causes of his dissatisfaction are given at length in his autobiography, which is easily accessible in English translation, and need not be repeated here.) He largely rewrote it, making numerous major and minor changes; contrapuntal 'interest' was introduced, the vocal writing was made less declamatory, the orchestration more 'classical', even with natural horns and trumpets. This version, never performed and not yet published, was completed early in 1878. Only the major changes in the action need be mentioned here:

B. — Prologue. Rimsky-Korsakov now composed a prologue based on Mey's First Act: five numbers (with a new, short overture), for the second of which he used his 1866 setting of Vera's lullaby.

Act I. The game of *gorelki* was extended. The insignificant part of Matuta's daughter Styosha was enlarged and a duettino, presumably for her and Tucha's friend Terpigorev, was inserted between Vlasyevna's tale and Tucha's song. The short second act of A now became the finale of Act I.

Act II. Essentially the same as Act III of A but with insertions, e.g. hubbub in the street before the *veche*, with boys playing *babki* (knucklebones), and a septet in the second tableau. Olga's D flat arioso was rewritten in a more lyrical style in G; against the back-

ground of the folk-song chorus of waiting-maids, a dialogue for
Styosha and the Tsar was inserted.

Act III (= Act IV of A). This now began with a new episode, born
partly from a whim of Balakirev's, partly from one of the composer's.
A short entr'acte depicts the 'thick forest'; pilgrims appear singing
an ancient 'Hymn of Alexey the Man of God'; the Tsar rides up
with a train of hunters overtaken by a storm and is denounced for
his cruelties by the *yurodivy* hermit Nikola Salos (as Boris by
the *yurodivy* in the St Basil's scene of *Boris*); Tsar, hunters, and
pilgrims go away and the storm subsides, the girls' chorus is heard
(as in A).—An aria or cavatina 'in Phrygian mode' for the Tsar was
inserted in the last scene and a new final chorus in D flat was
composed.

So much one gathers from Rimsky-Korsakov's own account in his
Letopis, from a sketch-plan published in the editorial preface to the full
score of A (pp. xii–xiii), and from a short article by V. V. Yastrebtsev.[6]
Though this version has not yet been published as a whole, some
portions have been printed in more or less altered forms:

(1) In the autumn of 1877 Rimsky-Korsakov decided to salvage from B
    a suite of 'Music to Mey's drama *Pskovityanka*', consisting of the
    overture to the prologue, entr'actes to Act I (of the play = the
    introduction to Act IV of A and the intermezzo between the two
    tableaux of II in C), to Act II (before the meeting of the *veche*), to
    III (the game of *babki*, naturally with the voice-parts omitted),
    and to IV (opening of Act III of B, on 'Alexey the Man of God').
    This suite was reorchestrated in 1882.

(2) In 1878 he published, as Op. 20, a concert version of 'Alexey the
    Man of God' for chorus and orchestra.

(3) In 1893 he dedicated to Shalyapin the cavatina 'in modo phrigico'
    and in 1898 published it separately; since 1898 it has been included
    in most, but not all, editions of the Bessel vocal score of C.

(4) In 1898 he partly rewrote the prologue and published it, with its
    overture, as *Boyarinya Vera Sheloga*, 'a musico-dramatic prologue
    to Mey's drama *Pskovityanka*' for performance either as an indepen-
    dent work or as prologue to his own opera.

For by this time he had produced yet another version, the definitive one.

C.– On 19 January 1889 Rimsky-Korsakov began a revision of the
    introduction to Act III and Olga's arioso, and between April 1891
    and April 1892 he made a third version of the whole opera though
    the final chorus was not added till 1894. In the main it is a complete
    rewriting of A, on the lines he was to follow later in rewriting
    Boris: vocal lines were revised, unorthodox harmony was cleaned
    up, everything was rescored 'sometimes with Glinka-ish forces,

sometimes with Wagnerian'. A few features were taken over from
B: notably the form in three acts, and the Tsar's hunt-and-storm —
though Nikola Salos and the pilgrims disappeared. (The hunt-and-
storm was to be performed as a 'musical picture' and, beginning
with the Maryinsky production on 28 October 1903, Rimsky-
Korsakov preferred it to be played with the curtain down.)

This is the form published by Bessel and first performed on 6/18 April
1895 by Petersburg amateurs. It had to wait till 31 December 1898
(12 January 1899) for its first professional production (in Moscow, by
the Mamontov company), and quickly became popular — thanks largely
to Shalyapin's marvellous Ivan. In 1909 Dyagilev introduced it to the
West in Paris under the title *Ivan le Terrible*. This is the only form in
which it has been known up to now and 'Rimsky-Korsakov's first
opera' has had to be discussed[7] in terms of a score dating from the
composer's maturity.

Thanks to the recent publication of A, we can at last see where he
really stood at the outset of his career as an opera composer and,
taking the score in conjunction with the original versions of the early
orchestral works already published in the Soviet Complete Edition,[8] to
get a clear first-hand picture of the young musician who was appointed
professor of composition in the Petersburg Conservatoire before he had
'learned harmony properly'. This is not the place to list the uncountable
changes of pitch or length of single notes, of tempos or tempo-markings,
of barring, of small details of scoring or choral layout, of underlay of
words, the small cuts or insertions, made in converting version A to
version C. Indeed it is far easier to draw attention to the very few
passages where nothing, or virtually nothing, was later touched up in
any way: Vlasyevna and the girls' folk-song chorus after the game of
gorelki; Vlasyevna's very Musorgskian tale of princess and dragon; a
passage in the choral reply to Tokmakov (Act I scene 2 of C) where
changes of key-signature are substituted for the changes by accidentals
in A; the opening of Act II (though here the orchestration was touched
up); and the passage in the last scene, where Matuta comes to the Tsar
with his story, rewritten in 6/8 instead of 3/8 but otherwise unaltered
even in details of scoring. Sometimes Rimsky-Korsakov adds little
touches of neat craftsmanship to music identical in substance: when
Olga is telling the Tsar of her abduction by Matuta, her part at Fig.
48 (C) was in A purely declamatory, rising in semitones; in C it twice
doubles an orchestral phrase (now dotted, instead of in even quavers,
as this phrase is throughout the opera in A) and the first part of her

'rising semitones' is placed an octave higher. There is a striking heightening of agitation.

Major changes include the fairly drastic rewriting of the overture in C minor instead of B minor, with recomposition of the passage after Fig. 8 (C) and extension of the end; the extension of the game of *gorelki*; the cutting of twenty-nine rather weak bars in the love-duet, for which were substituted the 9 bars before Fig. 49 (C); the rewriting of the striking B flat minor end of Act I (Ex. 1) into the beginning

Ex. 1

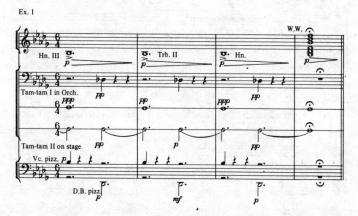

of the Intermezzo (Fig. 50)[9]; the insertion of the Intermezzo itself (on material from B); patches of rewriting in the *veche* scene, particularly as regards the chorus, and changes in the key-scheme (to which I shall return later); in Act II (= III of A) the Olga–Vlasyevna scene was taken over, and no doubt further rewritten, from the version in B. In A Olga's arioso begins as shown in Ex. 2, and when Vlasyevna

Ex. 2

replies there is an interesting example of Rimsky-Korsakov's total remoulding of his original material, a remoulding probably made first in B if we may judge from the contrapuntal nature of the orchestral writing (Ex. 3*a*, 3*b*).

The remainder of their dialogue (some 30 bars) is extremely feeble in
A; in C it is replaced by completely new music, with more melodic
interest and dramatic contrast. The ensuing crowd scene is substantially
the same but the two choruses are handled differently and A's brass
band on the stage, already heard at the beginning of the act, disappears
in C, its music being transferred to the orchestral brass.

The Intermezzo before the second scene of Act II (C), originally the
introduction to Act IV of A, is at present the only passage where —
thanks to the 'Music for Mey's play'—we can compare all three versions
in full score. A and B are both in E major, C in F major, but all three
are substantially the same. Yet Rimsky-Korsakov remoulds every detail
of the substance (Ex. 4a, 4b, 4c).

Here the composer obviously decided finally not to clutter the beautiful 'Olga' theme with a distracting counter-idea; the counter-idea now introduces it instead of accompanying it. Elsewhere he sometimes tightens things up. There is an instance of this later in this scene in Tokmakov's house, when the *posadnik* addresses Ivan as '*Gosudar!*' (sovereign), to which the Tsar replies sarcastically: 'Sovereign! We're all sovereigns here: great Pskov and Novgorod are sovereign too . . .' A brief quotation will show not only the tighter imitation of flute and oboe but the more subtle declamation and immensely greater orchestral sophistication of C (Ex. 5*a*, 5*b*).

Ex. 5b

With the advent of Tsar Ivan such changes become more and more marked. Rimsky-Korsakov clearly realized that he had originally drawn this powerful and complicated character in rather pallid musical colours. Thus the end of Act II (Act III in A), when Ivan realizes that Olga must be his own daughter and repents of his intention to destroy Pskov, was drastically rewritten, throw-away recitative being replaced by dramatic declamation and the scoring much strengthened. This applies also to Ivan's great monologue at the beginning of the last scene,[10] outstandingly at the moment when, after his vision of his people as 'a single flock with a single shepherd', he sees himself as the ruler who will bind Russia together with laws wise as well as stern. This went for little in A, whereas in C (with the sudden change of key emphasized by the voice taking over the melody, and the unexpected entry of the quartet of horns) it becomes one of the most impressive strokes in the musical characterization of the Tsar. Similarly the dramatic tension of Olga's arioso as she waits for Tucha in the wood is much heightened.

Perhaps the most astonishing change of all is in the final chorus of the opera, originally 28 bars long, in which the chorus—supported by a modest orchestra of strings, wood-wind, horns, and timpani—reflects quietly on Olga, who gave her life and beauty and youth 'for her native Pskov and her love'. The last five bars, for orchestra alone, must be the most 'ineffective' end of any opera in existence; they challenge—but do not, by a long way, sustain—comparison with the true end of *Boris*, the *yurodivy* alone on the stage lamenting (Ex. 6).

Ex. 6

Rimsky-Korsakov transformed this chorus in 1894, using the same material, into a sumptuously scored piece with an *ff* climax at the right point and an effective tutti crescendo curtain-chord. It is the right way to end a *grand opéra*, but one may be permitted to feel a little sad at the loss of the idealistic truthfulness of Ex. 6.

One might put it that in the final chorus musical considerations triumphed over drama. And, broadly speaking, the changes in *Pskovityanka* are more often musical than dramatic. While the declamation is made more telling and the part of the Tsar immensely strengthened, many of the alterations were aimed solely at making the score musically more effective. They may be roughly subsumed under the headings: change of key, change of harmony, change of scoring, additions to texture. But naturally these overlap – and the scoring is changed almost throughout, not so much in general colours as in refinement and weight. A few examples will indicate the general directions of Rimsky-Korsakov's second (or, rather, third) thoughts. One from the latter part of Act II (Act I scene 2 in C) shows all of them. Originally, from the point where Tokmakov finishes his speech to the end of the act, the music is almost entirely in the favourite 'Balakirev keys', B minor and B flat minor; only near the end, when Tucha addresses Tokmakov ('Prince Yury Ivanovich!': Fig. 86 in C), is there a modulation to G before the final stretch of B minor. In the final version, Rimsky-Korsakov introduces a much more marked key-change earlier and continues in keys a semitone lower to the end of the act, thus ending in B *flat* minor. The new version has more energy but the passage has lost its quasi-modal flavour; the bloom of 'Russianness' has been brushed off. There are other wholesale key-changes, as well as shorter ones, later: for instance, the 5/4 duet in the penultimate scene was moved up from B major to C (and the 12/8

middle section correspondingly to E), and in the ensuing abduction
scene – much rewritten – the passages of original music are transposed a
minor third down or a minor third or even diminished fifth up. But the
most drastic alteration here is in the practically atonal end of the scene
with its 25 measures of unrelenting ostinato bass, the – for 1872 – hair-
raising dissonances produced by the contrary motion of the bare oboes
and bassoons, the unresolved horn chord, and the final petering out
of the ostinato into a long-held G.

Ex. 7

Musorgsky himself never wrote anything more primitive. But there is a
characteristic difference between Musorgsky's empirical harmony and
Rimsky-Korakov's; Musorgsky's is essentially expressive, Rimsky-
Korsakov's – at any rate, in this case – essentially schematic. It is easy to
imagine with what relief he concealed the nakedness of the clashing
sixths by anchoring the passage in D flat, mitigated the ruthlessness of
the ostinato, and resolved the final chord. The 'nakedness', the primary
orchestral colours, are characteristic of early Rimsky-Korsakov scoring
in general. In re-orchestrating, he generally retains the same basic
colouring but subtilizes it; he adds instruments, seldom or never
subtracts; he strengthens by doubling and by inserting sustained notes

or chords or by filling out texture in other ways—perhaps no more than
the addition of four or five pizzicato notes echoing the voice, as at bars
13-14 and 16-17 after Fig. 30 in Act I (Ex. 8, voice and first violin

Ex. 8

only quoted) or the addition of a rhythmic figure on trumpets. It is
noticeable that originally unaccompanied or very lightly accompanied
choral passages were later given more support. But while most of these
strengthenings were motivated by purely musical or downright practical
considerations, at least one was due to Rimsky-Korsakov's original lack
of theatrical sense. In the first act, when Tokmakov and Matuta are
talking about Olga, the Prince's crucial confession, 'But we don't know
her father...', is completely thrown away. The meaning of the Tsar's
theme here is not yet apparent to the audience, but the overture has
already told them that this theme has *some* tremendous significance;
yet played like this on a single clarinet its appearance here might easily
pass unnoticed. There is no fear of its passing unnoticed in the final
version, played by all the violins tremolo, plus both clarinets and cor
anglais, intensified by its partial mirror-image in the cellos, supported
by the weight of full horn and bassoon harmony, and brought up from
pp in a *crescendo molto*.

Not only here but in almost every change C is the better version.
There can be no question of a campaign for the revival of A as there is
for the *Urfassungen* of Bruckner's symphonies or Schumann's D minor;
it is a fascinating score to study and one may feel little pangs of regret
here and there for the later loss of some true or bold touch by that
naïve young man of near-genius who managed to write an opera before
he had 'learned harmony properly'. One would like to hear it—once—
as a curiosity. But Rimsky-Korsakov was as right to make a better job
of his own early score as he was wrong in performing exactly the same
operation on his friend's *Boris*. *Boris Godunov* is a work of another
man's genius; the original *Pskovityanka* was a work of his own great
talent. He raised one and reduced the other to nearly the same level.

NOTES

1. Rimsky-Korsakov, *Letopis moey muzikalnoy zhizni*, 5th edn (Moscow, 1935), p. 84.

2. *Pisma A. P. Borodina*, i (Moscow, 1928), p. 109.

3. *Sovetskaya muzïka: tretiy sbornik statey* (Moscow and Leningrad, 1945), p. 122.

4. For Stasov's, which were totally neglected, see his letter of 11 November 1869 to the composer: Rimsky-Korsakov, *Polnoe sobranie sochinenity*, v (Moscow, 1963), p. 330. Musorgsky supplied texts for choruses.

5. In Mey's play she commits suicide on the stage.

6. 'Neskolko slov o II-ï i III-ï redaktsiakh "Pskovityanki". . .', *Russkaya muzïkalnaya gazeta*, ii (1895), col. 314, reprinted in an emended form in his reminiscences, *Rimsky-Korsakov: Vospominaniya* i (Leningrad, 1959), p. 114.

7. For instance, by myself in *Studies in Russian Music* (London, 1936).

8. See 'Rimsky-Korsakov as Self-Critic', *Slavonic and Romantic Music* (London, 1968), p. 195.

9. The way in which the join was originally made, in B, may be inferred from the opening of Entr'acte II of the 'Music to Mey's play'.

10. The so-called 'phrygian' aria which replaced it in B is infinitely inferior; the vocal line was curiously derived from an absolutely instrumental accompaniment figure in A: C restores the A version, with no more than readjustment of the string scoring, though with doubled note-values.

5. *Satire and Symbolism in* The Golden Cockerel

'If any one of them can explain it', said Alice . . . 'I'll give him sixpence. *I* don't believe there's an atom of meaning in it'. 'If there's no meaning in it', said the King, 'that saves a world of trouble you know, as we needn't try to find any. And yet I don't know', he went on, spreading out the verses on his knee . . . 'I seem to see some meaning in them, after all'.

Rimsky-Korsakov's last opera has something in common with the poem in the last chapter of *Alice*. Its meaning is not clear and it is not even clear whether it has one. Is it just a comic fairy-tale, a piece of delicious nonsense? Is it satire? Or has it some deeper, more elusive meaning? It is open to anyone to take it simply at the first level; perhaps most of us do. But the Russian authorities in 1908 were not content to do that, and no one has ever seriously challenged the correctness of their view that the opera had a political sting, that the foolish old King Dodon was a symbol of stupid autocracy. Rimsky-Korsakov had openly taken the anti-government side in the political upheaval of 1905 and been dismissed from the Conservatoire; performance of his works had been forbidden for two months by the police in St Petersburg and several provincial cities. When he interrupted the composition of the *Cockerel* in 1907 to visit Paris for Dyagilev's Russian orchestral concerts, two members of the Imperial family – the Grand Duke Paul Alexandrovich and the Grand Duchess Marya Pavlovna – made friendly advances to him and were snubbed for their pains.

It is hardly surprising that the censor of plays looked for trouble in the libretto of the *Cockerel* when it was submitted, though he might have been expected to do so with more intelligence; the considerable cuts and alterations he demanded included passages borrowed directly from Pushkin's poem, which was a familiar classic. And although the authorities gave way on some points, the composer had to make some concessions in the sung text although the original words remained in the published score. For instance, the censor insisted that the 'bloody denouement' should be changed to an 'unexpected' one and that the 'new dawn'—a phrase of terrifying political significance— must be a 'white' one.[2] The phrase which inspired the cockcrow theme itself, 'Cockadoodle-doo! Rule, lying on your side!', had worried the censorship even in Pushkin's time since it conveyed too clear an image of the ruler's indolence, and in 1908 the censor wanted the line changed to 'Sleep quietly on your side'. One consequence of this tussle with the censorship was that the production was delayed until after the composer's death. Even then Gershelman, the Governor-General of Moscow, insisted on the king being reduced to 'the Mighty Tsar's general' and the real general, Polkan, to colonel.[3] Incidentally, Dodon —or Dadon, as Pushkin spells the name—is called *tsar* in the poem and the opera, not *korol* (king), but Rimsky-Korsakov himself expressed a wish to the French translator of the libretto that '*Tsar* Dodon be translated *Roi* and not Tzar, and *Shemakhanskaya tsaritsa*, la *Reine* de Chemakha, and not Tzarine'. As for Shemakha*n*, as it is often spelled in the West: 'What's this *Chémakhan*? It must be la reine de *Chémakha*'.[4]

The element of political satire in the opera is indisputable, yet one has a feeling that there must be something more than this, something less obvious. Who is the mysterious Queen of Shemakha? Is she a symbol of youth or beauty or evil? There are all sorts of hints at inner meanings; Pushkin himself gives one in the last two lines of his poem, which the astrologer quotes in the prologue of the opera:

> The tale's not true, but in it there's a hint,
> A lesson for fine young fellows!

The Cockerel seems to symbolize something, but one does not know what. And at the very end the Astrologer comes before the curtain and tells the audience not to worry about the tragic conclusion, since he and the Queen—who seem to be the only two magical characters in the opera—are really the only two living ones: the rest are 'delirium, illusion, pale phantoms, emptiness'. But there is no suggestion of that in Pushkin.

'The Golden Cockerel' was one of a group of stories in verse written in the spirit of Russian folk-tales but with more sophistication. One of them, 'Tsar Saltan', originated in a traditional Russian story, but the 'Tale of the Dead Tsarevna and the Seven Heroes' was based on the Grimms' familiar 'Schneewittchen' (Snow White), and 'The Golden Cockerel' on two chapters of Washington Irving's *The Alhambra*. Pushkin read both Grimm and Irving in French, as we know from the

volumes preserved in his library. *The Alhambra* had been an immediate
success: in the very year (1832) of its first publication in London
and Philadelphia, two English editions appeared in Paris (A. and W.
Galignani, and in Baudry's Foreign Library) and H. Fournier brought
out *Les Contes de l'Alhambra . . . traduits de Washington Irving par
Mlle. A. Sobry* in two volumes. In the first volume of the Fournier
edition Pushkin found a short account of 'La Maison de la Girouette'
which is followed by the 'Légende de l'Astrologue arabe'. In 'The House
of the Weathercock' Irving describes how a building 'on the brow of the
lofty hill of the Albaycin . . . all that is left of what was once a royal
palace of the Moors' had borne that name for centuries, 'from a bronze
figure on one of its turrets, in ancient times, of a warrior on horseback,
and turning with every breeze'.

On lisait sur la girouette deux vers arabes, que l'on traduit ainsi en
espagnol:

> Dice el sabio Aben Habuz,
> Que asi se defiende el Anduluz.

C'est ainsi, dit le sage Aben Habuz, que doit se défendre l'Andaloux.

When, toward the end of his life, Washington Irving drastically revised
and rewrote *The Alhambra*, he expanded this chapter considerably,
offering other versions and explanations of the inscription, one of which
includes a phrase that seems as if it might have suggested Pushkin's
final couplet: 'This to a wise man reveals a mystery'. But Mlle Sobry
and Pushkin knew nothing of this. All Irving says in his first version is
that popular tradition explains things differently; the bronze horseman
was originally a talisman of great power which it lost in the course of
time, becoming a simple weathercock. He will relate these traditions in
the following chapter, 'Legend of the Arabian Astrologer' (which in the
definitive edition was revised only in insignificant details).

The 'Legend' begins, like Pushkin's *Skazka*, with an account of a
once warlike but now old and pacific monarch, Aben Habuz, Moorish
king of Granada, harassed by neighbours whom his armies are quite
unable to keep off. To him comes 'an ancient Arabian physician' who
by occult means has prolonged his life to the age of two hundred or so,
'though, as he did not discover the secret until well stricken in years, he
could only perpetuate his gray hairs and wrinkles'. He becomes the
king's friend and counsellor, and tells him of a marvel which will solve
the problem of defence. Many years ago he had seen:

On a mountain, above the city of Borsa, and overlooking the great valley of the Nile, was a figure of a ram, and above it a figure of a cock, both of molten brass, and turning upon a pivot. Whenever the country was threatened with invasion, the ram would turn in the direction of the enemy, and the cock would crow; upon this the inhabitants of the city knew of the danger, and of the quarter from which it was approaching, and could take timely means to guard against it.

He provides Aben Habuz with a figure of the same kind, placed on the top of a tower:

A bronze figure of a Moorish horseman, fixed on a pivot, with a shield on one arm, and his lance elevated perpendicularly. The face of this horseman was towards the city, as if keeping guard over it; but if any foe were at hand, the figure would turn in that direction, and would level the lance as if for action.

More than that: a room in the tower contained a magic quasi-chessboard by means of which Aben Habuz was able to destroy his enemies at his ease. Offered a lavish reward, the astrologer asks only 'the means of fitting up my cave as a suitable hermitage'. However, the fittings turn out to be vastly luxurious and expensive. When he is absolutely content and ready to devote all his time to study he tells the royal treasurer: 'Je ne désire rien de plus, excepté une bagatelle, une petite récréation pour remplir les intervalles entre mes travaux abstraits', and the treasurer is shocked when the *bagatelle* turns out to be 'a few dancing-girls'. ('And let them be young and fair to look upon, for the sight of youth and beauty is refreshing. A few will suffice, for I am a philosopher of simple habits and easily satisfied'.)

All goes well for a long time, with the bronze horseman keeping watch. Then one day the lance points toward the mountains of Cadiz, but the figures on the magic table do not move and the troops sent to scour the mountains find no enemy—only 'a Christian damsel of surpassing beauty, sleeping at noontide beside a fountain', who says she is 'the daughter of one of the Gothic princes, who but lately ruled over this land' (his armies have been destroyed by means of the magic table). The astrologer warns the king that she is probably 'one of those northern sorceresses' and suggests that she should be handed over to him, since he has had no share in the spoils of previous victories: being a magician himself, he will be able to cope with her if she is indeed a witch. But the king has already marked her down for his harem; they quarrel and the astrologer retires in a huff. The king is besotted and blissful, but a later trouble obliges him to turn once more to the astrologer for help. This time the magician offers to build him a most marvellous palace, and again asks for a very modest reward—'the first beast of burden, with its load, which shall enter the magic portal of the palace'. It is hardly necessary to say that the first beast of burden to enter the gateway is the princess's palfrey. King and astrologer quarrelled more bitterly than ever over the animal's beautiful load, who regarded both greybeards with equal contempt, until at last the astrologer

seized the bridle of the palfrey, smote the earth with his staff, and sank with the Gothic princess through the centre of the barbican. The earth closed over them, and no trace remained of the opening by which they had descended.

A thousand workmen dug in vain to get to them; the bronze horseman remained fixed, facing the hill, his spear pointing to the spot where astrologer and princess had disappeared, 'as if there still lurked the deadliest foe of Aben Habuz'; and the king was once more at the mercy of his enemies.

Pushkin turned Washington Irving's long-winded story, with its wealth of inessential detail proper enough to an oriental tale, into a relatively short poem. As in 'Saltan' he tells the story with mock simplicity in rhymed couplets, in a metre that enhances not only the naïveté but the charm and the light irony—a degree sharper than Irving's—of the telling. Nothing is more typical of his genius than compression and elimination of the inessential and merely decorative. The 'chess'-table is dispensed with altogether and, taking a hint from the brazen cock at Borsa, Pushkin replaces the bronze horseman with the golden cockerel—which he obviously thought of as a living thing, since it crows, raises its comb, ruffles its feathers, and flies. (It is not a weathercock, nor was the bronze horseman of Irving's story—only the supposedly once-existent figure which gave its name to 'La casa del Gallo de Viento' at Granada—and the 'corrected' title of the opera in the supplementary volume to the fifth edition of Grove's *Dictionary*, p. 190, is wrong.) Pushkin invented the Tsar's sons and the old general, but without giving them names as in the opera; the housekeeper Amelfa appears for the first time in the opera. The poet describes the astrologer as an 'old friend' of Dodon's, so that he is by no means the mysterious stranger of the opera, who only claims to have known Dodon's father. But the Russian astrologer differs markedly in one respect from Irving's: he is introduced as 'wise man, astrologer, and eunuch' and afterwards referred to more than once as 'the eunuch'—so that Dodon's question: 'What do you want the girl for?' is very reasonable. Rimsky-Korsakov evidently regarded him as a eunuch; the part is written for a tenor-altino, and when the King asks the same question in the opera and the astrologer, 'assuming a dignified air', answers: 'I confess I'm not hot-blooded, but now, come what may, after all, I want to pluck up courage and have a try at marrying', his voice goes up to a high E (Ex. 1), though Rimsky-Korsakov mercifully, or realistically, allows him C sharp as an alternative.[5]

Ex. 1

No reader of the poem in the 1830s can have failed to draw mental parallels between 'the famous Tsar Dodon' and his court,

>Somewhere, in the thrice-ninth kingdom,
>In the thirtieth country,

and contemporary Russian officialdom; and the final hint that the tale has a moral was commonly believed to be a reference to Nicholas I's liability to go back on solemnly given promises. Yet, while Nicholas was faithless and autocratic, and his political aggressiveness may well have been caused by fear, he was certainly no fool and he was anything but indolent. All in all, the element of political satire in the poem is slight and relatively harmless; in the opera it is much sharper.

It is difficult to determine precisely when Rimsky-Korsakov's attention was drawn to the poem as an opera subject. It first came to the surface in 1906, when on 15 October he noted down the opening theme, the Cockerel's crow, in his note-book.[6] But, while he must have been familiar with the poem all his life, it seems probable that his interest in Dodon as a political symbol was stimulated by a cartoon that had appeared on the cover of the second number of the periodical *Zhupel* at the beginning of 1906.[7] The cartoon showed the King standing at a window and staring stupidly at the moon, and the caption indicated that 'the most illustrious Tsar Dodon, sovereign of the entire earth, his magnificent belly filled with foreign foods', was contemplating the idea of rounding off his dominions by annexing the moon. It was an obvious attack on Tsarist 'expansionism'. The artist was Ivan Bilibin, one of the most delightful illustrators of Russian fairy-tales, and it can hardly have been pure coincidence that Bilibin was commissioned to design both the sets and costumes for the first production and the cover of the vocal score.

The librettist of the *Cockerel* was Vladimir Belsky, who had already helped Rimsky-Korsakov with the libretto of *Sadko* and provided those for two of his best operas, *Tsar Saltan* and *Kitezh*. He did a very skilful job in the adaptation of the poem. A great deal of the King's part is pure Pushkin, either word for word or third-person narrative turned into first-person speech; so is a good deal of the dialogue between King and Astrologer in the last act. Even some of the stage-directions are taken word for word from Pushkin. And Belsky caught the poet's style very cleverly on the whole in much of his own writing. But he also had to fill out the action, which he did by inventing the housekeeper and giving the princes names and ideas about national defence which he regarded as idiotic (although in our country—but not in Russia—they would nowadays be considered enlightened), and above all by making some sort of character out of the mysterious Eastern Queen. In Pushkin— compressing Washington Irving most drastically—she gets a mere 20 lines or so; we learn only that the King was infatuated by her beauty, was entertained by her for a week, and then took her home. She never utters a word, even when the Astrologer asks for her. She simply disappears when the Cockerel flies down and kills the King. The greater part of the second act, with her seduction and humiliation of Dodon, was entirely Belsky's invention and it was these additions that gave the greatest offence to the authorities. The behaviour of the troops in Act II was regarded, perhaps wrongly, as a satire on the misfortunes of Russian arms in the recent war with Japan. But although Belsky would hardly have mocked at the troops, he certainly intended to mock the administration and the high command: when the army is setting out at the end of Act I and Polkan assures his master that they have supplies 'for three years', a contemporary audience could hardly have failed to remember the repeated assurances that Port Arthur had 'supplies for three years'.[8] (Actually Port Arthur held out for only seven months.)

There are other points in the libretto which may have been unintentional but were taken at the time to be deliberate. The character of the housekeeper Amelfa was supposed to have been suggested by an English- woman who exercised too much influence at the court of Nicholas II; alternatively she was regarded as a caricature of the Empress herself. And Dodon's remark, near the end, that 'blood at a wedding' is a bad omen was held to refer to the accidental crushing to death of nearly a thousand people at Nicholas II's coronation.[9] One certainly deliberate, and very telling, point is the treatment of the King's promise. In Pushkin, Dodon 'promises mountains of gold' and adds: 'For such a service I will grant your first wish'—and the Astrologer seems to be satisfied. In the opera he is not; he knows his sovereign and respectfully asks for the promise to be put in writing 'according to the laws'. To which the autocrat significantly replies: 'According to what laws? What word? I never heard of such a thing. My whim, my command—that's the law every time'. There is thus no question that the treatment of Dodon and his court is political satire—satire as bitter as Belsky dared to make it. And Rimsky-Korsakov did his best to underline it in his music which he once said might be characterized by Mephistopheles's phrase in Berlioz's *Faust*: 'La bestialité dans toute sa candeur'.[10]

So much for the more or less 'real' characters—or, rather, the realistic puppets. The problematic characters are the magical ones, those which at the end of the opera the Astrologer declares are the only living ones: the Queen and himself. It is Belsky's Astrologer who says so, not Pushkin's, yet Belsky pretended to be puzzled by this dark saying. In his preface to the score he speaks of 'the mystery in which Pushkin has wrapped the mutual relationship of the fantastic characters of the tale—the Astrologer and the Queen'. It is true their relationship is not explained; reading the poem in the light of Irving's story, one sees there was no particular 'relationship' to explain. In any case, in telling a fantastic fairy-tale—which was Irving's sole object and Pushkin's main object—one is under no obligation to justify everything logically. But Belsky had got himself and Rimsky-Korsakov involved in something deeper than a fairy-tale and there had to be some justification. In his preface he goes on to speculate:

Are [the Queen and Astrologer] actually involved in a conspiracy against Dodon or have they come together only by chance to attack him? In Pushkin this is quite unexplained. A circumstantial scenic treatment of the story cannot be content with such a precarious basis, and it was necessary in the first place to find a definite solution of this riddle; and although the peculiar charm of the tale lies in what is not fully stated, nevertheless in order to make the action comprehensible the author feels obliged to convey in a few words the significance of what is happening on the stage. The audience is watching the desperate efforts of a still living magician who, some thousand years ago, tried to subjugate by his magic power the Daughter of the Air. Having been unable to do this by his own power, he has the idea of getting her through Dodon. But, as we are aware, he has been defeated—after which he is left with nothing but the consolation of showing the audience in his magic lantern the story of Dodon's black ingratitude.

If ever there were an incredible explanation of the incomprehensible, this is it. All it really explains is the passage in Belsky's own epilogue where the Astrologer says that he and the Queen are the only living persons.

The words of the epilogue are Belsky's, but the idea of having an epilogue was not his at all; he wanted nothing that would soften the impact of the satire. (Similarly he had already expressed his fear that Rimsky-Korsakov's orchestration might 'ennoble' the Queen's 'diabolical sensuality'[11] and destroy the sense of 'infinite evil' in Act II.) It was the composer who in August 1907, when the whole opera was roughed out and the first two acts were orchestrated, decided that he wanted an epilogue—for mainly musical reasons. He had just rewritten the prologue and decided to open the opera with the cock-crow on the muted trumpet; now he wanted a balancing piece at the end to 'make a marvellous frame for our tale' and 'round it off musically'. He wrote Belsky a wheedling letter:[12]

Dear, good, kind Vladimir Ivanovich, I want you to do this: at the end, after the last chorus with the words 'What will the new dawn bring' let the curtain down quickly, and out comes the Astrologer in front of it: turning to the audience, he says he has shown them some comic masks and they can go and sleep 'till dawn' and 'till the cock crows'. He disappears; loud Cockerel motive on the trumpets in the same key as at the beginning but harmonized and ending *ff* on an A♭ chord or an
        F♭
augmented one C. You will have to give the Astrologer 4, 6 or at most 8 lines.   A♭

He goes on to demonstrate the disarming effect on the authorities of such an epilogue, whether or not they cut it.

'Dear, good, kind Vladimir' grumbled:

I've always been against an epilogue in the 'Cockerel'. It was to avoid it that I purposely worked in the words 'The tale's not true, but in it there's a hint . . .' at the beginning of the opera. I counted on a serious (even weighty) impression from the final scene and chorus, and feared that any turning to the audience at the end would destroy the reality of what has just happened and turn it into a joke. And a bad joke at that. But obviously this idea doesn't correspond to your nature, which deeply understands the most gloomy things but always prefers the light; you have a positive need to wipe out the gloomy impression and end the opera with a facetious chord.

So the idea of the Queen and the Astrologer being 'the only living persons' in the opera was thought of at the last moment to provide a satisfactory musical rounding off—and to avoid ending with the chorus asking:

> What will the new dawn bring?
> What shall we do without a tsar?

(As it was, the censor objected even to the harmless text of the epilogue —which he took to be Dodon's words, not the Astrologer's—and it had to be changed.) The still more improbable idea at the end of Belsky's preface—the nonsense about the attempted abduction of the Daughter of the Air—was thought of still later in an attempt to justify the words of the epilogue. We are quite right in reading political satire into the *Cockerel*. But to look for deeper symbolism is useless; there is none.

NOTES

1. A part of this chapter was broadcast in the BBC Third Programme on 27 December 1969.

2. A. N. Rimsky-Korsakov, *N. A. Rimsky-Korsakov: zhizn i tvorchestvo*, v (Moscow, 1946), p. 151.

3. Anonymous introduction to the souvenir booklet published by Zimin, apparently soon after the production.

4. Letters to M. D. Calvocoressi, 23 December 1907 and 10 January 1908.

5. The passage is easily accessible in full score as Ex. 50 in the second volume of Rimsky-Korsakov's *Principles of Orchestration* (Paris, 1914).

6. V. V. Yastrebtsev, *Rimsky-Korsakov: Vospominaniya*, ii (Leningrad, 1960), p. 431, and A. N. Rimsky-Korsakov, op. cit., pp. 128–9, n. 1.

7. A. A. Gozenpud, 'Iz nablyudeniy nad tvorcheskim protsessom Rimskovo-Korsakova', *Rimsky-Korsakov: issledovaniya, materialï, pisma*, i (Moscow, 1953), p. 248.

8. M. F. Gnesin, *Mïsli i vospominaniya o N. A. Rimskom-Korsakove* (Moscow, 1956), p. 167.

9. Ibid., p. 169.

10. Yastrebtsev, op. cit., p. 407.

11. Her music was not all originally conceived for her. The 'hymn to the sun' is based on music (sketch in Gozenpud, op. cit., p. 200) for a projected one-act *Barber of Bagdad* in 1895: the lovesick Nureddin's aria in the opening scene. The Queen's melody at 'Kto-to dïshit, sam nezrimïy' (Jurgenson vocal score, p. 111, bars 10 f.) and the second theme of her dance with Dodon were first intended for the heroine, a Persian princess, of a more recent opera project, *Stenka Razin*; the sketches are printed in M. O. Yankovsky, *Rimsky-Korsakov i revolyutsiya 1905 goda* (Moscow and Leningrad, 1950), p. 70.

12. A. N. Rimsky-Korsakov, op. cit., pp. 143–4.

6. Arab Melodies in Rimsky-Korsakov and Borodin

In his *Letopis' moei muzïkal'noy zhizni* Rimsky-Korsakov tells us of the authentic Arab melodies he employed in his *Antar* Symphony:

Except the principal theme of Antar himself . . . and the theme of the *peri* Gyul Nazar with oriental florid ornamentations, the other purely cantabile themes (the F sharp melody 6/8 in the first movement and the melody in A major 4/4, the secondary theme of the third movement) were borrowed by me from some French edition of Arab melodies from Algiers which Borodin happened to have; the chief theme of the fourth movement was given me by A. S. Dargomïzhsky with his harmonization, taken by him from Christianowitsch's collection of Arab melodies. For the beginning of the *Adagio* of this movement I preserved Dargomïzhsky's original harmonization (*cor ingl.* and 2 *fag.*).[1]

The 'French edition of Arab melodies' was the *Album de Chansons arabes, mauresques et kabyles*, transcribed and provided with French words and piano accompaniments by Francesco Salvador-Daniel, published in Paris (originally by Richault, later by Costallat) during the 1860s. (Some of the songs had been published separately by 1863.) *Antar* was originally composed in 1868 but already by 1875, when he was making a revised version of the score, Rimsky-Korsakov had forgotten the name of his source, for we find him writing to Balakirev on 17 May, 'If you remember the actual title of those Moorish melodies and the author's name, please let me know'.[2] Christianowitsch's collection was the *Esquisse historique de la musique arabe aux temps anciens avec dessins d'instruments et quarante melodies notées et harmonisées par Alexandre Christianowitsch* (Libraire de M. Dumont-Schauberg, Cologne, 1863).

These particulars are well known to students of Rimsky-Korsakov, but up to now, so far as I know, no one has taken the trouble to look at his sources and study his treatment of them, though Miloš Velimirovič[3] has shown that, even in the earliest version of *Antar*, he did not 'preserve Dargomïzhsky's original harmonization' or the melody as Dargomïzhsky copied it. For that matter, Dargomïzhsky did not copy the melody quite faithfully from Christianowitsch, whose version I give here).

Ex. 1

As usual, Christianowitsch prints first the melody alone and then a clumsily harmonized version; in the latter in this case he smoothes out the first down-beat of the melody into even quavers and then, assuming the melody to begin in C major, he accompanies the whole of the first phrase with a dominant seventh. Rimsky-Korsakov's version is a vast improvement.

Ex. 2

And his indication *amoroso* suggests that he had seen not only Dargomïzhsky's copy but Christianowitsch's publication, with its French paraphrase of the text:

Toi, qui dans ton ignorance invoques l'amour, écoute, je vais te le faire connaître. — Au début il apporte la langueur, et à la fin le trépas. Songe à Medjenoun, l'amant de Leïla. Il consuma ses jours dans un espoir toujours déçu. — La mer de l'amour est une mer sans rivages. L'amant qui s'y plonge est toujours submergé. — Interroge la sagesse des proverbes. Elle te dit: On ne recueille le miel qu'avec le feu.

The two themes borrowed from Salvador-Daniel are called by him 'Yamina' and 'Chebbou-Chebban' and he says they are both 'chansons mauresques d'Alger'. The 'F sharp melody 6/8 in the first movement' is based on 'Yamina'.

Ex. 3

The first two bars provide the flute motive first heard at bar 13 of the *Allegretto vivace*, and afterwards with a triplet ornament added and other modifications. But bars 5–6 are given quite different treatment: played by the violins in octaves, *con delicatezza*, repeated and transposed, so that the listener takes them to constitute a fresh theme. And so indeed it is; from the first six bars of the melody — he made no use of the remainder — Rimsky-Korsakov extracted two themes which he used and developed separately. The treatment of 'Chebbou-Chebban' is quite different. The entire melody (Ex. 4) is borrowed though its tonal

Ex. 4

De Fath - ma   de Fath-ma la   bel - le Dont les yeux lan - cent des é -clairs

course is changed, but the languorous 6/8 *Andantino* is transformed into the trio section of a brilliant *Allegro risoluto* march celebrating 'the joys of power'.

Ex. 5

There is a third borrowing in *Antar* — if it really is a borrowing — from Salvador-Daniel's collection, which the composer did not mention in his autobiography for the very good reason that he had been unconscious of it and then, when it was pointed out to him, thought it not worth mentioning. His attention was drawn to it in a curious way. On 13 October 1891, his enthusiastic admirer V. V. Yastrebtsev tells us:[4]

talking to Nikolay Andreevich about *Antar*, I drew his attention to one curious circumstance, namely that the theme of the Peri Gyul-Nazar [Ex. 6] is almost identical with the 'Thème de la gazelle' recorded by

Ex. 6

Fétis in his 'Musical encyclopedia' in the section on Arab folk-songs. Nikolay Andreevich was, obviously, extremely surprised by this analogy.
   'You know', he said thoughtfully, 'it's very possible that at some time in my youth I saw that theme somewhere. I really don't remember.

It's hardly possible to explain it as simple chance; they have awfully much in common'.

Rimsky-Korsakov may well have been taken aback for he had possibly never set eyes on Fétis's *History*[5]— it is not an encyclopedia, of course — in his life; he certainly could not have seen it when he composed *Antar*, for it was not yet published. But neither he nor Yastrebtsev realized that Fétis had taken 'Ma gazelle', French text and all, from Salvador-Daniel (p. 26).

Ex. 7

That was where Rimsky-Korsakov must have seen it. His Gyul Nazar theme is first heard when the *peri* is transformed into a gazelle; moreover the pedal A on the horns and other points in his harmonization obviously echo Salvador-Daniel, though by no means exactly. But for these circumstances and the identity of key, one would be tempted to dismiss the merely melodic similarity, little more than the fioratura augmented second, as of little account. Even more than with 'Yamina' and 'Chebbou-Chebban', the composer has moulded the Arab *donnée* into something new and personal.

Borodin not only 'happened to have' a copy of Salvador-Daniel's collection; he also knew Christianowitsch's *Esquisse historique*. Stasov had drawn his attention to the copy in the St Petersburg Public Library,[6] no doubt the copy Dargomïzhsky had seen. He turned to it in 1881 in order to fulfil a promise to the well-known contralto Darya Mikhaylovna

Leonova, who had recently helped him in a fund-raising concert in aid of his Women's Medical Courses, to compose something specially for her jubilee concert in April. According to Dianin:[7]

Borodin had been looking through the Arabic Kasids in the Public Library with a view to adapting for his own use certain of their motifs, which he valued very highly, when he suddenly had the idea of writing an exotic love-song in a most subtle harmonic setting.

But this is not quite true. Borodin simply copied out the melody of Christianowitsch's 'Insiraf Ghrib' at the same pitch and note for note, except for the substitution in two places of acciaccaturas for double appoggiaturas, added a piano accompaniment with much more subtle harmonies than Christianowitsch's, and wrote a Russian text freely paraphrasing the French one in Christianowitsch:

O toi, qui me fuis! Si tu venais me visiter, ne fut ce qu'en rêve pendant mon sommeil, tu me rendrais la vie, tu guérirais le mal que j'endure. — Ah! prends pitié de moi! Je suis submergé dans la mer de ma passion. Et je ne puis me sauver du gouffre de l'amour.—Belle est ma mort,. c'est la mort d'un martyre!

Thus the title under which the song was posthumously published in 1889, 'Arabskaya melodiya', was absolutely accurate. It is not a composition but merely an arrangement. Having made it, Borodin had qualms about offering it to Leonova. In a draft for a letter to her, dated 5 February 1881,[8] he says:

I had done for you a little thing on an Arab theme, but on mature consideration it seemed to me hardly suitable for the concert and I've started on something else. In my opinion there are so many ordinary sentimental, amorous subjects that they're not worth it, besides who does not sing them? I want something special for you . . .

In the actual letter he sent her, of the same date,[9] there is no mention of the 'Arabskaya melodiya' but he describes the nature of the 'something special' which replaced it:

I have taken a genre subject, popular and humorous; there are not many things of this kind, nor are there any singers except you who can sing them. Your highly artistic performance of such genre-pieces tempts me to try my powers in this style. How it will turn out, I don't know but I shall exert myself and do my best. I only ask you to tell me your opinion and if I get your approval—I'll quickly orchestrate the thing for you.

The 'thing' was the well-known setting of Nekrasov's 'U lyudey-to v

domu'.Borodin did orchestrate it but, owing to the assassination of
Alexander II, Leonova's jubilee had to be celebrated by a domestic
concert (at which she sang Konchakovna's aria from *Igor*). However, it
duly figured in the postponed public concert on 22 January 1882,
when she sang it with orchestra.

One other point is worth making about the *insiraf* which Borodin
borrowed for his 'Arab Melody'. Even if he did not read carefully
through all Christianowitsch's *quarante mélodies*, the attention of even
a browsing Russian reader would be caught by the author's fatuous
footnote to the middle part of the melody—that to which Borodin has
set the words, 'O szhal'sya tï, szhal'sya nado mnoy':

Il y a une ressemblance frappante, entre la mélodie de l'Insiraf Ghrib,
avec celle de l'une des plus vieilles chansons Russes, connue par le
peuple, sous le nom de *'Podbludnaia pesnia'*, chanson des jeux de
Noël. Il serait difficile d'expliquer cette ressemblance si ce n'est en
supposant que cette mélodie eût passé en Russie en venant des Tatares
lors de leur invasion. Cette hypothèse est admissible, vu le rapport qui
existe entre la musique des Tatares et celle des Arabes.

Christianowitsch then quotes the 'Podbludnaia pesnia', which is none
other than the famous 'Slava Bogu na nebe!', familiar to everyone from
the Coronation Scene of *Boris Godunov* and the trio of the third movement of Beethoven's second 'Razumovsky' Quartet, to say nothing of
various works by Rimsky-Korsakov.

NOTES

1. *Letopis* (5th edn, Moscow, 1935), p. 86.
2. 'Perepiska N. A. Balakireva i N. A. Rimskavo-Korsakova', *Muzikal'niy Sovremennik*, i (1916), p. 85, and 'Rimsky-Korsakov: Literaturnïe proizvedeniya i
perepiska', v (Moscow, 1963), p. 103.
3. 'Russian Autographs at Harvard', *Notes* (2nd series), xvii (1960), p. 542;
quoted in my own *Slavonic and Romantic Music* (London, 1968), p. 197.
4. *Vospominaniya*, i (Leningrad, 1959), p. 38. He omits the sharp before the
F in bar 2.
5. *Histoire générale de la musique*, i (Paris, 1869). ' "Ma gazelle" (traduit d'une
kacidah arabe)' appears on pp. 82-3.
6. *A. P. Borodin: evo zhizn', perepiska i muzïkal'nïya stat'i* (St Petersburg,
1889), p. 33.
7. *Borodin* (trans. Robert Lord) (London, 1963), p. 264. The passage does not
occur in either of the Russian editions of Dianin's book.
8. *Pis'ma A. P. Borodina* (ed. Dianin), iii (Moscow and Leningrad, 1949), no.
706.
9. Ibid., no. 707.

7. *Vladimir Stasov: Man and Critic*

A recent English book on music refers in passing to 'a Russian music critic called Stassov'. This is rather like speaking of 'an Irish music critic called Shaw'. It is true that Stasov was not himself a creative artist, though he stimulated a vast amount of creativity in others, but his intellectual energy and the breadth of his interests, his love of controversy, sometimes even his wit and sarcasm, remind one of Shaw. Actually he was even less a 'music critic' than Shaw, for although he wrote occasional concert notices he was never engaged in regular concert criticism as Shaw was for years on *The Star* and *The World*. When the first collected edition of his writings – other than books – appeared in three large volumes in 1894,[1] the first two volumes consisted of art history and criticism, and biographical studies of architects, painters, and sculptors, while hardly more than half the third volume is devoted to 'Music and the Theatre'. And when a small fourth, supplementary volume came out in 1906, the year of his death, the most important study – a survey of 'Art in the Nineteenth Century' – gives 178 pages to painting as against 101 to music. Merely to glance at the titles of a few of the articles gives some idea of Stasov's wide-ranging interests: 'Notes on two ancient Asiatic bronze statuettes found near Lake Van', 'A new Raphael [the "Madonna del libro"] in Petersburg', 'Ornamentation in Russian folk art', 'A catacomb with frescoes found in 1872 near Kerch', 'The Representation of the Hebrew race in European art', 'European capitals and their architecture', 'An exhibition of V. V. Vereshchagin's pictures'. His book reviews, always substantial, sometimes Macaulayan in proportions, range from Alfred Butler's *The Ancient Coptic Churches of Egypt* to Zola's *L'Oeuvre*. In 1847, at the age of twenty-three, he reviewed Grote's *History of Greece*, Harris Nicolas's *Memoirs of the Life and Times of Sir Christopher Hatton*, Bulwer-Lytton's *Lucrezia*, Fenimore Cooper's *Ravensnest*, Disraeli's *Contarini Fleming* and *Tancred*, Dickens's *Pictures from Italy*, Lord Lindsay's *Sketches of the*

History of Christian Art, E. F. Apelt's *Die Epochen der Geschichte der Menschheit*, Heinrich Alt's *Theater und Kirche in ihrem gegenseitigen Verhältniss*, Niebuhr's *Vorträge über alte Geschichte*, W. A. Schmidt's *Geschichte der Denk- und Glaubensfreiheit im I-sten Jahrhundert der Kaiserschaft und des Christenthums*, and the first volume of Schiller's correspondence with Körner. Archaeology, history – not only art history but political history and the history of ideas – biography, contemporary writing: here already Stasov's main interests are revealed. And music as well: in 1847, besides the 'Review of the Year', he also published a seven-column review of Henselt's piano transcription of the *Freischütz* Overture, making detailed technical criticisms and particularly attacking Henselt for ignoring the contemporary methods of transcription as developed by Liszt.

It is only because the Western world is more interested in Russian music than in Russian painting, architecture, or archaeology that we read the lives of Russian musicians but not those of Russian painters, and so we know Stasov as the friend and propagandist of the Russian nationalist composers, the first biographer of Musorgsky and Borodin, the instigator and provider of programmes or scenarios for *Khovanshchina* and *Prince Igor* and Tchaikovsky's *Tempest*, but not as the friend and propagandist of Repin and Vereshchagin, Antokolsky and Kramskoy. He was not a propagandist of Tolstoy or Turgenev, but he was a valued friend. Aylmer Maude tells us in his *Life of Tolstoy* that 'his immense knowledge of books, as well as the great library at his command, enabled him to be of much use to Tolstoy when the latter wanted to read up any subject he was dealing with', and also that he was (typically) one of the first volunteers of information when Maude began to contemplate his biography.[2] Incidentally, Stasov makes one anonymous appearance in that *Life*:

When he [Tolstoy] was over seventy I remember taking a walk with him and a friend of his – a well-known literary man who was still older. The latter was saying that Tolstoy's assertions did not accord with his (the speaker's) own experience of life. He had a mistress and did not consider that it spoilt his life.[3]

The 'well-known literary man' was, as Maude himself told me, Stasov.

As a boy, Stasov had wanted to be an architect – which was very natural, since his father, Vasily Petrovich Stasov (1769-1848), was one of the greatest Russian architects of his day, held in high favour by

Alexander I and Nicholas I, and designer of the Trinity (Izmaylovsky) and Transfiguration (Preobrazhensky) Cathedrals, the Imperial Barracks and the Moscow Arch at St Petersburg, as well as an early masterpiece – the beautiful bell-tower on Arakcheyev's estate at Gruzino, near Novgorod.[4] The architect's fifth child, Vladimir Vasilevich, was born on 14 January 1824, just too late to be conscious of the Emperor Alexander who 'loved to meet and converse with' his beautiful mother when the family were living at Tsarskoe Selo. The mother died in 1831 and it was the father who fashioned the boy in his own image, for he was interested in very much more than his profession, 'highly cultivated, reading much, and (above all) of an enquiring mind'; at 79, during the last months of his life, he made Vladimir read to him *Faust*, Hegel's *Aesthetics*, and various travel-books. His favourite saying, 'A man is worthy of the name only when he is of use to himself and to others', became his son's lifelong motto.

The Stasov children, five brothers and two sisters, were at an early age taught foreign languages, drawing, and music. Their earliest music teachers were of little account but toward the end of the 1830s they had Anton Gerke, the best piano teacher in Petersburg – ten years later he taught Musorgsky – a Pole who introduced them to the music of Chopin and Schumann. Before this, in 1836, Vladimir had entered the new, so-called Law School (really a school for future civil servants founded by the Tsar's nephew, Prince Peter of Oldenburg) which was housed in one of his father's buildings. Thanks to its founder's passion for music, the School was a hot-bed of musical activity; the pupils were expected to study either a string or a wind instrument and become a member of its school orchestra, and from 1838 the principal piano teacher was Adolf Henselt. The fourteen-year-old Stasov actually studied with the classically inclined Henselt at the School on week-days and with the 'romantic' Gerke at home on Sundays; in 1840 he appeared at a School concert as pianist in Hummel's Septet and later as soloist in concertos with the School orchestra. His intimate friend was A. N. Serov, just four years older than himself, later to be famous as music critic and composer, already a good amateur pianist and like himself an enthusiast for art and literature, though Serov was more interested in painting and German literature, while Stasov preferred architecture and the French classics. Both tried their hands at musical composition. They heard every great performer who visited Petersburg: Thalberg, Pasta, Lipiński, Ole Bull, and, most impressive of all, Liszt. As we learn from Stasov's famous account of 'Liszt, Schumann and Berlioz in Russia', it was during Liszt's visit that he got to know the Russian musician who was his lifelong hero, Glinka.

In the field of painting Stasov then greatly admired K. P. Bryullov, the most famous Russian painter of the day,[5] and would visit the Kazan Cathedral in the early morning, waiting for the sun to light up Bryullov's 'Assumption', before which he would then sit for hours in adoration. 'Through another Bryullov picture, the 'Crucifixion' in the Lutheran Church of Peter and Paul, he made the acquaintance of the organ — unknown in Orthodox churches — and, more important, of the fugues of Bach which made not only a deeper but a much more lasting impression than the works of Bryullov.[6] Throughout his life he would visit the Lutheran Church to hear an oratorio or the *Matthew Passion*. (But the 'Herr von Stassoff' who appears among the early subscribers to the Bach-Gesellschaft edition was his brother Dmitry.) The contemporary Russian writers who influenced him most in adolescence were Belinsky, Gogol, and Lermontov; he read the complete works of Winckelmann in German and soon came across Heine, whose work he loved 'passionately, though well aware of his unevenness and his shortcomings'. All this meant much more to him than what he was actually taught at the Imperial Law School, where the — mostly German — teachers were sound but pedantic. Already at the School, too, he distinguished himself by his gift for sarcasm; on two occasions his victims retaliated with penknife attacks. For his part, during his very first days at the School, when another boy jeered at him he seized him by the ears and threw him to the ground.

Leaving the School at nineteen, Stasov entered the Survey Department of the Ruling Senate. But one reason after another would prophetically direct his steps in his spare time to the Imperial Public Library, first to study in the collection of prints in the art department, then to help a friend in the department of foreign books; and in 1847 another friend, who had been reviewing foreign books for the *Otechestvennïe Zapiski* and was now moving to Moscow, recommended him as his successor to the editor Kraevsky. Hence the astounding crop of reviews described above and hence, also, Stasov's first essay in musical criticism. Professionally, he moved from one government department to another until in 1851 he was offered, and joyfully accepted, a chance to escape. He took the post of Russian secretary to the immensely wealthy Prince A. N. Demidov, who had an estate at San Donato near Florence.

In May he resigned from the government service and next month travelled by way of Berlin and Cologne to London, where he stayed at Long's Hotel, New Bond Street, from 30 June (new style) till the end of July. He saw all the usual sights, including the Great Exhibition, and visited Windsor Castle and the House of Commons, where he saw Lord John Russell in action. Demidov's influence opened all doors to him. He heard *Elijah* at Exeter Hall and *Figaro* at the Queen's Theatre. But what impressed him most of all was the acting of Rachel in Schiller's *Maria Stuart*. She gave him some of the deepest artistic impressions of his highly impressionable life; he saw her afterwards in Paris and Italy in most of her great roles and wrote later: 'How many lands and cities I have traversed since those times, how much I have seen, how much I have changed! But one thing has not changed—my passion for Rachel'. From London he went to Paris and then by way of Basle to Florence, where he had a flat in the Palazzo Ricci Altoviti. Characteristically, he immediately hired a piano on which the first things he played were Beethoven's Sixth and Ninth Symphonies, in four-hand arrangements, with another of Demidov's young secretaries, brother of the then well-known pianist and composer Theodor Döhler. He played Bach's *Forty-eight*, as well as the Viennese classics, and before long he was writing to his favourite brother Dmitry:

What should I have done here without all my music? Sometimes I should have been completely lost. For me music is not simply a pleasure, like others, but the *sole medicine* for my spleen and my black days. Just like David's music for Saul. Only just as our music towers millions of versts above the poor and meagre music of David's harp, so much deeper and sharper is my pain compared with Saul's . . .

Stasov stayed in Italy until early in 1854, mostly in Florence but also visting Rome, Naples, Venice, as well as making an expedition to Vienna. The impression made on him by Italy, her people, her cities, and above all her incomparable art-treasures—many of which he had copied for Demidov—may be imagined. But he was by no means bowled over by every masterpiece; in the Sistine Chapel he found fault with Michelangelo's 'Last Judgement' though the 'Creation' was another matter—'that is where he is the *whole* Michelangelo'; as for the Colosseum, he regarded this as an 'architecturally clumsy elephant'. And while Italy opened his ears to older music, this did not happen at once; he was bored by Allegri's famous *Miserere* in the Sistine Chapel and a Gloria by Marcello he found 'good, but not particularly':

How far, for example, from the Haydn choruses in the *Schöpfung*, not to speak of the Choral Fantasia [of Beethoven], the final chorus of *Fidelio*, the Sanctus of the *Requiem* [Mozart's] and all our own things. (Letter to his family, 29 March/10 April 1852.)

But a couple of months later he had had copies made of Arcadelt's 'marvellous' (but, alas, spurious) 'Ave Maria' and a number of Palestrina motets, and his conversion was completed by his meeting with the Abbé Santini, the famous Roman collector of old music. His first thought on seeing Santini's wonderful library, he told his brothers (letter of 29 May/10 June), was to ask the old man to have copied for him *'all* Palestrina, who has now become absolutely my *passion*':

But then I judged it better to begin with those famous names which so far I don't know at all, and so I ordered from him the best things of *Durante, Leo, Scarlatti, Anerio, Benevoli, Bernabei, Pitoni*; then will come *Jomelli, Clari*, various printed things by *Marcello, Carissimi*, etc. But I'm awfully afraid this will make away with much of my travel money. What's to be done? I shall arrange things as best I can so as not to lose my present chance, which won't come again. . . . Santini lets me borrow and take home whatever I like. . . . Since I've been here I scarcely ever play either Mozart or Beethov[en] any more — always *Palestrina, Marcello*, and goodness knows whom else.

He was already thinking of having as much as possible performed in Petersburg by Lomakin, the director of Count Sheremetyev's then famous choir. (This was actually done after Stasov's return home.) It would help if Lomakin would send lists of what he has already and what he would like to have:

church things or secular, long or short, i.e. *motets* or madrigals; *Masses*, requiems, *lamentations* (there are hundreds of them), *cantatas*, with accompaniment or without, etc.

Later he became interested in still older music; before Lent 1853 Santini had had copied for him two Masses by Arcadelt, and *Lamentationes* and Magnificats by Carpentras, Goudimel, Févin, Festa, Lejeune, Cadéac, Certon, Claudin de Sermisy, as well as Handel chamber duets, Alessandro Scarlatti's *Missa in canone* and 'a fat book of Palestrina motets chosen by me'. And there was much more to come: duets by Steffani and Agostini, works by Lassus and Marenzio, Benevoli's 16-part Mass. . . . No wonder he could write to Glinka that he had had tons of music copied for him 'so that when I return to Russia a long caravan will have to accompany me'. Long before this he had been sending home smaller consignments of more ordinary musical purchases:

Handel, Gluck, Mozart, Beethoven – and a vocal score of Purcell's *King Arthur*,[7] in which he was impressed above all by 'Come, if you dare', to which he refers again and again in his letters. (I will say nothing of his non-musical purchases, which range from treatises on Egyptian obelisks and the manufacture of boric acid to architectural books and a volume of 'petits poèmes grecs'.) But it was the Santini collection which widened his musical horizon so vastly. He paid tribute to it in an article in the Petersburg *Biblioteka dlya chteniya* (April and July 1853),[8] a much extended French version of which, *L'Abbé Santini et sa collection musicale à Rome*, was published in a limited edition of 250 copies at Stasov's own expense in Florence in 1854 on the eve of his departure; he sent copies to Liszt, Berlioz, Fétis, and Ulybyshev among others; and more than half a century was to pass before a Western scholar – a German, Joseph Killing – was to write anything of comparable value on the contents of Santini's library. As for the manuscript copies, in 1870 Stasov presented the lot – some four hundred works from the fifteenth to the nineteenth centuries – to the St Petersburg Public Library.

Stasov began to work in the Library soon after his return to Russia in the spring of 1854. Demidov no longer needed him and he was at a loose end. He found that under a new director, Baron Korff, the Library had become a much more lively and attractive institution; he spent most of his time there, and before long V. I. Sobolshchikov, head of the department of art and *Rossica*, suggested that he should compile a systematic catalogue of the latter section. 'Systematization, arranging in categories, had always been my passion in everything', he wrote later, 'and here was my chance to set in order some tens of thousands of books concerned with practically every sphere of human knowledge, in this astonishing, unique section *Rossica*'. He did not catalogue without reading and it seemed to him that 'in a few months he had learned more new things than previously in many years'. He published articles – on a medieval Greek treatise on church song by a pseudonymous 'Hagiopolites' which he had found in Paris in the Bibliothèque Nationale, of which he presented a copy to the Petersburg Library, on the autograph manuscripts of musicians in the Petersburg Library, on the sumptuous 1855 French edition of the *Imitatio Christi* – and when in 1856 his catalogue of *Rossica* had been approved by the Academy of Sciences he compiled for Sobolshchikov lists of art books which should be acquired. Before the end of the year he was appointed personal assistant to Korff with the special task of collecting material for a history of the reign of Nicholas I (which had ended the year before);

beside this anonymous work, Stasov's labours in the Imperial archives produced a number of monographs, some published, others preserved in the Imperial Chancery and printed for official circulation only. He also arranged a series of exhibitions in the Library, beginning with one of all the engraved portraits of Peter the Great which occupied him for several months. His activity was already indefatigable and many-sided: through a sea-captain he got hold of an eleventh-century Georgian version of the Gospels, an emissary was dispatched to Athens to photograph Slavonic and Greek manuscripts, Prince M. A. Volkonsky was induced to collect for presentation to the Library 'Athenian popular woodcut pictures of sacred subjects'. When Glinka died in 1857, Stasov secured for the Library his musical autographs, his autobiography, and some two hundred letters.

In 1856 Stasov had made the acquaintance of the twenty-year-old Balakirev, and soon began to play that inspirational role in Russian music with which Western readers are familiar. And not only in Russian music but in Russian art generally. Repin and Antokolsky regarded him as their teacher, and he was closely associated with Kramskoy's Free Artists' Co-operative of 1863 and the Society of Travelling Exhibitions — the so-called *Peredvizhniki*, or *Ambulants* as French critics call them —which developed from the Co-operative in 1870. The period 1856-72 was that of Stasov's chief activity as a historian and of his greatest influence on the minds of his creative contemporaries. At the latter date he became head of the department of art in the Library and was more absorbed by official responsibilities. But he resisted. Twice there was question of his appointment as director of the Library, but he flatly refused. 'Neither by nature, by character nor by inclination am I capable of being an administrator or the *head* of anything', he wrote to the Minister. Besides, as he confided to his brother, 'there would be the impossibility of writing freely, *democratically*, controversially. ... Once I had taken on the directorship it would be goodbye to my bold, light-hearted, jolly polemics'. And this was in 1899, when he was 75.

Polemics were the breath of life to him. As a young man, he ruefully admitted his 'unfortunate habit' of quarrelling about matters of art, 'of which, it seems, I shall never cure myself and which has spoiled for me many a pleasant acquaintanceship'. He always wanted, indeed needed, to share his enthusiasms—'It is always absolutely essential to me that many others, that *everyone*, should be pleased by what pleases me', he wrote in 1852—and a failure to share his enthusiasms was unforgivable. Serov's lack of sympathy for Balakirev and his circle[9] and for Glinka's

Ruslan led Stasov to break with his oldest and closest musical friend, and with such bitterness that when in 1865 they met by the grave of Serov's mother, to whom Stasov had been devoted, he refused to take the offered hand of his former friend. But it was this passionate need to share his enthusiasms that made him such a wonderful source of inspiration to others. His ardent love of Russian legend, Russian literature, and Russian history made him send Rimsky-Korsakov—he had already tried to send Balakirev—to *Sadko*,[10] Borodin to *Prince Igor*, Musorgsky to *Khovanshchina*. He sent Tchaikovsky to Shakespeare's *Tempest* and provided him with the outline programme which he actually used, just as he had earlier sent Berlioz the programme for a symphony on Byron's *Manfred*—the very same programme that Tchaikovsky acquired from Balakirev many years later. (In 1852, in Italy, he had wanted to find a comic-opera libretto to wake the sleeping genius of Rossini.) These enthusiasms were twofold: for the subject and for the artist. And when he found an artist whose ideals were nearly, as with Balakirev between 1857 and 1864, or totally—as with Musorgsky and with Repin until the later years—identical with his own, he boiled over.

Gusto, in both senses, was the real keynote of his criticism: idiosyncratic *gusto* supported by vast learning and spiced with sarcasm. One must not expect from him cool, objective criticism, deep and subtle penetration, or even striking originality of thought. He loved *life* above all and was impatient with Tolstoy's insistence that he ought to be thinking about death, though he did think much of death in his last years, especially after a serious fall in the summer of 1904. 'He always thought only of life, activity and creativity', wrote one of his nieces with pardonable overstatement, and much of the value of his criticism lay in his infectious vitality; he is the archetype of the propagandist–critic.

He stated the basis of his critical beliefs very early, in a long letter to his father written on New Year's Day 1844, the eve of his twentieth birthday:[11]

Hitherto all criticism of the arts has consisted of saying: this is good, this is bad, this is not seemly, here are such-and-such errors in costume, here in proportion, etc. No talent is needed for such criticism as this, only a certain degree of *study* and *learning*, consequently *anybody* (for any untalented fellow can learn and know the technical parts with which such criticism deals—hands, feet, capitals) can *enounce* such criticism . . . and consequently all the criticism written up to this time can be quietly destroyed since it is helpful neither to the works themselves nor to those who look at them.

All 'so-called aesthetic criticism' falls under this condemnation, although 'Plato, Kant, Hegel and some others have said good things about the arts *in general*'; these critics look at works of art as at mirrors, finding only reflections of their own tastes and emotions.

But what should we demand from works of art, what are the arts for? They don't exist for their details but to state *a whole*, concentrated in one point, the product of all its parts, all its elements. . . . This whole . . . is closely connected with the most important questions of mankind, inseparable from universal history; for it doesn't exist for the satisfaction of refined feeling, it exists together with life, with which it decides questions whose origins cannot be separated from conscious life. . . .

Every real work of art . . . bears within itself its *meaning* and its *allotted task*; to reveal both of these for the human race is the task of criticism, and such criticism has not existed for the arts (however, it has begun for *the art of poetry*). So it is not for criticism to invent something new or to invent factual adornment of the existent; its duty is to extract from the work of art itself its vital idea, *by which* and *for which* the whole work exists with all its beauty and greatness; in short, criticism of the arts must show that works have been created in the world up to now . . . by what means they utter their inner thought, and the *meaning* of this thought for the world, i.e. criticism must show the indispensability of these productions to the world. . . .

This thought is so simple and clear that, once it has occurred to you, it seems impossible to take in works of art in any other way; but this has not been the case. . . . A difficult question awaits me on this point: for what have the arts existed for some thousands of years if their real significance was not known? This is one of the first questions of the philosophy of history . . . the inseparable connection between the history of the human race and the arts in this human race, and the examination of it, and likewise the attitude of the whole mass of people existing up to the present time with regard to the arts, all this must be decided by the history of the arts, if only these problems are soluble.

Thus workers in the arts are of two kinds: the *artist* and the *critic of art*. Feeling the inevitability of having to work to the best of my powers as the latter, I first of all had to find the limits of some extensive field lying before me for future cultivation, i.e. I had to *fix on certain products* (and consequently that which had produced them), throwing all else into the river of eternal oblivion; little remained, by way of reward, but that little comprises everything that *to this day* the world needs (it will go further, and therefore the art corresponding to it will be in equilibrium with it); between them exists the law of *inevitable consequence* or *succession*, and this again is a problem of art criticism.

I cannot accept existing appraisals and traditions; from the very start (because on different bases) I was obliged to begin my own appraisals, the result of different *demands*, and thus many former idols were burned. . . .

From what I have said about criticism it becomes clear that such criticism must embrace *all* the arts, absolutely without exception, since they are essentially different sides and means of one and the same general whole. . . . When one leaves off, there another begins. . . .

Another significant remark occurs near the end of the letter:

The greater the artist, the more he is a man, the more he feels himself connected with the world and his fellow-men. . . .

No doubt much of this, particularly the emphasis on the inseparability of art from humanity, was influenced by Belinsky, who had recently begun to write in this sense. These were the views later adopted more and more widely by Russian intellectuals, especially after the appearance of Chernïshevsky's *Aesthetic Relationships of Art to Reality* (1855) and the writings of Dobrolyubov, which absolutely dominated Russian thought during the 1860s, which Tolstoy developed to absurdity in *What is Art?* in 1898 (by which time they had become 'old stuff', as Chekhov said), and which are the foundation of the Soviet doctrine of 'socialist realism'. But Stasov must have been one of Belinsky's earliest disciples. The remarkable thing is that he never modified his creed. Balakirev and Repin fell victims to mysticism, as Gogol and Perov (the first notable realist–nationalist Russian painter) had done before them; in fact, mysticism in one form or another, with artistic cosmopolitanism, 'decadence', aestheticism, *art nouveau*, impressionism, had supplanted the ideals of the 1860s in the Russia of Stasov's later years. But he went on till his death in 1906, fighting faithfully for his old beliefs, in the Russia of Chekhov, Skryabin, Merezhkovsky, and Dyagilev's *World of Art*. In 1903 he astonished Rimsky-Korsakov by pronouncing his 'realistic' *Mozart and Salieri* to be a masterpiece 'side by side with *Snowmaiden*'. And his last published article, 'A Friendly Commemoration', shows him once more in his early role of Schumann's champion.

Next to realism, Stasov placed nationalism; it was the combination of both in Musorgsky and Repin that specially endeared their work to him. His English disciple, Mrs Newmarch, has put on record his remark that 'if you strip a Russian of his nationalists, you leave a man several degrees inferior to other Europeans'[12] and in some cases—for instance, that of the architect Viktor Hartmann, who would hardly be remembered if Musorgsky had not immortalized the posthumous exhibition of his sketches—he over-valued inferior artists on account of the Russianness of their work. He interested himself in the collection of Russian lace-work and old Russian textiles, and in the totally unrealistic field of ornamentation—provided it was Russian or had Russian connections.

Indeed, he was an authority on it and his *Slavonic and Oriental Ornament according to Manuscripts of Ancient and Modern Times* (1884) is a landmark.

'Romanticism' mattered to Stasov mainly in a negative sense, as opposed to classic beauty, beauty for its own sake, and art smelling of the conservatoire. He preferred the irregular townscape of Florence to the classical monuments of Rome, the medieval to the Renaissance, and the Renaissance to the Baroque — for which he had no sympathy at all: 'How can one compare the soulless, cold and stupidly correct buildings and churches of the 17th or (still worse) 18th century with the bold, always original, always different, always unexpected, always irregular and hence always beautiful forms of medieval architecture'. Even the Russian neo-classical architecture of the late eighteenth and early nineteenth centuries ceased to please him. He equated originality and irregularity with life, and not only in art; wherever he went, he was more attracted by the lower classes who behaved freely and naturally than by polite and conventional society. He was acutely conscious of the frequent failure of art to match itself against life and, faced as a young man with the experience of Rome and the efforts of the minor artists who sketched and painted it, could exclaim, 'How happy I am that I *don't know how to draw*!' His scorn for Goethe in Italy, more interested in pseudo-Greek statues than in the marvellous Italian peasant women, was profound.

Yet other indications that in the end life mattered even more to him than art were his relationships with Balakirev, Repin, and Antokolsky. All three drew away from him in their artistic ideals and there were consequent strains in their personal relationships; but there was no bitter break as there had been with Serov. In his last letter to Antokolsky,[13] written in 1902 not long before the sculptor's death, he says, 'Maybe we differ in our opinions about art. So be it! There's no harm nor sin in that. There's not the slightest need for everyone in the world to hold one and the same opinion about art . . .' This is very different from the intolerant Stasov of forty years earlier. Not that he had moved an inch from his old positions, but an old friendship was now too valuable to lose for an old opinion. He was delighted when Balakirev in 1900 sent him his First Symphony, begun many years before, but he did not spare him some adverse criticism, and when the still earlier *King Lear* music was printed at last in 1904 he rather touchingly hoped 'you didn't destroy and won't destroy the dedication of *Lear* to me. Repin, once being angry with me, destroyed on his marvellous picture "Liszt" (a full-length) the dedication of this picture to me'. But 'dear, dear, dear, a hundred times dear Mily' had let the *Lear* dedication stand, and when the score arrived as an eighty-first birthday present, Stasov sent him in return his latest book, *Shakespeare's 'Merchant of Venice'* (St Petersburg, 1904) and wrote:

How happy I am that you still remember me and those happy days when I lived in the whole orchestra of life, and when you began and composed *Lear*. So that time and our then still young relationships and transports remain engraved even in music, its sounds and poetry!! How grateful I am![14]

Some years before, he had written to Rimsky-Korsakov's wife that he was 'like a bulldog, in that I hold on hard with my teeth to anything I've once got hold of firmly and affectionately': herself, her husband, Pargolovo where he had spent his summers for nearly fifty years. And his mind kept going back to 'poor, unhappy' Gussakovsky, one of the minor members of the *kuchka* who, like Lodïzhensky, never fulfilled the high hopes aroused in his youth. He wanted to arrange for the publication of Gussakovsky's works—they are still in manuscript—and his very last letter to Balakirev (25 January 1906) ended with a request to be told

What can you remember of our poor talented Ukrainian, untimely dead *Gussakovsky*? How I should like to preserve his image! To this day I can't forget, it's as if it were yesterday, how he burst into tears when I read you both one evening the sixth book of the *Iliad* (Hector's farewell to Andromache). Ah, how marvellous was that time!!!

NOTES

1. *Sobranie sochineniy V. V. Stasova: 1847-1886* (St Petersburg, 1894).
2. 'World's Classics' edn, ii, pp. 428 and 436.
3. Ibid., ii, p. 281.
4. The Gruzino tower and Moscow Arch are illustrated in G. H. Hamilton, *The Art and Architecture of Russia* (London, 1954), pl. 137.
5. In the long letter to his father (1 January 1844) quoted from below, he brackets Bryullov with Mozart, Shakespeare, Homer, and Beethoven. His admiration for Bryullov did not last, however.
6. Glinka was so amused by Stasov's passion for Bach that he nicknamed him 'Bach', and the name was used for many years by his intimate friends. Balakirev usually converts it into an affectionate diminutive: 'Bakhinka'.
7. Some passage in one of Walter Scott's novels led him to believe that Purcell was an Elizabethan.
8. Reprinted in the *Sobranie sochineniy*, iii, col. 1.

9. For whom Stasov inadvertently in 1867 coined the nickname by which they
    have since been known: 'the mighty handful'. His article in the *St Peterburg-*
    skie Vedomosti on 'Mr Balakirev's Slav Concert' (reprinted in the *Sobranie*
    sochineniy, iii, col. 217) ended with the wish, 'God grant that our Slav
    guests may never forget today's concert, God grant that they may forever
    preserve the memory of how much poetry, feeling, talent and intelligence are
    possessed by the small but already mighty handful of Russian musicians (*u*
    malenkoy, no uzhe moguchey kuchki russkikh muzïkantov)!' But the
    Russian musicians actually represented in this programme were not the
    so-called 'five' but Glinka, Dargomïzhsky, Balakirev, and Rimsky-Korsakov.
10. He exercised strong influence on both *Sadko*s. The original 'programme' of
    the early orchestral piece was his and when, more than a quarter of a century
    later, Rimsky-Korsakov first thought of using the subject for an opera, Stasov
    pounced on the first, very limited scenario by N. M. Shtrupp, which the
    composer had sent him, and enthusiastically urged all sorts of additions –
    notably the crowd scenes in Novgorod, which are the making of the opera –
    and the introduction of Sadko's wife. (See Rimsky-Korsakov, *Literaturnïe*
    proizvedeniya i perepiska, v (Moscow, 1963), particularly Stasov's letter of
    7 July 1894: Rimsky-Korsakov's account in his autobiography, which most
    biographers and critics–including myself–have followed, is very inaccurate.)
    When the libretto was completed, he vigorously criticized verbal ineptitudes:
    one phrase sounded like 'Tatar or Mongolian or Kirgiz' and one mustn't
    speak of 'pothouse beggars' because there were no 'pothouses' (*kabaki*)
    in Russia before the sixteenth century: to use the word 'in Russian antiquity'
    was 'the same as introducing *cannon, rifles, carriages, French quadrilles* and
    polkas', so he offers twenty-two alternatives 'and 100 others' if necessary.
    But Korsakov kept to *kabaki*.
11. Printed in *Pisma k rodnïm*, i (Moscow, 1953), pp. 33–45.
12. Rosa Newmarch, *The Russian Arts* (London, 1916), p. 261.
13. *Pisma k deyatelyam russkoy kulturï*, i (Moscow, 1962), p. 96.
14. Ibid., p. 149.

8. Some Eighteenth-Century Polish Symphonies

Whereas the symphonies of Czech-born composers of the eighteenth century—though, it is true, more those of the emigrants to Mannheim, Paris, and Italy than those of their compatriots (such as J. A. F. Miča) who stayed at home—are historically famous, the Polish symphonies of the same period remain almost unknown in the West. Indeed they have until recently been largely unknown even to Polish musicians. When in 1932 Henryk Opieński was writing about eighteenth-century Polish symphonists,[1] he was able to name in addition to the two he was dealing with—Wojciech Dankowski (*c*. 1762–*c*. 1820) and Jan Wański the elder (1762–after 1800)—only two others: Jakub Gołąbek (*c*. 1739–89) and Antoni Milwid (dates unknown). Since the War, thanks very largely in the first place to the researches of Tadeusz Strumiłło, who died tragically young, the picture has altered enormously. At a Round Table of the Congress of the International Musicological Society at Salzburg in 1964 Hieronim Feicht spoke of the great number of early Polish symphonies now known and of the employment in some of them of Polish folk themes. And at Bydgoszcz two years later Jan Węcowski read a paper[2] summing up the then state of research, with a valuable appendix in the form of a catalogue of non-Polish eighteenth-century symphonies preserved in Polish libraries. At the same time reliable publication began. In 1951–2 the conductor Jan Krenz had published 'practical' versions of one of Dankowski's two D major Symphonies, and Milwid's in C major as a 'Sinfonia concertante' for oboe and symphony orchestra, but the first Polish symphony to appear in a scholarly text was one (dated 1771) by a totally unknown composer, A. Haczewski, which Strumiłło printed in the musical appendix to his *Źródła i początki romantyzmu w muzyce polskiej* (Cracow, 1956). Then three of Gołąbek's symphonies and two of Wański's were published in Szweykowski's series *Źródła do historii muzyki polskiej* (Cracow, 1962) and in 1964 the same general editor embarked on a special series of *Symfonie polskie* in which works by Paszczyński, Pietrowski, Pawłowski, Orłowski, Namieyski, Bohdanowicz and others appeared.

Not one of these names is likely to be familiar to any Western musician who has not interested himself in Slavonic culture. These were not composers working in the wider context of European music and contributing to its main stream, like Mysliveček and Jírovec (Gyrowetz) and Vaňhal. Some, like Haczewski and 'Giacomo' Pasczyński, are totally unknown, surviving only in single symphonies to which their names are attached. Karol Pietrowski has left a 'Veni Creator' for three solo voices, two violins, two trumpets, and continuo and a 'Jesu Corona Virginum' for soprano and the same instruments in addition to his two symphonies, but neither his dates nor anything else about him is known. Milwid is slightly less shadowy; he was a member of the church *kapela* at Czerwińsk and composed Masses and other church music. Gołąbek belonged to the *kapela* of Cracow Cathedral. Wański was a violinist at Poznań and wrote operas and church music. Dankowski was a prolific composer of church music, which turns up all over the place, and in 1792 played the viola in the orchestra of the German theatre at Lwów under Elsner. Practically all were local musicians who composed for the local vocal/instrumental *kapela*. And according to J. Kitowicz,[3] symphonies were sometimes played by the *kapele* in church, at aristocratic houses before balls, and at marriages and other festivities. Symphonies thus written by the local composer for the local band for the great house in the neighbourhood must clearly not be judged by international standards, but if studied sympathetically for what they are, these unpretentious—sometimes quite primitive—works of art offer a great deal of interest.

Two of the most primitive are the already mentioned D major Symphony of Haczewski and the Symphony in the same key by Bazyli Bohdanowicz,[4] found in the library of the Theological Seminary at Sandomierz and probably also dating from the 1770s since Bohdanowicz emigrated to Vienna in 1780 and became a viola-player at Karl Marinelli's Leopoldstadt Theatre. Haczewski's is scored for 2 flutes, 2 horns, and strings, Bohdanowicz's for 2 oboes, 2 horns,[5] and strings. In both the weakest movement is the first; the invention is extremely poor, though Bohdanowicz's second subject shows that he was acquainted with Mannheim idioms and to keep it going he employs a device he uses later almost *ad nauseam*: the echoing of first-violin phrases by the seconds at the same pitch or an octave lower. The pseudo-development is no more than a brief, pointless modulation in Haczewski, practically non-existent in Bohdanowicz. But both become a little more interesting in the later movements, which in each include a polonaise. Indeed Haczewski's central movement – he has only three – is the *alla polacca* (Ex. 1), in the middle section of which the flute, mostly solo, has an independent part. The flutes in thirds dominate the entire minor middle section of the finale, a 2/4 ternary *allegretto* which suggests a krakowiak.

Ex. 1

In Bohdanowicz's Symphony the 'Polonese' is an additional movement to the usual scheme: slow movement (without tempo marking) for strings only; minuet and trio; 'Polonese'; and 3/8 *presto moderato* finale in sonata form, with a substantial development of 45 bars. The second strain of his polonaise (Ex. 2) shows a striking relationship to

Ex. 2

Haczewski's, and the syncopated openings of most of the melodic phrases of his slow movement are related rhythmically to those of the polonaise and melodically to the second strain of its trio.

Pietrowski's two symphonies[6] and Namieyski's[7] – all three in D – represent a rather more sophisticated type of symphony, though the clinging to D major, an easy key for the violins as well as the brass (which are always crooked in D, although the horns appear in F in the modern scores), suggests that they were written for not particularly skilful players. Indeed the only score of Namieyski's Symphony known for a long time was in the parish church music at Grodzisk in Poznańia, though another, anonymous, copy (dated 1834) turned up later in the library of the Monastery of the Pauline Fathers at Częstochowa; an inscription on the Grodzisk manuscript tells us that the church acquired it 'from the papers of Stanis. Ścigalski', presumably a relative of Franciszek Ścigalski, himself the composer of a 'Symphonia grande' (as well as a number of liturgical works), from which Strumiłło published the slow movement in the musical appendix to his *Zródła i poczatki romantyzmu*. We know even less of Namieyski than we do of Pietrowski, not even his Christian name or other compositions by him, though the making of a copy as late as 1834 suggests that his Symphony enjoyed some little reputation. The existence of two copies also provides an association, if not exactly a link, with a composer of whom we know rather more: the Silesian-born Jakub Gołąbek, member of the Cathedral *kapela* at Cracow from about 1774 until his death on 30 March 1789.[8] For his Symphony (II) in D was also 'offered to the Church in Grodzisk by Stani. Ścigalski', a copy of his C major Symphony was found in the Pauline Monastery at Częstochowa, and a list of symphonies—also dated 1834—in the same Monastery includes both Namieyski's Symphony and symphonies in D and C by Gołąbek, no doubt the Grodzisk D major and the C major we know.

Of these three—Gołąbek, Namieyski, and Pietrowski—Gołąbek was probably the oldest. He writes for the same orchestra as Bohdanowicz, except that in the finale of the C major Symphony he exchanges the oboes for flutes, but with much more enterprise. His wind are more independent of the strings and in the finale of D major (I), for which he provides a bassoon part, he has a long passage for wind only. That he had a penchant for the wind is apparent also from his C major Partita for clarinets, horns, and bassoon.[9] Thematic invention was not his strong point; his first subjects are all fanfare-like and, as Muchenberg points out, all his insipid second subjects are cast in the same rhythmic, and nearly the same melodic, mould. Muchenberg has no difficulty in finding a number of Mannheim affinities; indeed Węcowski's catalogue shows that the Mannheimers and Czechs—and early Haydn—were well known in Poland ('Hayden is a very good composer', someone has written on one of the Grodzisk scores), but not Sammartini or Monn, the Bach brothers hardly at all, and not Mozart. (Mozart's operas were known but not his symphonies.) Gołąbek's first movements are typical of the mid-century formal experiments before the general acceptance of sonata form. In his D major (I) the first subject is extended and followed by wandering modulations which return to a fresh tonic theme before the dominant second subject appears; the 'development' is hardly more than a tonal interruption and the recapitulation is a mere 24 bars in which the second subject never reappears at all. Indeed Gołąbek never does bring back the second subject in his recapitulations. In the exposition of D major (II) it is the second subject which is allowed to expand, but the recapitulation is even shorter, a mere 8-bar reference to the first subject, followed by a 34-bar coda which refers back at one point in the bass to a passage heard twice in the development. In the C major occurs something like a true development, in the sense of ideas being worked through a series of harmonies; the recapitulation is, as usual, very brief.

Gołąbek's slow movements differ considerably: a short binary *andante* (still in D major), a *rondeau andante* so-called (really a binary-form theme with two variations), and in the C major an extended binary movement on a theme of a much less conventional type, rather suggesting a sentimental song of the day, with an odd little imitative interruption. So with the finales – for all three symphonies are three-movement compositions: D (II) ends with an *allegro molto* in binary form, the C major with a 3/8 *prestissimo* sonata-rondo, while D (I) concludes some conventional *presto* variations with a highly unconventional coda.

Ex. 3

Namieyski's five-movement symphony, with two minuets-and-trios, employs pairs of flutes and horns; clarinets in D may be substituted for the flutes but they are treated exactly like oboes, being written almost entirely in their upper register, with total neglect of the chalumeau sound and of all the instrument's other special qualities. Namieyski's themes are more shapely than Gołąbek's and the whole symphony shows a much more assured command of technique; it could easily take its place beside all but the best Mannheim or J.C. Bach symphonies

—and would pass unnoticed among them, since it lacks personal or national traits. The opening theme of the sonata-form finale is

Ex. 4

particularly attractive; the 28-bar development is entirely based on a scale idea from the second member of the first subject.

Pietrowski can be associated with Namieyski and Gołąbek in that one of his symphonies, both again in D major, was found in the Grodzisk archives. But he differs from them by betraying the unmistakable influence of Mozart. The opening theme of the *allegro* of (I), the Grodzisk symphony, has a likeness to that of the *Zauberflöte* overture which was pointed out by Strumiłło[10] and is too close to be accidental. This *allegro*, moreover, has a 12-bar *grave* introduction which is far from Mozartean but could have been suggested by Mozart, and the development begins by taking up an idea from the codetta as Mozart so often does. Something like *durchbrochene Arbeit* occurs later

Ex. 5

and real harmonic tension is built up before the recapitulation. One curiosity of the exposition is that, while arrival in the dominant area is marked by the appearance of a new theme, most of the 'second subject' is built on the first theme. The *andante* variations on a binary theme the minuet-and-trio are much more Haydnish, but the very attractive *presto* sonata-form finale has a distinct flavour of *Nachtmusik*.

Pietrowski's Symphony (II) has no slow introduction and the chief interest of the material of the first *allegro* is that the second subject is a sort of free inversion of the first (Ex. 6).

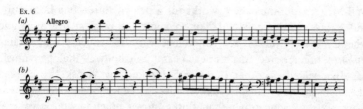

But the development has all the features of that in (I), except that the recapitulation is less skilfully approached, and both slow movement and minuet run on parallel lines to the companion work. The finale is a *prestissimo* in a free form obviously modelled on the finale of Haydn's no. 70 (1779). It begins in the tonic minor (Ex. 7), passes through a fugato in F major, travels as far afield as E minor, and reaches the tonic major only at bar 142—rather more than half-way through the movement. One idea after another is picked up and discarded until, just before the end, the first violins (always unaccompanied) begin to throw out the first two bars of Ex. 7 in the major; finally they do it twice, *pp*, and the symphony ends with tutti tonic chords.

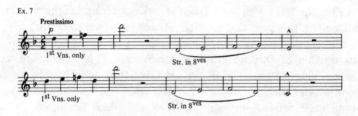

Such breaks with custom and the 'farewell' end of Gołąbek's D major (I) are naturally rare. But by no means all these early Polish symphonies run on conventional lines. Milwid's lost Symphony in B flat minor was entitled 'Bieda ruska' (Russia's woe) and is said to have been based on Belo-Russian folk melodies; the second movement was a *dumka*. The two symphonies by Wański, in D and G, published by Florian Dąbrowski,[11] are as the autograph title-page tells us 'Two Symphonies from Opera Overtures', the operas in question being his *Pasterz nad Wisłą* (The Shepherd by the Vistula) (1791) and *Kmiotek* (The Peasant), produced at Radomicko in the winter of 1786-7, which was not mainly his composition though he may have written the overture for it. The main *allegro* theme of the *Pasterz* Symphony again has a whiff of *Die Zauberflöte* and again there is a short *adagio* introduction. Both are well-written four-movement works for a pair of flutes, one horn only, and strings, but one would like to know the original overtures and whether the conversion to symphonies was effected simply by adding *andante*, minuet, and finale in each case; unhappily all the opera music has disappeared. Another D major Symphony by Wański,[12] preserved like them in the Archiepiscopal Archives at Gniezno, a four-movement work with no wind other than flutes, shows much less resource, and Opieński wrote very unenthusiastically[13] about yet another D major Symphony in three movements, now apparently lost. Dankowski's E flat Symphony[14] is unusual in several ways: e.g. the substitution of fresh material for the original first subject in the recapitulation (an area in which the Poles were often unorthodox – Wański's G major Symphony recapitulates the first subject after the second). But its most striking feature is the free treatment of the wind (two clarinets, bassoon, and two horns): the antiphony of strings only and wind only at the very beginning and in several later passages, the interplay of clarinets and violins at the beginning of the *adagio*, the predominance of clarinets and horns in the minuet, the episode for wind only in the *rondeau* finale. In fact Dankowski treats the wind as a self-contained group equally important with the strings; it was not for nothing that he indicated on his title-page that the clarinets and horns were '*obligée*'.

Although Opieński could justly claim that the *adagio maestoso* introduction of Dankowski's D major Symphony is a polonaise, and one can point to examples of the old folk-polonaise in Haczewski and Bohdanowicz, none of these – nor Haczewski's krakowiak – has a very pronounced national flavour. For that, the Polish symphony had to wait for a foreign-born musician, though one who became a very true and loyal Pole: Elsner, the future mentor of Chopin. Of Elsner's eight symphonies, the earliest that has survived is the seventh, in C major, Op. 11, performed in Warsaw on 22 April 1805, and published by André of Offenbach the same year. Here, as the trio of the minuet, he inserted a true mazurka – with the sharpened fourth of the major scale which is one of the hallmarks of Polish folk-melody.[15]

Ex. 8

That is the historic link between Poland's early symphonists and her greatest composer.

NOTES

1. 'Symfonje A. Dankowskiego i J. Wańskiego', *Kwartalnik muzyczny*, xvi (1932), p. 685.
2. 'La musique symphonique polonaise du XVIIIe siècle', *Musica Antiqua Europae Orientalis: Acta Scientifica Congressus* (ed. Zofia Lissa) (Warsaw, 1966), p. 334.
3. *Opis obyczajów za panowania Augusta III* (Wrocław, 1951). Quoted by Wecowski, op. cit., p. 342.
4. *Symfonie polskie*, vi. The earliest recorded Polish symphony is one by Jacek Szczurowski (1718–after 1773), dating from about 1740 but still undiscovered; the earliest surviving one is an anonymous *Symphonia a 2 Violini Alto Viola con Organo* which Węcowski discovered at Raków Opatowski (Węcowski, op. cit., p. 335).
5. In D, not F as in the printed score.
6. *Symfonie polskie*, ii.
7. Ibid., v.
8. The highly condensed English, French, German, and Russian summaries of Bohdan Muchenberg's admirable and extensive preface to the scores of Gołabek's three surviving symphonies, *Źródła do historii muzyki polskiej*, iii (Cracow, 1962), all give the wrong date, 27 March. At least one other Symphony of his – in D and dated 1783, mentioned by Opieński, op. cit., p. 687 (footnote) – disappeared during the last war. Wecowski discovered two more, in B flat and D.
9. *Źródła do historii muzyki polskiej*, iv, and *Music in Old Cracow* (ed. Szweykowski) (Cracow, 1964), p. 288.
10. 'Do dziejów symfonii polskiej', *Muzyka* (1953), 5–6, p. 38.
11. *Źródła do historii muzyki polskiej*, v.
12. Printed in *Muzyka staropolska* (ed. Hieronim Feicht) (Cracow, 1966), p. 289.
13. Op. cit., p. 690.
14. *Muzyka staropolska*, p. 322. Unfortunately the D major work described by Opieński is available only in Krenz's modernization which makes serious consideration impossible.
15. Quoted from Alina Nowak-Romanowicz, *Józef Elsner* (Cracow, 1957), p. 49.

9. The Early Development of Opera in Poland

In different political conditions Polish opera might well have got away to a very early start. In February 1625 the future Władysław IV, an Italophile and music-lover like his father, was regaled by the Tuscan court with an opera-ballet, *La Liberazione di Ruggiero*. The libretto was by Ferdinando Saracinelli, the music by Francesca Caccini, and both libretto and score were published in Florence the same year; the title-page of the score reads:

La Liberazione/Di Ruggiero/Dall' Isola d'Alcina/Balletto/Composto in Musica dalla Francesca / Caccini ne Signorini / Malaspina / Rappresentata nel Poggio Imp.le / Villa della Sereniss.ma / Arcid.sa d'Austria / Gran Ducessa di Toscana / Al Sereniss.mo / Ladislao Sigismondo / Principe de Polonia / e di Suezia / In Firenze . . . 1625

The work is—unflatteringly—described by Hugo Goldschmidt,[1] who also prints six excerpts in his musical appendix.[2] But the prince seems to have been duly impressed, for one of his retinue, Stanisław Serafin Jagodyński, made a Polish translation of the libretto which was published at Cracow in 1628, a fact which suggests that a Polish production was contemplated. There is no record that any such performance took place, but Jagodyński's version, *Wybawienie Ruggiera z Wyspy Alcyny* . . . *Komedia tańcem z muzyką*, is considered to have some literary merit. It was reprinted in 1884, and an excerpt published by Zdzisław Jachimecki[3] in parallel with Saracinelli's original shows that it could have been fitted without much trouble to the music.

While in Florence, Władysław was also present at a performance of Marco da Gagliano's *sacra rappresentazione, Le Regina Sant'Orsola* (1624), and after his return to Poland he lost little time in introducing this novel form of art; in 1628 the court at Warsaw were given a *Galatea*, of which neither the poet nor the composer is known. It was a 'fisher idyll, diversified by numerous intermedi, with brilliant machine effects devised by a leading theatrical engineer brought from Mantua'.[4] Immediately on his accession to the throne in 1632 Władysław had a theatre constructed on the first floor of the royal palace, which was opened the following year with a *dramma per musica, La Fama reale, ovvero Il Principe trionfante Ladislao IV, monarca della Polonia, re di Suezia* (this branch of the Vasas still clung to the fiction that they were the rightful kings of Sweden). Either the words or the music, perhaps both, were by a Pole, Piotr Elert (d. 1653), a violinist or violist in the Royal Chapel and a man of considerable learning and substance, but it was clearly an Italian opera, not a Polish one. So were its successors. The new king's enthusiasm for opera was probably encouraged by his younger brother, Aleksander Karol, for whose benefit Landi's *Sant' Alessio* (1632) was revived in Rome in 1634, and during the next thirteen years the royal brothers commanded a whole series of new operas, mostly for Warsaw but also for special occasions at Gdańsk, Wilna, and Cracow. First came a *Dafne* (1635, repeated 1638), possibly Gagliano's, and in the same year a *Giuditta* that, judging from the Polish synopsis which is all that survives, was a scenic oratorio rather than an opera; it was performed as part of the festivities marking the conclusion of a peace treaty with Russia, in the presence of the Papal nuncio and the Muscovite ambassador. The libretto was by Virgilio Puccitelli, the king's secretary and also a singer in the Royal Chapel, who supplied the texts of all but one of the later works of the reign. Władysław's marriage to his first wife, Cecilia Renata, was commemorated on 23 September 1637 by an 'Italian comedy, called *recitativa*, about St Cecilia, which pleased everyone vastly; it cost 15,000 gold pieces'. The ballet of gladiators which followed, with 'dances of soldiers and silver-covered chariots', cost 35,000. This time we know the composer of the opera, if not of the ballet: Marco Scacchi, master of the Royal Chapel from 1628 to 1648. Then came *Il Ratto d'Elena* (1638), *Narciso trasformato* (1638), also composed by Scacchi, *Armida abbandonata* (1641), and *Andromeda* (1641). Scacchi's last opera, *Le Nozze d'Amore e di Psyche* (1646), greeted Władysław's second queen, Maria Gonzaga, when she landed at Gdańsk, and was subsequently performed at Warsaw and at Cracow for her coronation. A Frenchman in the queen's train, Jan le Laboureur, has left us in his *Histoire et relation du voyage de la Royne de Pologne* (Paris, 1648) his impression of the Royal Chapel:

La musique du Roy ... est estimée la première de l'Europe, et composée particulièrement des meilleures voix de l'Italie, et couste extrèmement, tant en pension qu'en récompenses et en liberalitez au Roy, à qui la passion qu'il a pour ce plaisir véritablement Royal, ne fait rien espargner pour attirer à son service tous ceux qui excellent.[5]

There was one more *dramma per musica*, a *Mars ed Amore* by Michelangelo Brunerio, 'basso del Rege cappellano della Regina', but then the curtain fell. Władysław's reign ended in the middle of the terrible rebellion of Bohdan Chmielnicki; his successors had to cope with Swedish invasion, Russian invasion, Turkish invasion; and the first great flowering of Italian opera outside Italy was cut off before it could strike native roots. It actually disappeared without leaving traces, for not a note of these operas survives. All we have is a handful of librettos by Puccitelli, which, as Jachimecki says,[6] were 'entirely based on Florentine models':

there were passages in madrigal style and free forms in the solo parts, ariosos and recitatives, dialogues between soloists and between soloists and chorus, and then favourite echo effects introducing word-play involving anacolutha, antonyms and puns.

As for the instrumentation, we gather from the librettos at least that in *Il Ratto d'Elena* Paris sang to the *lira da braccio* and that the shepherds in *Narciso* were accompanied by the bagpipe (*zampogna*) (or perhaps instruments imitating it).

It is not obvious why Polish composers did not try their hands at opera composition; the Royal Chapel included at least two gifted men familiar with contemporary Italian music, Marcin Mielczewski and Adam Jarzębski, but they displayed their gifts only in instrumental music and *concertato* church music. Ironically, Jarzębski – who also had literary talent – has left an account of the 'comedies with singing', ballets and so on at court[7] in his narrative poem *Gościniec albo Krótkie opisanie Warszawy* (The Highway, or A Short Description of Warsaw) (1643). Operas were occasionally given at court under Jan Kazimierz and Jan Sobieski to enhance special festivities, but to the end of the century they were written and composed by Italians: for instance, *Per goder in amor ci vuol constanza*, written by Giovanni Battista Lampugnoni, secretary to the Papal nuncio, composed by Augustino Viviani, a member of the Royal Chapel, and performed by the Italian members of the Chapel at Warsaw on 28 March 1691 to celebrate the marriage of the king's son Jakub.

The accession of Augustus II, Elector of Saxony, to the Polish throne in 1697 certainly gave a fresh impetus to opera performance in Poland but did nothing to nationalize it. The Dresden Court Opera was distinguished long before the appointment of Hasse in 1731 and commanded much greater resources than Władysław IV's almost domestic performances can have done; it visited Warsaw and Cracow, but naturally spent most of its time in Saxony; in any case, its repertory was still Italian. However, in 1725 the first public theatre in Warsaw was opened with the performance of a ballet, *Proserpina*, conducted – and presumably composed – by Augustus's Dresden *Kapellmeister*, Johann Christoph Schmidt. And in the same year the nobility began to take a hand; a *Venceslao* (probably Carlo Francesco Pollarolo's setting of Zeno's libretto) and *La Fede ne'tradimenti* (perhaps also with Pollarolo's music) were performed in the Lubomirski Palace in Cracow, and two years later a *Griselda* was given there (possibly by Domenico Sarri, who also composed a *La Fede ne'tradimenti*). Some of the nobility actually had Italian opera composers in their service, as the Rzewuskis had the Bolognese Giuseppe Maria Nelvi (1698–1756), who composed four operas while he was in Poland. The heyday of the public opera in Warsaw came later, in the reign of Augustus III, a greater lover of opera than his father: he not only ordered in 1748 the construction of a bigger and better theatre, but, when expelled from Saxony by the misfortunes of the Seven Years War and obliged to settle in his Polish capital for five whole years, consoled himself and entertained his subjects with a splendid series of Hasse productions, ten in all, of which at least two, *Il Sogno di Scipione* (1758) and *Zenobia* (1761), were first performances.[8]

All this came to an end soon after Augustus's death in 1763, and the company dispersed. But the next reign, that of Stanisław August (Poniatowski), which suffered the Partitions and ended in 1795 with the Third Partition, was to see the belated beginning of genuinely Polish opera. (A five-act comedy translated from the French and produced in 1749 at a country palace of the Radziwiłłs had included a 'pastoral opera' intermezzo consisting of 'arias, dialogues and choruses' sung in Polish and composed by an anonymous musician; but this was hardly a beginning.) Native opera was by no means the consquence of the election of a native king or even of an immediate eruption of patriotic feeling produced by the First Partition of 1772. During the first thirteen years of Stanisław Poniatowski's reign, Italian opera was challenged only (as elsewhere) by *opéra comique*, beginning in 1765 with an *Annette et Lubin* (to Favart's libretto) by Gaetano Pugnani, which thus antedates his Italian version, *Nanetta e Lubino* to Carlo Francesco Badini's text, by four years. But of course *opera seria* had mostly given

way to *opera buffa*, and there was a new generation of Italian composers
–Piccinni, Sacchini, Galuppi, Salieri. Besides them and the composers of
opéra comique – Duni, Monsigny, Philidor, and later, Grétry – Germans
and Austrians were performed: Haydn's *Der krumme Teufel* (1774),
Gluck's *Orfeo* (1776), Gassmann, and Johann Adam Hiller.[9] It was
against this background that the earliest opera composed to a Polish
text made its appearance in 1778: *Nędza uszczęśliwiona* (Misery Made
Happy), a text by Franciszek Bohomolec originally intended for a
cantata but now expanded into a two-act opera libretto by Wojciech
Bogusławski (1757–1829) and set to music by a composer of Slovak
origin, Maciej Kamieński (1734–1821). It was dedicated to the king,
who had interested himself in the work, and it was produced in the
theatre of the Radziwiłł Palace in Warsaw on 11 July 1778.[10]

The plot of *Nędza uszczęśliwiona* could hardly be more simple. A
poor countrywoman, a widow, Anna, has a daughter, Kasia, with two
suitors. One, Antek, is poor; the other, Jan, is well off – and, needless
to say, Kasia loves the poor one. 'Misery' is 'made happy' by the
intervention of a kindly and generous landlord.[11] The music[12] – eleven
solo songs, a duet for Kasia and Antek to end Act I, a quintet for all the
soloists to end Act II, with an overture to each act – is equally artless,
though Kamieński expected his soloists to tackle showy coloratura, and
there is some fire in the two overtures, for instance the opening of
that to Act II.

Ex. 1

Kamieński's orchestra consists of two violins, viola and bass, pairs of
flutes, oboes, and horns. There is little local colour, even in Kasia's
sparkling 'Tempo di Pollacco' in the second act, or the krakowiak-type
songs of Anna and Jan in the first. The general flavour is mildly Italianate.
Nevertheless some of the songs enjoyed considerable popularity for a
time, and Kamieński strengthened his Polish accent in his later works:

Prostota cnotliva (Virtuous Simplicity), in three acts with libretto by
Bohomolec (1779); *Zośka czyli Wiejskie zaloty* (Zośka, or Rustic
Courtship), a one-act vaudeville, libretto by Stanisław Szymański (1779);
Balik gospodarski, a three-act vaudeville on Franciszek Zabłocki's
translation of Favart's *Le Bal bourgeois* (1780); *Tradycja dowcipem
załatwiona* (Tradition Settled by Ingenuity), one-act libretto by Zabłocki
(1789); and *Słowik czyli Kasia z Hanką na wydaniu* (The Nightingale,
or Kasia Persuaded by Hanusia), two-act libretto by G. Witkowski
(1790).[13] In these there are hints of the Lydian mode and much more
flavour of popular song. Jan's first song in Act I of *Tradycja*, 'Listen,
Barbara!', is a quite respectable polonaise (Ex. 2),[14] and a little later in

Ex. 2

the same act Szczepanowa begins her song 'Sługa, sługa' with two bars
which present the kernel of the opening of Chopin's A major Polonaise,
Op. 40 No. 1, identical even in key.[15] Like *Nędza uszczęśliwiona*, both
Tradycja and *Słowik* are *Singspiele* with the slenderest of plots.

Kamieński was not left alone in the new field. Foreign operas,
including *Die Entführung* in 1783, began to be performed in Polish, and
foreign-born composers produced new works: Gaetani (sometimes
spelled Kajetani and possibly not an Italian), conductor of the Royal
Opera from 1780 to 1793; the Hanoverian Johann David Holland
(1746–*c*. 1825), who conducted the Radziwiłłs' opera at Nieświez;
Gioacchino Albertini (1751–1811), who served first the Radziwiłłs and
then the king and composed a *Don Juan czyli Libertyn ukarany* to a
libretto which Bogusławski translated 'from the Italian',[16] produced in
Warsaw in 1783; and Antoni Weinert (1751–1850), of Czech origin,
flautist in the Royal and other opera orchestras in Warsaw for more
than 60 years (1778–1839). Weinert married Kamieński's daughter and
composed the overture to his father-in-law's *Tradycja*.[17] But all their
works have been destroyed in the wars that have devastated the unhappy
capital—with one exception. This is a setting of *Żółta szlafmyca albo*

Koleda na Novy Rok (The Yellow Nightcap, or A Present for New Year),
a three-act libretto which Bogusławski–who as playwright, director,
actor, and bass singer long played such an important part in the Polish
theatre that he has been called its 'father'–had translated from a French
comedy, *Les Etrennes de Mercure* by Pierre Barré and A. de Pils. It
was produced in 1788, and the music has been variously attributed to
Kamieński, Gaetani, and one Ertini,[18] who was master of the court
chapel of the Chancellor, Stanisław Małachowski. Prosnak seems to
accept that two settings of the same libretto were performed in 1788,
Gaetani's and Ertini's.[19] Kamieński's claim appears to rest solely on an
entry in Andrzej Zalewski's *Krótka kronika teatru polskiego 1764-1807*
(Warsaw, 1814). But the fragmentary manuscript copy, luckily made in
1938 from the since destroyed original in the library of the Warsaw
Opera, and now in private possession, firmly ascribes the music to
Gaetani. Possibly the score was a collective work; it would not be the
only Polish opera of the period with 'musique de plusieurs auteurs,
principalement de Mr. Gaetano'.

The music of the *Żółta szlafmyca*, whoever wrote it, is notable for
its links with popular music. Prosnak has no difficulty in demonstrating
the relationship between the trio in Act I and a popular song of the day,
that the *kolęda* at the end of Act I has a genuine oberek accompaniment
(the word *kolęda* has two meanings: Christmas or New Year present, as
in the sub-title, or carol), that the first two bars of the duet for Zofia
and Żona in Act II[20] are practically identical with the corresponding
bars of 'Dąbrowski's Mazurka' (later adopted as the Polish national
anthem) and that the 3/4 section of the duet for Fircyk and Czesław at
the beginning of Act III, with its rhythmic patterns and melodic motives
and sharpened fourths, is very close to more than one folk mazurka–
though he is perhaps straining a point when he claims that a phrase in
Czesław's song in Act II is based on the old Christmas lullaby 'Lulajże,
Jezuniu', where the partial identity seems to be fortuitous. And it is
hazardous to suggest that the composer always borrowed from 'the
people'; judging from dates, it seems more likely that 'Dąbrowski's
Mazurka' was suggested by the opera melody rather than vice versa–
though, naturally, both may have had a common prototype.

The national element is even more prominent in another work to a
Bogusławski libretto, with music by the Czech-born Jan Stefani (1748
or 1746-1829), member of the royal orchestra[21] and conductor at the
National Theatre: *Cud mniemany czyli Krakowiacy i Górale* (The
Supposed Miracle, or Cracovians and Mountaineers), which like Mozart's

Il dissoluto punito is known solely by its alternative title. Although the plot is only an elaboration of the almost inevitable one of divided lovers brought together or reconciled by or through a third person – the kindly landlord in *Nędza uszczęśliwiona*, Szczepanowa in *Tradycja*, Hanusia in *Słowik*, Mercury in *Szlafmyca* – the elaboration includes one feature so unexpected that it deserves to be described. Nor is the end altogether without significance.

The action takes place in a village in the Cracow district, not far from the Tatra mountains. A village lad, Stach, loves Basia, daughter of the miller Bartłomiej by his first wife; the miller has no objection to the match but Basia's stepmother, Dorota, has – she is attracted by Stach herself and would like to get the girl out of the way by marrying her instead to a mountaineer, Bryndas. The lovers are in despair, for Bartłomiej is a weak character unable to stand up to Dorota, but their conversation is overheard by a wandering student, Bardos, who happens to be passing through the village carrying on his back his books and an 'electrical machine'. Moved by their distress, he promises his help. When Bryndas and his friends come down from the mountains for the betrothal festivities, Bartłomiej – egged on by Bardos and emboldened by his presence – retracts his long-promised consent and says he leaves the choice to Basia. Bryndas is furious and swears he will be avenged for the injury, and Bardos fails to appease him; with his friends he seizes the Cracovians' cattle and makes off for the mountains. Once more it is Bardos's intervention that is decisive. Taking a short cut through the forests, he gets ahead of the mountaineers with his electrical machine and stretches an electrified wire across their path; before they have recovered from their surprise and shock the pursuing Cracovians come up and set about them with sticks. Bardos stops the fight, however, and the mountaineers, still bewildered and frightened by the 'supposed miracle' of the electrified wire, not only surrender the stolen cattle but even agree to go back to the village and take part in celebrating the betrothal of Basia and Stach. Dorota is likewise persuaded by the benevolent young scientist to abandon her designs on Stach and reconcile herself to the marriage. Finally, amid the general rejoicing, he announces that having 'corrected Dorota, prevented bloodshed and reconciled the obstinate', he has no wish to return to Warsaw, where 'perverse fashion' reigns and people like himself who 'live from the inkstand' often have to go hungry, but intends to stay there in the village among the simple, decent countryfolk.

Krakowiacy i Górale was first performed on 1 March 1794, barely a month before the national uprising led by Kościuszko, provoked by the outrages of the Second Partition. In this atmosphere of intense patriotic excitement the music in itself, closer to the national idiom than any earlier opera,[22] with krakowiaks such as the one sung by the male villagers in Act 1 (Ex. 3) and at least one genuine song from the Tatras, was bound to make a particularly strong effect. But the libretto must have made an even stronger one. The figure of Bardos, the very up-to-date intellectual, embodied many current ideals; his appeal for the renunciation of internecine conflicts, which had been the curse of Poland, had direct and urgent meaning. Indeed many passages in the text allude unmistakably to the political situation. It was not solely for its artistic merits, which are modest, but because it was 'the opera of the Kościuszko rising'[23] that *Krakowiacy i Górale* won and long kept its place in the hearts of the Polish people.[24]

Ex. 3

Nie u - wa - zaj,   mi - ła   Zo - siu,   lep - sy   chło - pak   świe - zy

There was no more royal opera. Freedom shrieked and Kościuszko fell — though he survived the fall for nearly a quarter of a century. In the Third Partition Warsaw came under Prussian rule and remained under it until in 1807 Napoleon set up his 'Grand Duchy of Warsaw' (with his cat's-paw Friedrich August, King of Saxony, as duke), which in turn became in 1815 the so-called 'Congress Kingdom', with Alexander I of Russia as king and his brother, the Grand Duke Constantine, as viceroy. Bogusławski, the key figure in the National Theatre, left Warsaw for some years, and most of his colleagues dispersed. However, temporary companies were got together to perform comedies and operas. The first of these companies revived an old opera of Gaetani's in 1795, and the following year another company put on two new works by Stefani, *Drzewo zaczarowane* (The Enchanted Tree) and *Wdzieczni poddani panu* (The Master's Grateful Slaves), neither of which was successful and both of which are lost. He continued to compose unsuccessful operas, one of the last of which, *Rotmistrz Gorecki czyli Oswobodzenie* (Captain Gorecki, or Liberation), produced on 3 April 1807, appears from its title to have been concerned with recent events: French troops had entered Warsaw four months before.

These political events naturally resulted in a certain amount of emigration, and Poland lost two very gifted amateur composers, both aristocrats: Michal Kleofas Ogiński (1765-1833) and Prince Antoni Radziwiłł (1775-1833). Having taken a prominent part in the Kościuszko rising, Ogiński, who has an honoured place in Polish musical history as a composer of instrumental polonaises, fled to the West and spent most of his life there; like so many Poles, he built great hopes on French Republican help and to that end wrote in 1799 the words and music of a one-act opera, *Zélis et Valcour, ou Bonaparte au Caïre*, in which the lovers—harem-favourite and French prisoner—are saved by Napoleon himself. Bonaparte sings an aria in praise of liberty, which he calls the 'seul but de mes travaux', and then in a recitative invites Valcour:

> Sous mes drapeaux, servez votre patrie!
> Combattre les méchants, les rois, la tyrannie
> De tout Français, c'est le devoir![25]

But Ogiński's opera was not produced in Paris, as he expected, or anywhere else. Radziwiłł, on the other hand, opted for Prussia in 1795 and the following year married the sister of a still more distinguished amateur, Prince Louis Ferdinand; all the same, as governor-general of the Grand Duchy of Posen after 1815, he opposed Prussianization. Radziwiłł composed no operas, but the music for *Faust*, on which he worked for many years, shows great dramatic power.[26]

The principal composer of Polish opera during the first decades of the nineteenth century was not a Teutonized Pole but a Polonized German, not an aristocratic amateur but the son of a Silesian carpenter and a thoroughly professional composer, violinist, conductor, and teacher: Joseph Xaver Elsner (1769-1854), of whom older editions of *Grove's Dictionary* say that 'his surest claim to remembrance is the fact that he was the master of Chopin'. He has other claims. He founded various schools and societies, including a Society for the Cultivation of Religious and National Music (1815) and the Warsaw Conservatoire of Music, of which he was the first director (1821). He was a prolific composer of music of almost every kind, editor of Polish popular songs, author of numerous theoretical and didactic writings. But above all he was a composer of operas. While theatre *Kapellmeister* at Lemberg (Lwów) in Austrian Poland (1792-9) he had already composed two German operas—one to his own libretto—when he met Bogusławski, who was now directing the theatre there, and provided incidental music for a French tragedy which Bogusławski had translated. Then came three other works in collaboration with Bogusławski: two three-act melo-dramas and a two-act 'heroic-comic opera', *Amazonki czyli Herminia*

(1797).[27] When in 1799 Bogusławski returned to Warsaw as director of the National Theatre, he invited Elsner to accompany him as principal conductor, a post he held for 25 years, becoming a patriotic citizen of his adopted country and even publishing in 1818 a treatise on the rhythms and metres of the Polish language 'with special reference to Polish verse from the point of view of music'. In 1810 Bogusławski appointed a native Pole, Karol Kurpiński (1785-1857), as second conductor; he succeeded Elsner in 1824 and held the post till 1840. Like his colleague, Kurpiński was highly literate; he was the founder and editor of the first Polish musical periodical, *Tygodnik Muzyczny* (1820-21), and wrote not only on musical but on non-musical subjects (such as 'the moral state of humanity'). It was these two, Elsner and Kurpiński, who developed Polish opera most fully before the advent of Stanisław Moniuszko (1819-72), with whose *Halka* (first version, in two acts, 1848) (see pp. 157 ff.), *Straszny dwór* (The Haunted Château, 1865), and other works it may be said to have reached maturity.

Some of the 'operatic works' listed in the article on Elsner in the fifth edition of *Grove's Dictionary* are really melodramas,[28] others are trivial or of slight interest. His first Warsaw opera was the two-act *Sultan Wampum* (1800), based on an adaptation by Bogusławski and Augustyn Gliński of Kotzebue's *Sultan Wampum, oder Die Wünsche* (for which, in its original form, Kamieński had composed music six years earlier). This is a comic-fantastic piece set in Persia, though Elsner's local colour does not go much deeper than conventional janissary music, and the overture actually has a mazurka-like opening theme and a *Ländler* second subject, while the second-act finale begins 'alla polacca'. Hussein's 'Ach! ten Królow król prawdziwy, Pan' in Act I[29] is a good Italianate patter aria, as Irena's 'Niech ręka najsroższych wrogów' in *The Amazons* is a fine Italianate rage aria. In both, as in his music generally, Elsner shows a command of technical resource decidedly superior to that of his predecessors; but they lack marked individuality. In 1804 came two one-act operas to librettos by Ludwik Dmuszewski: *Mieszkańcy Wyspy Kamkatal* (on a French original, *Les Sauvages de Kamkatal*, which had provided the subject for a ballet in Warsaw in the early 1790s) and *Siedem razy jeden* (Seven times one), a skit on the Parisian dress and manners then fashionable in Warsaw, with a sparkling overture and one of Elsner's best vocal polonaises sung by a character who is 'a friend of old ways'.[30] A third two-acter followed the next year: *Stary Trzpiot i Młody Mędrzec*, on a translation of *Le Jeune Sage et le vieux fou* by François Hoffman (pardonably confused by Alina

Nowak-Romanowicz with Elsner's friend E. T. A. Hoffmann, who was then living in Warsaw),[31] The three-act *Wiesczka Urzella* (1806) was a new setting of the Polish translation of Favart's *La Fée Urgèle* which had been made for the Warsaw production of Duni's opera in 1783.

In the course of 1807 Elsner produced – in addition to two three-act melodramas – three operas in connection with the French 'liberation' and the setting up of the Duchy. First came a one-act *Andromeda*, later named *Perseusz i Andromeda*, to a libretto by Ludwik Osiński which left no doubt that Napoleon was the Perseus who had freed the Polish Andromeda; it was produced on 14 January 1807 and repeated four days later, with a cantata also composed by Elsner, in the presence of the emperor himself, who followed with the help of a French libretto. History does not record what he thought of it. Then on 1 May, a month after Stefani's *Rotmistrz Gorecki*, came *Pospolite Ruszenie, czyli Bitwa z Kozakami* (The *Levée en masse*, or The Battle with the Cossacks) in two acts, with a libretto by Dmuszewski demonstrating the charity of the Poles towards the now distressed Prussians in their country – Hoffmann was among the distressed Prussians – and showing the young hero enlisting in Napoleon's Polish Legion. And on 5 December the new Duke, Friedrich August, attended the first performance of a two-act historical work, *Karol Wielki i Witykind* (Charlemagne and Witikind, text by Tekla Lubieńska)–also with cantata –which drew a parallel between Charlemagne's relationship to the Saxon Prince Witikind II and Napoleon's to Friedrich August.

These works give a general idea of Elsner's output, which continued on the same lines as long as the Duchy lasted, though the only important work was the two-act *Leszek Biały czyli Czarownica z Łysej Góry* (Leszek the White, or The Witch from the Bare Mountain, 1809), text by Dmuszewski. After the withdrawal of the French, Elsner abandoned the theatre for five years, partly because of disagreements with Bogusławski, partly because of Kurpiński's successes, partly because of other preoccupations. But on 3 April 1818 he reappeared with the best of all his operas, *Król Łokietek czyli Wiśliczanki* (King Dwarf, or The Girls of the Vistula, two acts: Dmuszewski). His last opera, *Jagiełło w Tenczynie* (King Jagiełło in Tenczyn, 1820), was a complete failure. All three of these works are quasi-historical. Leszek 'the White' was an early thirteenth-century prince whose love for a Galician princess gave Elsner a pretext for introducing that national element which always lights up his otherwise rather colourless scores: in fact two national elements, for the Poles, characterized by polonaises – the overture is a

really symphonic treatment of the polonaise – and a mazurka, are
contrasted with the Ukrainians, who are characterized by a dumka
(Ex. 4) which proved so successful that he introduced similar ones in
both *Król Łokietek* and *Jagiełło*.[32]

Ex. 4

Cdzie sze - ro - kim   nur - tem pły - nie   Dniepr jak mó - wią   mio-dem mie - kiem   na
(szcześliwej Ukrainie)

The little patriot king, Władysław I, affectionately nicknamed 'King
Dwarf', spent much of his early life as a fugitive and exile before in
1306, with peasant help, he freed his country from the Bohemian over-
lordship invited by the nobles, and the 'adagio' opening of the *Król
Łokietek* overture[33] reflects the tragic gloom of Poland under the
Bohemian yoke. Then comes a quasi-symphonic treatment of krakowiak
themes comparable with that of the polonaise in the overture to *Leszek*,
suggesting the popular element which was to carry Władysław to
victory. Indeed krakowiak melodies and rhythms recur throughout the
opera from the first chorus to the last; one in Act II is characterized by
the sharpened fourth and drone-fifth accompaniment so characteristic
of Polish folk music. Elsner caught both letter and spirit of folk music
so well that one of the mazurkas from this opera, sung by two of the
'girls of the Vistula', became adopted as a folk-song and was included
by Kolberg, with different words, in the first series of his great collection
of 'Songs of the Polish people';[34] this was the mazurka on which
Paganini composed variations[35] which he performed at his last concert
in Warsaw, on 14 July 1829. The figure of the king himself is musically
lost amid the wealth of popular melodies; except for one song, his part
is entirely in recitative.

There is one curious episode in *Król Łokietek* foreshadowing Libuše's
vision in Smetana's opera: one of the Czech characters, Hinkon, falls
asleep and in his dream beholds a series of scenes from Polish history,
from the time of the Dwarf King's reign to the then comtemporary. For
this Elsner selected a series of musical quotations – from popular music
(such as the so-called 'Dąbrowski's Mazurka'), from his own works
(including a polonaise from *Karol Wielki* and a march from *Leszek*), and
from other composers – which, even without words, would be strongly

evocative to a Polish audience. In an article on musical expression, Kurpiński referred to Hinkon's dream as an outstanding example of the expressive power of instrumental music:

You hear only two bars and already you understand everything; the heart throbs, you are involuntarily enthralled; and if you can for a moment regain your senses and turn your attention to the whole audience, you will be astonished that all at the same time are possessed by only one emotion.[36]

Kurpiński himself had begun his operatic career in 1808 with a setting of a translation of Rousseau's *Pygmalion*, probably for one of the private theatres; but, like the handful of operas of Franciszek Lessel, Karol Lipiński (the violinist) and Józef Deszczyński composed for provincial or private theatres, it has disappeared. His substantial activity began after his appointment as *Konzertmeister* and second conductor at the National Theatre in July 1810. And quite substantial it was. Although some of the '24 operas' listed in the fifth edition of *Grove's Dictionary*[37] consist of no more than an overture and half a dozen vocal numbers, like *Dwie chatki* (Two Huts, 1811), or are melodramas, like *Ruiny Babilonu* (The Ruins of Babylon, 1812), he did write no fewer than fifteen genuine operas and operettas during the period 1811-21. After that date he wrote only one opera, the two-act *Cecylia Piase-czyńska* (libretto by Dmuszewski) produced in 1829.

Like Elsner's idiom, Kurpiński's was essentially cosmopolitan but with an even stronger admixture of Polish elements. One of his last operas, the two-act *Kalmora czyli Prawo ojcowskie Amerykanów* (Kalmora, or The Paternal Law of the Americans, libretto by K. Brodziński, 1820), is said to show the strong influence of Rossini, but the main Western influences were Viennese and French. Indeed from his earliest successful opera onwards—the four-act *Pałac Lucypera* (Lucifer's Palace, libretto by A. Żólkowski, 1811)—he showed a marked predilection for librettos translated from the French; one, *Łaska Imperatora* (The Emperor's Favour, one act, by Dmuszewski, 1814), is based on Kotzebue (*Fedora*). Nevertheless nationalism keeps breaking in. The one-act melodrama *Marcinowa w seraju* (Marcinowa in the Seraglio, from the French, by Pękalski, 1812), has an overture in sonata form 'sur le thème de Mazurek',[38] the development section of which consists of a 50-bar fugato on the mazurka theme (Ex. 5). And the mayor in *Szarlatan czyli*

Ex. 5

Wskrzeszenie umarłych (The Charlatan, or The Resurrection of the Dead, two acts, Żółkowski, 1814) has a lively 'tempo di polacca' aria.

Kurpiński's most enduring operas are *Jadwiga, królówa Polski* (Jadwiga, Queen of Poland, three acts, J.U. Niemcewicz, 1814), *Zabobon czyli Krakowiacy i Górale albo Nowe Krakowiaki* (Superstition, or Cracovians and Mountaineers, or The New Cracovians, three acts, J. N. Kamiński, 1816), *Jan Kochanowski w Czarnym Lesie* (Jan Kochanowski in the Black Forest, two acts, Niemcewicz, 1817), and *Zamek na Czorstynie czyli Bojomir i Wanda* (The Castle of Czorstyn, or Bojomir and Wanda, two acts, J. W. Krasiński, 1819).[39] The title which at once catches one's attention is of course *Nowe Krakowiaki*; it is in fact a complete reworking of the old Bogusławski libretto with the same characters but entirely new music. The very opening of the overture (Ex. 6), on an open-fifth pedal, strikes the authentic note, and the score

Ex. 6

as a whole is the most thoroughly Polish that Kurpiński ever wrote. The opera is still revived occasionally, kept alive by its pretty mazurka songs.

Ex. 7

The two operas to texts by Niemcewicz, a distinguished man of letters, are on historical subjects. The character and sacrifice of Jadwiga, the queen who renounced her Austrian lover and married the Lithuanian prince Władysław Jagiełło for the sake of her country, offer obvious opportunities, and Kurpiński seized them in the best musical character-drawing he ever achieved; Jadwiga's first aria in itself earns him an honourable place among the Mozart-epigones. There is a fine choral conclusion to the first act, and the second is preceded by a striking imitative entr'acte suggesting dramatic tension.[40] That *Jan Kochanowski* is less successful was not altogether Kurpiński's fault. Kochanowski was the greatest poet of the Polish Renaissance – and more than a poet – but the lives of great men do not necessarily provide good operatic material (as Spontini found with Milton), and Niemcewicz did not gain much by giving his hero a daughter torn between two lovers. Nor was Kurpiński's idea of evoking a long-past age by suggestions of eighteenth-century idioms altogether happy. *Zamek na Czorstynie* is also set in the past; the year is 1683 and the hero is on his way home from the Turkish wars. But he belongs not to history but to the Gothick novel. The haunted castle in which he insists on spending the night is – unknown to him – the prison of his beloved Wanda, shut up there by a cruel father, out of her mind for love, and from whose nocturnal wanderings has originated belief in a ghost. Bojomir has a mournful dumka, Wanda a pretty but not at all tragic cavatina, which provides the second subject of the allegro of the overture. But the most interesting figure, musically, is Bojomir's peasant guide, who is characterized by a striking melody which he sings in Act II and which is introduced in the 'lento' intro-duction to the overture.

Ex. 8

Compared with Weber and Spohr, Boieldieu and the young Rossini, Elsner and Kurpiński seem insignificant. Compared more fairly with Weigl and Paër, Morlacchi and Cavos, they seem much less so. Considered simply in the context of their place and time, they are seen to be important. It was not for nothing that Bogusławski wrote in his *History of the Polish Theatre*[41] of his pride that 'the foundation of Polish opera, the attraction of Mr Elsner to the service of the nation and the development of Mr Kurpiński's talent, which has brought honour to the Poles, belong to that period when I directed the National Theatre'. Their interest in subjects from Polish history is highly significant; it really began after the establishment of the 'Congress Kingdom', when Warsaw first came under the Russian heel—however gently it pressed at first. But, as we have seen, opera in Poland always had been conditioned by political history. The early stops and starts—quasi-Florentine opera under the Vasa kings, *opera seria* under the Saxons, *opera buffa* and *opéra comique* and the beginnings of genuinely Polish opera under Stanisław Poniatowski—would be inexplicable apart from the political background.

NOTES

1. *Studien zur Geschichte der italienischen Oper im 17. Jahrhundert*, i (Leipzig, 1901), pp. 29–32.
2. Ibid., i, pp. 174–9. Published complete, ed. Doris Silbert (Smith College Music Archives, vii) (Northampton, Mass.. 1945).
3. *Muzyka polska w rozwoju historycznym* (Cracow, 1948–51), pp. 189–90.
4. Hieronim Feicht, 'Muzyka w okresie polskiego baroku', *Z Dziejów polskiej kultury muzycznej*, i (ed. Zygmunt M. Szweykowski) (Cracow, 1958), p.175.
5. Quoted from Jachimecki, *Historja muzyki polskiej* (Cracow, 1920), p. 87.
6. *Muzyka polska*, i, p. 198.
7. Quoted by Jachimecki, ibid., i, p. 195.
8. For a complete list, and further particulars of the Warsaw opera under the Saxon kings, see Jan Prosnak, *Kultura muzyczna Warszawy XVIII wieku* (Cracow, 1955), pp. 28 ff.
9. For a chronological list of operas produced in Warsaw during the reign of Stanisław August, see Prosnak, op. cit., pp. 103–13 (based on Ludwik Bernacki's monumental *Teatr, dramat i muzyka za Stanisława Augusta*, Lwów, 1925).
10. The date 11 May, given by Aleksander Poliński (*Dzieje muzyki polskiej w zarysie*, Lwów, 1907, p. 170), who has been followed in *Grove's Dictionary* (5th edn), art. 'Kamieński', and other authorities, is incorrect.
11. Full details of the plot, the genesis of the work, and musical incipits are given in Prosnak, op. cit., pp. 145 ff.
12. Full score, ed. Alina Nowak-Romanowicz and Piotr Pózniak, *Opery Polskie*, ii (Cracow, 1978).
13. Details and incipits of *Tradycja* and *Słowik* in Prosnak, op. cit., pp. 153 ff.; the others are lost, except for a few fragments. The manuscript materials of all three of Kamieński's surviving operas are now in the possession of the Warszawski Towarzystwo Muzyczne.

14. Quoted from Tadeusz Strumiłło, *Zródła i początki romantyzmu w muzyce polskiej* (Cracow, 1956), p. 39.

15. Two other numbers, the quintet and the quartet-finale, are printed in the musical appendix to Prosnak, pp. 115 and 126.

16. Mozart's *Don Giovanni* was given at Warsaw in Italian in 1789, but Albertini's survived this competition at least until 1805. Other librettos translated by Bogusławski include *Die Zauberflöte, Der Freischütz, Lodoïska, La Dame blanche*, and *L'Italiana in Algeri*.

17. Printed in Prosnak, musical appendix, p. 108.

18. It is tempting to identify this shadowy figure with Albertini, master of the Royal Chapel from 1784 to 1795, but the dates are inconsistent.

19. Op. cit., p. 114. In a note on p. 287 he says it was 'unquestionably' Ertini's opera that was produced at the National Theatre in November 1788.

20. Musical appendix, p. 143.

21. A list 'des Personnes qui composent l'Orchestre de Sa Majesté', dated 22 February 1784, headed by 'Mr Albertini' as *Maître de Chapelle* and 'Mr. Gaetano', *Directeur de la Musique*, shows 'Steffan de Prague' as one of the three first violins. The string complement was small: four seconds, one viola, three cellos, and two basses. But the rest of the orchestra was 'Classical', with a third flute and a pair of clarinets.

22. See Prosnak's parallel quotations from folk music and Stefani's score, op. cit., pp. 140–2.

23. Strumiłło, *Zródła i poczatki romantyzmu*, p. 45.

24. The statement in *Grove's Dictionary* (5th edn, art. 'Stefani') that it was 'performed in Warsaw over 200 times within a couple of years' seems hardly credible. Alfred Loewenberg (*Annals of Opera*, 2nd, rev. edn., Geneva, 1955, i, p. 513) says 'given at Warsaw 144 times until 1859' but mentions no authority.

25. Quoted from Jachimecki, *Historja muzyki polskiej*, p. 115. The score is preserved in the Bibljoteka Jagiełłońskia, Cracow.

26. *Compositionen zu Goethes 'Faust'* (Berlin, 1835); the overture, based on Mozart's C minor Adagio and Fugue, K. 546, was published separately in piano arrangement, Berlin, *c.* 1840; the very fine cathedral scene is given complete in the appendix volume to Strumiłło, op. cit., pp. 71–95 – but Strumiłło (p. 145) takes Mozart's Adagio to be a composition by Radziwiłł. Chopin was greatly impressed by the *Faust* music (cf. *Selected Correspondence*, tr. and ed. Arthur Hedley, London, 1962, p. 37), Schumann less so (cf. *Gesammelte Schriften*, ed. Heinrich Simon, Leipzig, 1888–9, ii, p. 103) – but he also took the opportunity to say of Mozart's fugue that 'no one can call it a masterpiece, if one knows Bach and Handel'.

27. Autograph full score in Warsaw, Bibljoteka Narodowa, MS 6319 (vocal score MS 6320). Alina Nowak-Romanowicz gives copious musical examples, some in full score, in her definitive work, *Józef Elsner* (Cracow, 1957), pp. 60–8, and Irena's aria in Act II complete in full score in the supplementary volume of musical examples, p. 14.

28. An excerpt from a four-act melodrama, *Ofiara Abrahama* (Abraham's Sacrifice, 1821), is given in Nowak-Romanowicz, supplementary vol., p. 58.

29. Complete full score, ibid., p. 22. Locations of Elsner's operatic autographs etc. are given in the main volume, pp. 288–95.

140 *Essays on Russian and East European Music*

30. Complete vocal score, ibid., supplementary vol., p. 34.
31. E. T. A. Hoffmann sang the tenor solo in Elsner's cantata *Muzyka* on 3 July 1806. They had been friends since the Posen days.
32. The dumka in *Król Łokietek* is given in vocal score in Nowak-Romanowicz, supplementary vol., p. 56.
33. Complete full score, ibid., p. 38.
34. *Pieśni ludu polskiego*, series 1 (Warsaw, 1857), No. 461.
35. Presumably this is the unpublished *Sonata Varsavia*, 'seven variations on a Polish theme', which Geraldine de Courcy (*Paganini the Genoese*, Norman, Oklahoma, 1957, ii, p. 382) tentatively dates 1838 and says 'there is no record of his ever having played this work'.
36. 'O ekspresji muzycnej i naśladowaniu', *Tygodnik Muzyczny i Dramatyczny* (1821), Nos. 1–6.
37. One of them, *Kazimierz Wielki*, is probably not by Kurpiński.
38. Complete full score in Strumiłło, appendix vol., p. 30. A considerable amount of Kurpiński's opera music – overtures and separate numbers in piano arrangements – was published during his lifetime.
39. Full score, ed. Włodzimierz Poźniak, *Opery Polskie*, i (Cracow, 1969).
40. Facsimile of the first page of the autograph score in *Z dziejów polskie kultury muzycznej*, ii (Cracow, 1966), facing p. 113.
41. *Dzieje teatru narodowego w Polsce* (Przemyśl, 1884; modern edn, Cracow, 1951), p. 119.

10. *Polish Song*

The history of the art-song in Poland[1] in some respects is parallel to that of the Czech lands. Here again is an age-old musical culture closely related to that of the rest of Europe – though not confused by wholesale emigration and the intrusion of a foreign tongue – and here again the secular solo song, apart from folk-song, seems to be a relatively modern phenomenon inheriting little or nothing from the rich past. All through the seventeenth and early eighteenth centuries we find aria-concertos for church use. Mikołaj Zieleński's *Communiones totius anni* (Venice, 1611) include fifteen solos for soprano, tenor, or bass with organ and this type of work continued to be written by such composers as Mielczewski (d. 1651), Szarzyński (d. c. 1700), Kaszczewski (late seventeenth century) and Damian (d. 1729).[2] But no secular vocal solos, other than the melodies of vocal mazurkas,[3] have been preserved from before the last two decades of the eighteenth century, when the history of Polish opera opened with Kamieński's *Nędza uszczęśliwiona* (Misery Made Happy) in 1778. At this period French songs predominated – at first *bergerettes* and *opéra-comique romances* with Polish words, later revolutionary songs with patriotic texts – and the native patriotic pieces tended to imitate them, though the Constitution of 1791 and Kosciusz-ko's rebellion evoked a number of vocal mazurkas and polonaises. The broader foundations of a consciously Polish vocal style were laid in 1794 by another opera, Jan Stefani's *Krakowiacy i górale* (Cracovians and Mountaineers). (Incidentally, Kamieński was of Slovak origin and Stefani a Czech of Italian descent.) But, although Stefani wrote some songs with piano, it was left to another opera composer, the Silesian Joseph Elsner (1769-1854), to become the real founder of the Polish art-song.

Elsner was a fairly prolific composer of songs with piano,[4] of which twenty-five of the earliest appeared in the periodical publication *Wybór pięknych dzieł muzycznych i pieśni polskich* (Selection of Fine Musical Works and Polish Songs) for 1803 and 1805, side by side with piano polonaises by Ogiński and Polish dances by Stefani. They are rather weak and sentimental essays in the style of the lyrical songs of Zumsteeg and J. F. Reichardt.[5] In 1811 Elsner published nearly a score of Masonic songs. Though his songs seem artless, he gave a good deal of thought to the problems of Polish prosody and in 1818 published a *Rozprawa o metryczności i rytmiczności języka polskiego* (Treatise on the Metrical and Rhythmical Treatment of the Polish Language, with special reference to Polish verse from the point of view of music); in 1830 he returned to the subject in a second treatise of which only a fragment was ever published. By way of illustration to the *Rozprawa* Elsner published six songs, to words by Kazimierz Brodziński, of which the first, 'Pasterka' (The Shepherdess), must be quoted since it 'points directly to the style of Moniuszko's songs'[6].

Ex. 1

'Who will tell my heart . . .'

The last of these *Sześć pieśni*, 'Muza wiejska' (The Rustic Muse), is one of the best of Elsner's vocal polonaises.

Elsner's later compositions include German *Lieder* – one or two Schiller settings among them – and *Tre arie ed un duettino* for soprano. But his songs, and those of his contemporaries Kurpiński, Lessel, and Kaszewski, were thrown into the shade by some of those of his pupil Józef Nowakowski (1800-65). Nowakowski was no master of the song: like Elsner's his melodies tend to be sentimental, his accompaniments to be stereotyped and conventional, but when he touches the life of the people he becomes really attractive and thoroughly Polish (e.g. in the mazurka song 'Cóż ja winna') and he set the pattern for a good many of the most popular Polish songs of later times.[7] In many respects his position is comparable with that of his Russian contemporaries Varlamov and Gurilev.

Like his friend Nowakowski, Chopin (1810-49) was a pupil of Elsner, and the earliest of his songs to be preserved are those which he copied into Elsner's daughter's album at some time before he finally left Poland in November 1830; of all Chopin's works of this date, these are the only ones that still show anything of his master's influence. They are 'Życzenie' (The Wish), 'Gdzie lubi' (Where she loves), 'Poseł' (The Messenger), 'Wojak' (The Warrior), 'Hulanka' (The Carouse), and 'Czary' (Charms)—all from the *Piosnki sielskie* (Country Songs) of the composer's friend Stefan Witwicki—and 'Precz z moich oczu!' (Away from my sight!) by Poland's greatest poet, Adam Mickiewicz. With the exception of 'Czary', they were published posthumously as Op. 74, Nos. 1, 5, 7, 10, 4, and 6. Two other Witwicki songs, 'Smutna rzeka' (The Mournful River), Op. 74, No. 3, and 'Narzeczony' (The Bridegroom), Op. 74, No. 15, and a setting of a translated Lithuanian folk poem 'Piosnka litewska' (Lithuanian Song), op. 74, No. 16, were composed in 1831. Thus more than half of Chopin's nineteen songs[8] are comparatively early works. Two of these early songs, the familiar 'Życzenie' and 'Hulanka' are mazurkas; the first part of 'Precz z moich oczu!' is a sort of dramatized slow mazurka (though the ensuing *andantino espressivo* is Bellinian) and there is a curious little mazurka interlude for piano in the 'Lithuanian Song'. 'Wojak' and 'Narzeczony', the former undistinguished, the latter really dramatic, are in ballad vein and might have been written by Loewe. Of the others, 'Poseł' is notable for the sharpened fourths in its melody (a feature of Polish folk music which appears in other of Chopin's songs), 'Smutna rzeka'—beautifully plaintive—for its three-bar phrases.

Four more songs came during 1836-8, two of them Chopin's best vocal mazurkas, Op. 74, Nos. 12 and 14. And the mazurka rhythm plays an important part in 'Śpiew grobowy' (Grave Song), Op. 74, No. 17, the most complex in structure of all Chopin's songs and perhaps the finest; his country's tragic fate moved him deeply and the middle section of the song, beginning with the words 'Bili zimę całą' (They fought the whole winter), first sixteen bars of monotone on E flat, then a chromatically ornamented E flat ('Some rot in the ground and others are captive'), with the release of the tension in the outburst 'O Polska kraino!' is most impressive. The four settings of the Ukrainian poet Bohdan Zaleski, spread over the years 1840-5, are unimpressive; the earlier of the two *dumki* is a scrap of only eight bars and was not included in Op. 74, where the three others figure as Nos. 8, 11, and 13. Chopin's last song, 'Melodya', Op. 74, No. 9, composed in 1847, is a curious and striking piece in arioso style, quite different from the rest of his songs.

Although Chopin's pieces rise above the level of earlier Polish song, they are markedly inferior to most of his piano compositions and are much more closely related to the style of contemporary Polish song than to his personal style; most surprisingly, the accompaniments show little evidence of his skill in writing for the instrument. According to his friend Fontana, who contributed a preface to the posthumous collection of sixteen songs which he published as *Zbiór śpiewów polskich* (Collection of Polish Songs), Op. 74, in 1857,[9] Chopin simply improvised his songs at the piano, singing the words and accompanying himself.

By 1857, however, a better song-writer if lesser composer had emerged in the person of Stanisław Moniuszko (1819-72). As early as 1838 Moniuszko – then a pupil of K. F. Rungenhagen, Zelter's successor at the Berlin Singakademie – published in Berlin three settings of Mickiewicz: 'Sen' (Dream), 'Niepewność' (Uncertainty) and 'Moja pieszczotka' (My darling) (which Chopin had composed the year before, Op. 74, No. 12).[10] All three appeared first with German words only, though they were re-issued with the original texts in the *Śpiewniki domowe* (Song-Books for the Home) in which Moniuszko published his later songs, more than three hundred in number if we include those issued posthumously.[11]

The first *Śpiewnik domowy*, containing eighteen songs, appeared in 1843.[12] Moniuszko published five more volumes in his lifetime and six came out posthumously – a corpus of work which established him as the classic master of Polish song. It is difficult, if not impossible, to establish anything like a chronological order, for Moniuszko seldom dated his manuscripts or mentioned his songs in his correspondence; even the publication dates of the first six *Śpiewniki* give us only *termini ad quem*, for songs originally intended for one book were published in a later one or even transferred after publication. (The ballad 'Czaty' (The Ambush), for instance, was published in the third book but omitted from its third edition and transferred to the sixth *Śpiewnik*.[13]) However this matters less in Moniuszko's case than it would with most composers, for even his early songs are mature. 'In the first three songs of 1838 and those of the first *Śpiewnik*', as Jachimecki says,[14] 'Moniuszko's talent as a song-writer makes its début in forms already crystallized'. The best way, therefore, to begin to convey some idea of the wealth and variety of his output[15] is to examine this early group.

They may be roughly divided into four categories: narrative, more or less dramatic ballads; lyrical pieces sometimes showing the parentage of the *Lied*, less often of the French *romance*; light, often playful songs; and short songs with a specifically Polish flavour, mazurkas, krakowiaks, and the like. Naturally no firm lines can be drawn between the categories.

Two of the four ballads in this group are settings of Mickiewicz: 'Świtezianka' (The Nymph of the Świtez—a Lorelei story) and 'Panicz i dziewczyna' (The Young Master and the Girl) (though that is only partly by Mickiewicz). The ballads of Mickiewicz inspired the ballades of Chopin; translated, they have inspired the song composers of both Germany and Russia. In 1835, two years before Moniuszko went to Berlin, Loewe had published there two sets of Mickiewicz ballads, Opp. 49 and 50, including both 'Świtezianka' and 'Panicz', and, while the extent of Loewe's influence on the earlier Russian ballad is doubtful, there can be little doubt that it stirred the young Moniuszko to emulation and it is clear that emulation first took the form of imitation — though of general style, not of specific models. Moniuszko's 'Świtezianka' far surpasses Loewe's; it is the first masterpiece of Polish song. In 'Panicz i dziewczyna', however, as elsewhere in Moniuszko's early songs, his declamation has been criticized. The other two ballads illustrate other aspects of his work: humour in 'Dziad i baba' (Grandpa and Grandma), which anticipates a genre cultivated by Musorgsky, and even faintly his style; essential Polishness in 'Żal dziewczyny' (A Girl's Lament) with its mazurka opening, not really a ballad but ballad-like in structure.

All three of the songs published in Berlin show affinities with Loewe's more lyrical songs: 'Sen' might be a companion-piece to Loewe's Goethe 'Canzonetta'; 'Niepewność' and 'Pieszczotka' are in the vein, though not in the style, of 'Niemand hat's geseh'n' and 'Mädchen sind wie der Wind'. The once-popular 'Barcarolle' in the first *Śpiewnik* is naturally rather Italianate; 'Triolet', with a harmonic surprise which is charac-teristic, and 'Kukulka' (The Cuckoo: not to be confused with the vocal mazurka with the same title but different words in the fifth *Śpiewnik*) are essentially *romances*. More in the style of the *Lied*, robust, naïve, or lyrical, are 'Pielgrzym' (The Pilgrim), 'Pieśń żeglarzy' (Sailor's Song), 'Przyczyna' (The Reason), 'Zawód' (Deception), and 'Morel' (The Apricot) with its beautifully integrated voice and piano parts and (again) a harmonic surprise.

In lighter mood the delightful 'Dalibóg' (Upon my life!) stands beside 'Niepewność' and surpasses 'Pieszczotka'. 'Kochać' (Make haste to love) has a more markedly Polish flavour, and the first and third of *Trzy piosnki* (Three Country Songs from across the Niemen, from Jan Czeczot's volume of that name) are mazurkas, while the second might be a nursery-rhyme. These frankly national songs are generally, and of course appropriately, very lightly accompanied. But, although there is plenty of conventional figuration, Moniuszko's piano parts are extremely varied and generally well wrought; they are far superior to those of any earlier Polish song-composer, even (astonishingly) to Chopin's.

To consider the bulk of Moniuszko's songs at all closely is of course impossible; one can only glance at a few noteworthy examples in each category. Two of the best of the other ballads are the grim and dramatic masterpiece 'Czaty' which, in Pushkin's translation, inspired Tchaikovsky's 'symphonic ballad' 'Wojewoda', Op. 78, and the happier tale of the 'Trzech Budrysów: (The Three Budrys), three Lithuanian heroes who are ordered by their father to bring back, respectively, plunder from the Germans, plunder from the Russians, and a daughter-in-law from Poland, but who actually return with three Polish brides. Both of these, and most of the others, are settings of Mickiewicz but the Lenartowicz 'Maciek' and the Béranger–Syrokomla 'Stary kapral' (Le vieux caporal)[16] are hardly inferior. To illustrate the ballads adequately one would need a host of musical examples, which would still not convey their real power. But one can give some idea of Moniuszko's lyrical work by quoting the opening of 'Do oddalonej' (Grzymałowski's translation of Goethe's 'An die Entfernte').

Ex. 2

'So hab' ich wirklich dich verloren,
Bist du, o Schöne, mir entflohn?'

As for his setting of Mickiewicz's translation of 'Kennst du das Land?', Jachimecki has made out a reasonable case for preferring it to the versions by Beethoven, Schubert, and Schumann;[17] it certainly deserves a place among the finest compositions of Mignon's song. There are some other Goethe songs, including a pleasantly Schubertian 'Heiden-röslein' – though the words ('Polna różyczka') are commonly attributed to the translator, Józef Grajnert, as an original poem. (Rather similarly, 'Wieczorny dzwon' is acknowledged as a translation of Kozlov's 'Vecherniy zvon', but nothing is said of Moore's 'Evening Bells' though as a matter of fact Moniuszko's music is better suited to Moore than to Kozlov.)[18] Schubertian influences also show themselves in the composition of original Polish poems, especially slighter pieces such as 'Kotek sie myje' (Pussy is washing) and 'Wiosna' (Spring) which outclasses Chopin's setting (Op. 74, No. 2). More individual, though also in the *Lied* tradition, are 'Kraśna góra' (The Beautiful Mountain), 'Ksiezyc i rzeczka' (The Moon and the Rivulet), with its *Rheingold*-like suggestion of flowing water (though its date is not later than 1846), and the lullaby 'Luli'.

Some of the best of the lighter songs are compositions of poems by Jan Czeczot, probably the most popular of all being 'Prząśniczka' (The Spinner), with its effective, though conventional, humming-semiquaver accompaniment. (Another spinning song, 'Prządka', seems to have been an attempt to repeat this success.) But the most delightful of the songs in this category is 'Wybór' (The Choice). (The pianist's left hand continues its descent for two more octaves.)

'Three young men of this village: are coming to see me;
one counts his money . . .'

As for the mazurkas and krakowiaks, they are innumerable and one can only draw attention to a few specially interesting or attractive ones: among the krakowiaks, 'Nigdy serca krakowiaka' with its one-sharp signature yet largely poised on, and ending on, a dominant seventh in C, 'Kłosek' (The Little Ear of Rye), 'Sołtys' (The Bailiff), 'Kozak' (The Cossack) (a sort of slow krakowiak); among the mazurkas, the delicious E major 'Mazurek', 'Hulanka' (The Carousal) which again challenges a comparison with Chopin (Op. 74, No. 4), the brilliant 'Stary hulaka' (The Old Rake)' And then there is the most striking 'Mogiła' (The Tomb), a painfully expressive slow krakowiak composed in June 1862: sounding like a premonition of the insurrection of the following year. Another song dating from the same year, the lament 'Macierzanka' (Thyme), sounds the same note and is more explicit in its expression of passionate patriotism, though the music is less specifically Polish than that of the very beautiful setting of Czeczot's 'Dąbrowa' (The Oak Wood), which has the quality of an elegiac folk-song.

The titles of Moniuszko's publications — *Song-Books for the Home* — indicate that he had the needs of amateurs foremost in his mind, and his example in this respect as in others was followed by his contemporaries and successors. Among the first of these were Ignacy Komorowski (1824-57) and Kazimierz Kratzer (1844-90). Neither had anything like Moniuszko's talent; like Nowakowski, they were sentimentalists. But their melancholy strains harmonized with the prevailing mood of the Polish people and such songs as Komorowski's 'Kalina' (Guelder Rose) (1846) and Kratzer's 'Skrzypki swaty' (The Matchmaking Fiddle) and 'Piosnka o piosence' (A Song about Song) were, as Jachimecki said of the first, 'taken to the hearts of nearly three generations'. Less popular but musically superior are the songs of Ignacy Krzyżanowski (1826-1905).

The songs of Władysław Żeleński (1837-1921) and Moniuszko's pupil Zygmunt Noskowski (1846-1909) are on an altogether higher artistic plane. Żeleński is at his best in his songs, which are much more markedly Polish than the bulk of his work, while Noskowski's are essentially the songs of a good all-round craftsman. One of Noskowski's most successful songs, the krakowiak 'Skowroneczek śpiewa' (The Lark sings), is said to have been sketched out in a few minutes when he needed money from a publisher;[19] his *Śpiewnik dla dzieci* (Songbook for Children), Op. 34 (1890), contains some of his most delightful music. But both Żeleński and Noskowski were also important as teachers; between them they trained nearly all the next generation of Polish composers, passing on to them the tradition of Moniuszko. Żeleński's pupils include Felicjan Szopski (1865-1939) and the musicologist Henryk Opieński (1870-1942), who was also a song-writer, while Noskowski was the teacher of Szymanowski (1882-1937), Karłowicz (1876-1909), and Różycki (1884-1953).

Before we consider their work, however, something must be said about three late nineteenth-century song-composers: Jan Gall (1856-1912), Stanisław Niewiadomski (1857-1936) and Eugeniusz Pankiewicz (1857-98). Of this trio, Gall was the least important; he has little to offer beyond copious melodic invention but, as Jachimecki says,[20] 'the charm of his ideas, the smoothness of his phrases, the really Italian sweetness of his melody, and the light and skilful accompaniments earned for Gall's songs enormous popularity'. Similar in character and equally popular, but wider in range and more substantial in achievement, are the songs of Niewiadomski. Niewiadomski was a very prolific but very unequal song-composer. His workmanship is impeccable: prosody and general handling of words, well-written, light-handed accompaniments testify to his craftsmanship. He had a genuine lyrical gift; but his taste was unsure, so that he sometimes lapses into the amiably Mendelssohnian, as in the eleventh song of the cycle *Piosnki z różnych stron* (Songs from Different Regions), or into the downright commonplace, as in 'Dziewczę z buzią jak malina' (a translation of Heine's 'Mädchen mit dem roten Mündchen'), the first song of *Z wiosennych tchnień* (From Breaths of Spring), and the name-song of the Mickiewicz cycle *Kurhanek Maryli* (Maryla's Grave). Even the delightful mazurka 'Otwórz, Janku!' (Open, Janek!) comes perilously near banality in the — admittedly catchy — refrain lines, which would have been the making of an Edwardian drawing-room ballad. But on the whole Niewiadomski's salon vein is more perceptible in the quiet songs than in the livelier ones, which often have a more markedly Polish flavour. Such songs as 'Zosia' (quite a different conception from Moniuszko's popular setting) and 'Grzeczna dziewczyna' (The Polite Maiden), both from *Kurhanek Maryli*, or the breathless mazurka 'Malowany wazonik' (The Painted Vase), from *Piosnki starodawne* (Old-time Songs), are delightful. One of Niewiadomski's most attractive sets is the *Humoreski*, which contains a worthy counterpart of Moniuszko's 'Wybór' (Ex. 3) in 'Między nami nic nie było' (There was nothing between us), the charming *quasi parlato* 'Rezeda', and 'Wiem ja coś . . .' (I know something . . .) where the archness is of the *Lied*, not of the Edwardian ballad (Ex. 4).

Ex. 4

Whereas Niewiadomski may be said to have slightly debased the Moniuszko tradition, Pankiewicz refined it—with the result that he was sometimes accused of over-intellectualism. Of his forty-odd songs,[21] only eight had been published at the time of his tragic death in a mental hospital in 1898: the four of Op. 5 (1887), the two Adam Asnyk *Sonnets*, Op. 6 (1887), and in 1888 Nos. 2 and 8 of the *Osiem pieśni ludowych polskich* (Eight Polish Folk-Songs) posthumously issued as Op. 14. (They consist of slightly sophisticated settings of melodies and words from Oskar Kolberg's various collections.) His most important set, the cycle *Z miłosnych dziejów* (From Love Stories), Op. 19, to poems by Michał Bałucki, composed in 1888 for the singer Maria Bohte, whom he afterwards married, was not published until 1930.[22]

Pankiewicz's very first song, Op. 5 No. 1, is marked by the harmonic asperinties which annoyed contemporary cirtics, and No. 2 shows a distinctly unusual approach to 'Du bist wie eine Blume' (marked *allegretto giocoso*); but the other two songs of the set, another setting of translated Heine and a cradle-song for the infant Jesus, are very beautiful in their different ways. The second of the *Sonnets* shows what Pankiewicz could achieve in very simple terms. But his masterpiece is undoubtedly 'Poranek' (Dawn), Op. 19 No. 2. He sometimes reminds one of Chopin, the Chopin of the piano music (e.g. in Op. 19 No. 6 in the Rejnsztejn 'Kołysanka' (Lullaby), and the 'Mazurek' in C sharp minor). Harmonically and by his finely-wrought piano parts, he may be said to have paved the way for the generation of which Szymanowski is the outstanding figure.

With Szymanowski we at last reach a Polish song-composer of European importance, whose work can no longer be measured by the partly 'domestic' standards of the Moniuszko tradition.[23] Not that his earliest songs, dating from 1901–2, the six Tetmajer songs, Op. 2, are very successful; they depend overmuch on the harmonic basis; but the *3 Fragmenty*, Op. 5 (three fragments from poems by J. Kasprowicz) and 'Łabędź' (The Swan), Op. 7, show an advance in the handling of the poetic texts although the declamatory element is still over-important. The style is still not very individual but by 1907 in the sets Opp. 11, 13, and 17 Szymanowski had already achieved some real successes. He was then living in Germany and most of the songs of this period are settings of contemporary German poets: Dehmel in particular, Bodenstedt, Birnbaum, Mombert, and others. Op. 13 Nos. 2 and 4 – 'Kołysanka Dzieciątka Jezus' (The Christ Child's Lullaby) and the Bodenstedt 'Suleika' – and 'Verkündigung' and 'Liebesnacht' (Op. 17 Nos. 6 and 12) are outstanding lyrical pieces. (Two compositions for voice and orchestra from this early period, 'Salome', Op. 6, and 'Penthesilea', Op. 18, have never been published.) The Polish set, Op. 20, and the *Bunte Lieder*, Op. 22, of *c.* 1910, are also more vocal – and more individual in style. Szymanowski at the time considered the *Bunte Lieder* 'the favourites out of all my songs. Their intelligibility depends entirely on the (only now) complete mastery of the song form from the point of view of declamation and the style of the voice and piano parts – which one could hardly say of Op. 17, which is good music rather than good songs. They are tremendously decided and unambiguous in expression. . . .'[24]

This was the period when Szymanowski was finding his true creative self in all directions. Hitherto he had been a typical late romantic, an admirer of Reger and Richard Strauss; now more advanced harmonic idioms and new techniques fascinated him increasingly – French Impressionism, Skryabin above all, later Schoenberg and Stravinsky – fertilizing his art without smothering his creative personality. Already in such songs as Op. 17 No. 9 and Op. 20 No. 3 Szymanowski had stood on the brink of atonality, and now in the poetry of other cultures he suddenly found a catalyst which precipitated a new style. The first impulse came from Hans Bethge's German translations of Hafiz and the first fruits were the first set of *Des Hafis Liebeslieder*, Op. 24 (1911). (The second set of Hafiz songs, Op. 26, includes orchestral versions of three of these, together with five new settings for soprano and orchestra.[25]) Then, in turn, came *Pieśni księżniczki z baśni* (Songs of a Princess of Legend), Op. 31 (to quasi-oriental verses by the composer's sister) (1915), four settings of Rabindranath Tagore, Op. 41 (1918), and *Pieśni Muezzina Szalonego* (Songs of the Crazy Muezzin), Op. 42 (1918). These are songs of extreme difficulty for both singer and pianist: works of infinite delicacy and polished detail. The piano 'breathes and flutters' as in late Skryabin, and the singer has to perform similar feats, with much coloratura vocalization. The Fairy-Tale Princess begins most of her songs and ends her cycle with vocalises on 'Ah!'; the Muezzin keeps on vocalizing on 'Allah' and 'olali' and 'olio'. The final vocalise of the Princess's second song. 'Słowik' (The Nightingale) is typical. It is highly artificial art, but exquisite of its kind.

Ex. 5

This idiom is still more deeply but less exuberantly exploited in the five *Słopiewnie*, Op. 46 *bis*,[26] of 1921, but fresh aspects of Szymanowski's art are revealed in the three sets of *Rymy dzieciece* (Children's Rhymes), Op. 49 (1923), and the four settings of James Joyce, from *Chamber Music*, Op. 54 (1926). Here the technical difficulties are much less for both voice and piano; the accompaniment of 'Sleep now', Op. 54, No. 2, is even rather heavy-footed in a curiously Musorgskian way; but the

Joyce songs are very singable – and well worth singing. Yet the *Children's Rhymes* are much better. Here again one is sometimes reminded of Musorgsky, e.g. in No. 8, 'Święta Krystyna' (St Christine), and No. 18, 'Zły Lejba' (Naughty Lejba); but much more often one is reminded of Bartók, the Bartók of the miniatures. Here everything is economical and, while the harmony is as pungent as one could wish, the voice parts – indeed the textures generally – are essentially diatonic, with the sharpened fourths and other characteristics of Polish folk-song. (Szymanowski's last work for voice and piano, the three sets of *Pieśni kurpiowskie*, Op. 58, are actually folk-song arrangements.) The subjects of the *Rhymes* are what one expects in pieces for or about children – lullabies (for Christine herself, for her dolls, 'for the brown horse'), games, visits to the cowshed, 'The Little Pig' whose adventure is narrated in a slow mazurka, 'Bumble-bee and Beetle', and so on – but they are treated with freshness and originality, with astringent objectivity and absence of sentimentality.

Compared with Szymanowski's songs, those of his contemporaries are rather tame. The early songs of Mieczysław Karłowicz, Opp. 1, 3, and 4, show that their composer could have become a notable song-writer, but Karłowicz turned to the orchestra and the larger forms and, in any case, died young. The songs were written in Berlin, where he finished his musical education after studying with Noskowski, so it is hardly surprising that some of them, e.g. Op. 1 Nos. 1, 4, and 5 (settings of Kazimierz Tetmajer, who also inspired Szymanowski's Op. 2), are *Lied*-like. On the other hand, the mazurka 'Na śniegu' (On the snow), Op. 1, No. 3, and 'Najpiekniejsze piosnki' (The best of my songs), Op. 4, might have been written by Moniuszko himself. Most characteristic are three melancholy songs in 4/4 time – 'Skąd pierwsze gwiazdy' (From where the first stars), Op. 1 No. 2, 'Nie płacz nademną' (Do not weep in vain), Op. 3 No. 7, and 'Pod jaworem' (Under the sycamore) – but they are manifestly immature.

It would be unjust to omit mention of the names of Feliks Nowowiejski (1877-1946), Ludomir Różycki (1884-1953), Stanisław Lipski (1880-1937), and Adam Sołtys (b. 1890). The mild influence of French impressionistic harmony is apparent in their songs; several of those by Nowowiejski – notably 'Sobótka w czarnym lesie' (St John's Eve in the Enchanted Wood), Op. 40, and the three charming ones that make up his Op. 59 – echo the sonorites of early Ravel. Różycki produced four or five sets of songs, including some Nietzsche and Ibsen settings, about 1906, and here again one can detect French influence, e.g. in the translucent 'Akwarela', Op. 16 No. 6; the two best pieces in his later cycle *Z erotyków*, Op. 51 (1923), are the first, 'Baśń' (A Tale), and third 'Pieśń weselna' (Bridal Song), the words of which appear to be a very long way after Hymen's song in *As You Like It*. But Różycki was essentially an operatic and instrumental composer; indeed most of the Polish composers now living appear to belong to the class with whom song-writing is a rather marginal activity, though between them they have given us some notable things: Szeligowski's *Pieśni zielone* (Green songs) (1921), Maklakiewicz's *Pieśni japońskie* for soprano and orchestra (1930), based not only on Japanese poems but on Japanese scales and employing a somewhat Debussyish orchestral technique,[27] Panufnik's *Suita polska* (*Hommage à Chopin*) (1949) for soprano and piano, based on folk-tunes but wordless. But, as with all contemporary or near-contemporary art, one is too near the picture to see it clearly. The music of one's age is a proper subject for the critic; the historian does wisely to leave it alone.

NOTES

1. I have been unable to consult Seweryn Barbag, 'Polska pieśń artystyczna', *Muzyka* (1927), which is said to be an important study.
2. Examples by Mielczewski. Szarzyński, and Damian in *Wydawnictwo dawnej muzyki polskiej*, ed. Chybiński, ii, v, x and xiii. Such works are usually described as 'Concerto a 4' or 'a 3', the other solo parts being taken by specified instruments.
3. See Jan Prosnak, *Kultura muzyczna Warszawy XVIII wieku* (Cracow, 1955), pp. 67–72.
4. Complete list in Alina Nowak-Romanowicz, *Józef Elsner* (Cracow, 1957), p. 302.
5. Two songs in the supplementary volume of musical examples to Nowak-Romanowicz's book, pp. 5 and 7.
6. Nowak-Romanowicz, op. cit., p. 140; printed complete in the supplementary volume, p. 9.
7. Zdzisław Jachimecki, *Historja muzyki polskiej* (Warsaw, 1920), p. 134.
8. Published complete in the *Dzieła wszystkie Fryderyka Chopina*, xvii (Warsaw).
9. Not 1855, as is commonly asserted; see M. J. E. Brown, 'The Posthumous Publication of Chopin's Songs', *Musical Quarterly*, xlii (1956), p. 51. The seventeenth song, 'Śpiew grobowy', was added to the set only in 1872 when Fontana himself was dead.
10. The poem was later set by Cui (Op. 11 No. 2) and numerous Polish musicians, and in different Russian translations by Glinka and Rimsky-Korsakov (Op. 42 No. 4).
11. See the thematic catalogue compiled by Erwin Nowaczyk, *Pieśni solowe Moniuszki* (Cracow, 1954).

12. Moniuszko published an interesting prospectus in the Petersburg Polish paper, *Tygodnik Petersburski* (No. 72, 1842); reprinted in Witold Rudziński, *Stanisław Moniuszko*, i (Cracow, 1955), pp. 94–6.

13. The contents of all twelve *Śpiewniki* are listed in Jachimecki, *Stanisław Moniuszko* (Warsaw, 1921), pp. 47–57.

14. *Historja*, p. 176.

15. In 1862 the Paris publisher Flaxland issued thirty-seven of Moniuszko's songs, under the title *Échos de Pologne*, with French translations and titles that make them sometimes hardly recognizable. Otherwise, with a few exceptions, his works are – for Western musicians – locked behind the barrier of an unknown tongue. The most useful, easily accessible selection is the two-volume *Wybór Pieśni* edited by Bronisław Romaniszyn and published by the Polskie Wydawnictwo Muzyczne (Cracow, 1951), but it has only Polish words.

16. Published in 1857, several years before Dargomïzhsky's not altogether deservedly more famous Russian setting (see p. 16).

17. *Moniuszko*, pp. 40–2.

18. Moniuszko's other 'English' songs, settings of direct Polish translations, are 'How should I your true love know', from *Hamlet*, Medora's song from Byron's *Corsair*, three songs from *The Lady of the Lake*, and one from *The Lay of the Last Minstrel*.

19. Józef Reiss, 'Zygmunt Noskowski w stulecie urodzin', *Ruch muzyczny*, ii (1946), p. 26.

20. *Historja*, p. 211.

21. Thematic catalogue in Włodzimierz Poźniak, *Eugeniusz Pankiewicz* (Cracow, 1958), pp. 76–100.

22. By Gebethner and Wolff (Warsaw), with German translations; the reprint in the Polskie Wydawnictwo Muzyczne edition of the *Pieśni zebrane* (Cracow, 1956) has only the Polish text.

23. His songs are much more easily accessible than those of most Polish composers, being mostly published by Universal Edition with German translations.

24. Letter to Stefan Spiess: quoted in Stefania Lobaczewska, *Karol Szymanowski* (Cracow, 1950), p. 230.

25. Only two of these have been published, No. 1, 'Das Grab des Hafis', only in piano version as a posthumous work.

26. A good deal of close analysis has been devoted to this remarkable cycle: see J. M. Chomiński, 'Studja nad twórczością K. Szymanowkiego. Cz. 1: Problem tonalny w "Słopiewniach"', *Polskie rocznik muzykologiczny*, ii (1936), p. 53; S. Łobaczewska, op. cit., p. 464 ff. and 'O "Słopiewniach" Karola Szymanowskiego', *Ruch muzyczny* (February 1948), p. 2; S. Gola-chowski, 'W sprawie "Słopiewni" K. Szymanowskiego', *Ruch muzyczny* (March 1948), p. 15.

27. See Z. Mycielski, 'Pieśni japońskie J. A. Maklakiewicza', *Ruch muzyczny* (October 1947), p. 13.

11. *The Operas of Stanisław Moniuszko*

In August 1941, one of the blackest periods of the war, the Poles in Britain made a characteristic gesture. 'It would seem that one cannot cultivate at this time works of peace such as the arts, especially music', wrote Jadwiga Harasowska. 'But this only appears so. The Poles now in Great Britain have learned to regard the continuation of one's daily work in spite of war . . . as the first step towards victory. Such an attitude . . . has allowed us to continue on British soil the Polish cultural life so ruthlessly oppressed in Poland. We publish Polish newspapers, books and music'. Mrs Harasowska was introducing a rather curious publication, a reproduction by the Polish Library in Glasgow of two scores now bound together: one a complete full score of the overture to Moniuszko's opera *Halka*, the other a drastically simplified and shortened piano score – not even a vocal score – of the opera itself with Polish words and not very English translation. It was a splendid but Quixotic gesture though it never fulfilled Mrs Harasowska's hopes that 'British singers might include these melodies in their repertoire' and that conductors would 'certainly give an enthusiastic welcome to the full score of the overture'. My point is, of course, that in that very dark hour *Halka* was put forward as a Polish national symbol in a strange land, as the Russians might have put forward *Ivan Susanin* or the Czechs *The Bartered Bride*. Indeed, *Halka* has the same place in Polish operatic history as the works of Glinka and Smetana in their countries.

There had been Polish operas before Moniuszko, as there had been Russian and Czech ones before Glinka and Smetana, but *Halka* caught on as none of its predecessors had done – even outside Poland – and impressed non-Polish musicians. Hans von Bülow, a Prussian and no Slavophil, contributed a long article on Moniuszko and his opera to the *Neue Zeitschrift für Musik* (12 November 1858),[1] ending with a Polish tribute:

C'est un poète slave; il rend avec un sentiment profond et vrai la mélancolie, l'exaltation, la passion sauvage, la résignation pieuse de la race lithuanienne. Son opéra *Halka* renferme des beautés très saisissantes pour nous autres Polonais . . .'

which he endorses 'and for us Germans too'.

But the *Halka* Bülow knew was not the original *Halka*. This had first been heard ten years earlier (1 January 1848) at Wilno [Vilnyus] in a concert performance by amateurs. Moniuszko was then twenty-eight. After completing his musical education at the Berlin Singakademie under Zelter's successor, Rungenhagen, he had settled at Wilno where he was organist at St John's Church. He had already published two of his twelve *Song-Books for the Home*[2] which were to establish him as the classic master of the Polish solo song, and he had composed a number of operettas, mostly for the Wilno amateurs, one or two for the professional theatre. The original *Halka*, his first opera, was more ambitious—but not very much more. It was in two acts, on a libretto by Włodzimierz Wolski based on a dramatic sketch by K. W. Wójcicki: essentially the same subject as those of other Central and East European operas of the mid-century—the peasant girl who drowns herself when her lover deserts her for a social superior.

In the original Act I the action is concise. It opens with the festivities of the betrothal of Zofia, the daughter of the big house, to Janusz, a young nobleman. A terzetto for Zofia, her wealthy father, and Janusz is interrupted by the distant voice of the unhappy Halka. When father and daughter go indoors Janusz is left to console the girl he has deserted; he swears he still loves her and even makes an assignation, then goes into the house, closing the doors. Halka is overjoyed and when a peasant lad from the village appears—Jontek, who has always loved her —she rounds on him for having maligned Janusz. But she soon learns the truth from the chorus of guests in the house; she runs to it and beats frantically on the door. Everyone comes out and Janusz orders Jontek to take the girl away. Act II is set in a village on Janusz's estate in the mountains, a pretext for some local colour. The wedding procession appears; Janusz is startled to find Halka near the church, Zofia puzzled but compassionate. They go into the church and from time to time we hear the music of the ceremony while a melodramatic scene is enacted outside, Halka repulses Jontek's attempts to console her, sings a lullaby to her baby (Ex. 1), contemplates vengeance by setting fire to the wooden church but thinks better of it, and then throws herself into the

Ex. 1

'Who will rock you in your eternal sleep'

river. As people begin to come out of church the steward orders the crowd outside to sing a merry song for the gentlefolk.

In this two-act form *Halka* was given its first stage-performance at Wilno on 16 February 1854, six years after the concert performance. It still had to wait four more before it was staged in Warsaw (1 January 1858). Moniuszko had from the first been fishing for a Warsaw production but it was not until May 1857 that the prospect brightened — thanks to the efforts of the critic and publicist Józef Sikorski and of Giovanni Quattrini, conductor of the Warsaw Opera. (Although an Italian, Quattrini was always a champion of Polish music; he had conducted Moniuszko's operetta *Loterja* (The Lottery) at Warsaw in 1846.) But in 1857 *Halka* was still a rather short two-act work and Moniuszko wrote to Quattrini (4 June 1857) that

having looked through the opera, I feel the need for *total* recasting though without changing the original ideas. Thus: (1) the role of Jontek, really one of the chief characters, must be not a baritone as now but a tenor; (2) a duet for Jontek and Janusz must be added to the finale of Act I; (3) transposition of the introduction, terzet, and Jontek's aria in Act I; (4) the polonaise at the beginning of the opera must of course be danced, as is customary at a ball; (5) after the first number of the second act there will have to be a mountaineers' dance which I will see to.

The part of Jontek had originally been written for a baritone, Moniuszko's friend Józef Bonoldi, singing teacher at the Nobles' Institute at Wilno, where he had sung it in 1848. But this meant that among the male soloists there was a preponderance of baritones or basses and Jontek was probably sung by a tenor even in 1854. Now, for Warsaw, the changes in the part went far beyond transposition; instead of a secondary character he became a principal. Another major change was the insertion of a long scene after Halka's exit in Act I, leading to the ballet: a new chorus, a polonaise aria for Zofia's father, and then a mazurka. Act I was now so long that it had to be bisected, and the second half, with a change of scene to the garden at night, now became Act II. This is opened by Halka with a fine new recitative and Italianate aria written to appease the elegant soprano Pauline Rivoli who had not been too happy at taking the part of a peasant girl.

The original second act was also bisected, the first scene – now Act III – being set in a mountain village with the 'mountaineers' dance' mentioned in Moniuszko's letter to Quattrini. The remainder became Act IV, opening with a scene for Jontek with a bagpiper, and including another fine addition to the score: a *dumka* for Jontek. Even the names of some of the characters were changed: for instance, Zofia's father, originally Cześnik, became Stolnik. Wolski, the librettist, cheerfully provided the additional text needed. (He collaborated with Moniuszko again soon afterwards in another, much less successful, three-act opera *Hrabina* (The Countess).) Composer and librettist toyed with other ideas. At one point they considered the possibility of ending the opera with a peasant rising but realized that this would never be tolerated by the censorship. And apparently the first Wilno version had ended not with Halka's suicide but with her rescue by her faithless lover, a *dénouement* approved of by such an authority as Henryk Opieński[3] and which Moniuszko's publishers Gebethner and Wolff preserved in a libretto of 1860. But the suicide has remained the accepted version.[4]

Halka had now become a full-length opera, slightly Italianized – perhaps in awareness of the Italian prima donna, for whom the composer sent an Italian translation of part of Act II 'for better understanding' – but thoroughly Polish in its employment of mazurka and polonaise rhythms and in Jontek's *dumka* in Act IV (Ex. 2).

Ex. 2

'The fir-trees murmur on the mountain peaks, murmur
to themselves far away . . . and to a sad young life
when it has sorrow in its heart!'

Another authentic touch: Moniuszko begged the *régisseur* that in the
mazurka which ends Act I there should be, after the introduction, two
bars of rhythmic stamping. 'It seems to me that this is bound to have a
pretty good effect when the brilliant orchestra then begins the dance
proper'.[5] But he came nearest to genuine folk elements in the bagpiper's
tune with its sharpened fourth and drone accompaniment just before
Jontek's *dumka* (Ex. 3) and in the mountaineers' dances in Act III.

Ex. 3

Between the two versions of *Halka* Moniuszko had composed two
more insignificant operettas for Wilno; *Cyganie* (later re-named
Jawnuta) and *Bettly*, based on a translation from the Scribe factory. He
now wanted to compose a big historical opera, *Król chlopków* (The King
of the Peasants), the nickname of Casimir III. But the Warsaw Directorate
wanted a one-act opera and he responded at once with *Flis* (The Raftsman). It was begun during a hot summer holiday in Paris (1858) and,
according to his friend the baritone Aleksander Walicki, he shut himself
up in his completely shuttered lodgings and wrote the whole opera by
candlelight in four days! Presumably this was only the sketch, but the
score was finished in Warsaw in time for the first performance on 24
September.

Stanisław Bogusławski's libretto could hardly be simpler. Zosia, a
peasant girl living in a village on the Vistula, is in love with a young
raftsman, Franek. But he has gone away on a barge and her father,
Antoni, has promised her to a well-to-do barber from Warsaw. The

barber, Jakub, appears—a caricature of a town dandy—and although Franek returns with the other raftsmen, Antoni insists that Zosia must marry the rich dandy, not the poor raftsman. She is in despair until at the very end it is accidentally revealed that Jakub is Franek's long-lost brother; they embrace and Jakub, who has always been a lukewarm lover, cheerfully resigns his claim to Zosia. As in *Halka*, the heroine was sung by Rivoli. (The parts of Franek and his brother were taken by the Jontek and Janusz of *Halka*.) Her first solo is a *dumka* but she then takes part in an Italianate duet allowing a display of coloratura near the end; indeed, a great deal of the score is close to *opera buffa*; the native note is sounded best in the clarinet solo which heralds Franek's *kujawiak* when he comes ashore (Ex. 4), in the song itself, and in the following chorus of raftsmen.

Ex. 4 Allegretto

Hrabina, Moniuszko's last collaboration with the librettist Wolski, produced at Warsaw on 7 February 1860, has already been mentioned. With it they turned their backs on peasant heroes and heroines. The Countess of the title is a beautiful young widow in the ephemeral Napoleonic Duchy of Warsaw with a Saxon prince as French puppet-Duke and the time is half a century before the opera was written. The hero, Kazimierz, is a young lancer officer who temporarily loses the Countess's favour by accidentally tearing her magnificent ballgown with his spurs; the young girl Bronia, whom he wins in the end, is the Countess's guest. The background of Act II which quite overshadows the foreground, is a grand entertainment in the Countess's palace: a ballet, 'Flora pursued by Zephyrus'; a showy Italian coloratura aria sung by the Italian prima donna at the Opera; and another ballet scene, in which Neptune rather surprisingly appears on the Vistula and satyrs dance a polka. Bronia is asked to fill the gap left by a singer who has fallen ill and offers a simple little song. Act III takes place in Bronia's grandfather's house in the country, where Kazimierz returns after fighting Napoleon's battles in Spain to find Bronia, and where the Countess turns up in vain pursuit of him. It is introduced by one of a set of six piano polonaises Moniuszko had published in 1845, now arranged for three cellos, viola, and bass. The overture to *Hrabina* – a potpourri introducing the final chorus, a waltz from Act II, and two of Bronia's songs – includes a passage in which Moniuszko comes probably nearer than anywhere else to Chopinesque chromaticism.

Ex. 5

The Countess's own music – her duets with Kazimierz, the aria as she tries on her new dress in Act II, her Act III aria 'On tu przybywa, wiem niewzawodnie' (He is here, I know for sure) – is charming but rather characterless.

All Wolski's characters are stereotypes. But whereas in *Halka* the setting had given Moniuszko opportunities to bring the puppets to musical life by the injection of Polish idioms, the conventional characters and complicated, artificially inflated plot of *Hrabina* offered him little incentive Fortunately he had already found a new and more skilful collaborator in Jan Chęciński, an actor who had recently become *régisseur* of the Warsaw Theatre. Chęciński had translated Italian and French opera librettos – *Figaro, Puritani, Favorita, Rigoletto, Traviata, Ernani, La Juive, Le Prophète*, and many more – with outstanding skill, and even before the completion of *Hrabina* Moniuszko had asked him to provide a libretto on Casimir Delavigne's tragedy *Le Paria*, a drama of the Portuguese landing in India in the early fifteenth century. When *Parja* was at last produced in 1869 Chęciński published in his introduction to the libretto[6] an account of how, years earlier, Moniuszko had come to him 'wreathed in smiles, his eyes shining, carrying under his arm a thick beautifully bound book'. Here, as the composer saw it, was the ready-made opera subject needing only translation and versification. Chęciński knew the task was not as simple as that, but Moniuszko was not to be balked, and Chęciński did his best to cook up a libretto, boiling down Delavigne's five acts to three and slashing thousands of his Alexandrines. Moniuszko actually composed the introduction (based on the music of a cantata of 1847), an aria for the Indian commander Idamor, some choruses, and a song for the crazy pariah Dżares, but was then distracted by the need to complete *Hrabina* and then by two other operatic projects. However, some years later an excellent straightforward translation of *Le Paria* by Wacław Szymanowski was performed in Warsaw; Moniuszko supplied incidental music and interpolated some of the choruses he had composed for Chęciński's libretto. And before long he demanded words for a duet for Idamor and the Brahmin high priest's daughter Neala:

'What? You're writing music for *Parja* again?' I asked in astonishment. 'Yes'—'And how far have you got?'—'It's nearly finished.'

In vain Chęciński protested that after ten years he would want to revise and improve what he had written; he no longer had even his rough drafts. But Moniuszko brushed aside all his objections: 'You don't need rough drafts; the opera is complete; I've cut out a few unnecessary scenes and shortened some overlong ones, and as for the rest, you'll see when it's finished'. 'So', says Chęciński, 'In a month or two I at last saw the end of the libretto of *Parja*, for which the music was already complete'. Of course, operatic masterpieces are not concocted like that and in any case the exotic was right outside Moniuszko's range; *Parja* is one of his feeblest operas. But in the years between the first work on it and its production on 11 December 1869 Moniuszko and Chęciński had collaborated in two thoroughly Polish compositions, the one-act *opera buffa, Verbum nobile,* produced on New Year's Day 1861; and the four-act *Straszny dwór* (The haunted château) written against the background of the patriotic insurrection of 1863-4[7] and produced on 26 September 1865.

Verbum nobile is only a trifle, but it is a charming trifle. The plot is as slight as that of *Flis* and even more improbable. Pan Serwacy Łagoda and Pan Marcin Pakuła, two old friends, have agreed that when the son of one of them grows up he shall marry the other's daughter. The two young people do grow up, unknown to each other, meet by chance, and of course fall in love. But the hero, Michał Pakuła, stupidly and inexplicably, tells Zuzia that his name is Stanisław. When they meet again in Serwacy's garden they are found by her father, who has to tell them their marriage is impossible since he has given his *verbum nobile*, his word as a nobleman, that she shall marry another young man. Even the appearance of Marcin and the revelation that 'Stanisław' and Michał are the same are not a final solution, for Serwacy has given his *verbum nobile* again: that whomever Zuzia marries it shall not be Michał. Zuzia resolves the dilemma by declaring that the second *verbum* really applies to the bogus 'Stanisław', whom she doesn't love, not to her Michał.[8] The *opera buffa* note is struck immediately in the opening of the sparkling overture (Ex. 6), and the series of short choruses of

Serwacy's villagers. Michał-Stanisław's polonaise on his entrance, though conventional, became very popular. And Moniuszko was careful not to allow anything too serious to intervene; he had first set Zuzia's sad *dumka* elaborately with passionate feeling (Ex. 7i), but replaced this with much simpler music (Ex. 7ii). The next number, Marcin's

'If you keep sorrow under control, talking to yourself,
is that crazy?'

polonaise, in which he comforts the 'little bird' with the offer of his son, who has few worldly goods but 'a fine figure and a handsome little moustache', also became a popular hit.

More than four years passed after the production of *Verbum nobile* before the next Chęciński–Moniuszko collaboration could be staged. They were terrible years for Poland, for the 1863 rising was repressed even more savagely than that of 1830–1. But in a letter of 28 November 1863, before the rebellion had been finally crushed, Moniuszko told a friend in Wilno that his only consolations were health and work, 'to which as the only comforter I have returned with relish after a long rest and yesterday in one spurt I finished Act III of *Straszny dwór* from beginning to end.' He began to orchestrate on 4 June 1864, and the Warsaw Opera took the work in hand on 5 January 1865, nearly eight months before the first performance.

The subject was suggested by one of the stories in the *Stare gawędy i obrazy* (Old talks and pictures) (Warsaw, 1840) of Kazimierz Wójcicki, the same book from which Wolski had got a hint for *Halka*. But Chęciński considerably elaborated Wójcicki's story, altering some of the names of the characters and adding fresh ones; further changes were made in the course of composition. The hero of *Verbum nobile* had been a young noble returned from the wars; *Straszny dwór* has two, the brothers Stefan and Zbigniew, and the glorification of Polish arms worried the Russian censor. (For instance, in old editions of the score the reference in Stefan's Act III aria to the heroes' father firing them with warlike 'Sarmatian songs' is altered so that the old man sings only of peaceful things; the Austrian censor at Lemberg (Lwów) had no such qualms; the Galician Poles had not rebelled in 1863.) In the first scene of Act I of *Straszny dwór* we see the brothers with a crowd of their men drinking in the courtyard of an inn after a victorious campaign. They agree never to marry, so as not to come under a woman's thumb. The scene changes to their estate where the old servant Maciej is factotum and house-keeper. Their aunt, Cześnikowa, has already secretly looked out two sisters who would make them excellent brides, and she is very disappointed by their misogamy. However, it is necessary for them to visit their late father's debtors, among others Miecznik at Kalinowa whose daughters the aunt has had in mind. She cunningly tries to dissuade them: the old château is ugly, haunted, and buried in inaccessible country.

Act II opens with the sisters, Hanna and Jadwiga, and their maids on New Year's Eve amusing themselves with such customary games as trying to see the faces of future husbands in a bowl of water; they are watched by their father's factotum Damazy who aspires to Hanna's hand. Country girls sing at their spinning-wheels; their chorus is charming and very Polish.

Ex. 9

The maids leave and Cześnikowa enters to a light dancing theme that has accompanied her appearance in Act I (but it never becomes a *Leitmotiv*). Her nephews have not yet arrived and she loses no time in revealing their intention never to marry. Before long the young men themselves appear and, despite their resolution, it becomes clear during the finale that the couples are mutually attracted.[9] Even before this finale Hanna has shown signs of a tendency to coloratura; she is the lively sister. Jadwiga has already established her gentler nature in a *dumka* and in her quartet, where she sings—to an accompaniment reminding one of a theme Wagner wrote probably at nearly the same time—that 'helmet and visor are only fine feathers' to compensate for something lacking.

Ex. 10

Act III takes place at night in a room under the tower; a great chiming clock stands between two huge windows; on each side of the stage are hung two life-size portraits. First there is a comic scene in which Miecznik's porter Skoluba frightens Maciej, who is to sleep there, with tales of the clock which strikes when a stranger dwells in the house and of the pictures of Miecznik's ancestors which come to life. (Skoluba's exit aria was one of the hits of the opera.) Left alone, Maciej's fears are confirmed when the two girls who have been hiding behind the pictures

speak and move their faces. He is rescued by his masters and goes off
with Zbigniew, but Stefan remains. His accompanied recitative and aria
provide the finest scene of the opera. He is meditating on his situation
and his resolution to remain unmarried when the clock strikes twelve
and its mechanism plays what Moniuszko calls a *kurant*, though it is
really an old-style polonaise.

Ex. 11

It has already been heard, also on the flute and in the same key, in the
Act I *terzetto* when the brothers remember their parents – a point which
is explained only now, when Stefan recalls how their father 'often used
to sing this Sarmatian song' when they were children. Zbigniev returns,
and in a *duettino* the brothers try in vain to dismiss the girls from their
minds, though in the end they stick to their resolution. There follows
a fine quartet, for the pictures are pushed aside revealing recesses in
which the girls stand in the costumes of their portraits; the men do
not notice them, despite Hanna's coloratura. Damazy then emerges
from the clock where he too has been concealed and runs toward the
'pictures', but the girls escape by a hidden staircase. He denies having
anything to do with the clock and the pictures, saying he has hidden
in order to learn the truth about the haunting, of which he now claims
to be convinced. He also explains why the house has acquired its
reputation: it was paid for with 'shameful services' which brought on it
'curses and tears' – and 'divine wrath'. The brothers decide to 'leave the
accursed house'.

By Act IV Hanna no longer believes the young men have been making
a cowardly excuse to avoid matrimony; Cześnikowa has explained that
they have taken this pledge 'so as not to give way to wifely tears' when
honour calls them to go and fight for their country. Though she is

horrified at the thought of dying an old maid, Hanna applauds this
noble resolution in a recitative and aria in which her coloratura reaches
new heights.

Ex. 12

Damazy enters gleefully to announce the departure of the heroes;
Stefan comes to say goodbye and Miecznik accuses them of cowardice.
But the stage is filled with New Year revellers; Damazy's lies and
intrigues are exposed, and Miecznik explains that the real reason why
his house is known as *straszny* (which means 'awful' as well as 'haunted')
is that his grandfather had twelve daughters and got them all married,
so that the continual noise of festivity enraged the entire neighbourhood.
He then blesses the young couples, the heroes having forgotten their vow
of celibacy, and the opera ends—in the second version, for the original
conclusion was longer and weaker—with the whole company singing a
brief chorus on the theme to which, in Act I, Stefan had sworn never to
have women in their house (Ex. 13a). Indeed, it might be described as a
'celibacy theme', for it is heard in the orchestra when Stefan thinks of
Hanna's lovely eyes during his vigil in the haunted room (Ex. 13b) and
is sung by each brother in the *duettino*.

Ex. 13
(a)

'Good comrade! Excellent plan, to have no women
in our house, *vivat! Semper* bachelorhood!'

'Careful, Stefan! You promised yourself a life without
a wife.'

Moniuszko was not altogether content with the libretto, which he
described as 'a lifeless trudge to a solution foreseen in the beginning'.[10]
All the same, he clothed it in some of his best music, though he could
do little with the fourth act. And he was happy to collaborate again
with Chęciński in the already mentioned *Parja* and in the one-act
operetta *Beata*, produced in 1872 just before his death and, like *Parja*,
a failure.

Moniuszko's reputation as a stage-composer rests on *Halka, Flis,
Verbum nobile,* and *Straszny dwór. Halka* was given abroad, first in
Prague, Moscow, and St Petersburg, and after the composer's death in
Vienna, New York, and Milan but neither *Flis, Hrabina,* nor *Verbum
nobile* made its way beyond Poland, though *Straszny dwór* was produced
in Vienna and Prague in the early 1890s. In 1849 Moniuszko had given
lessons in 'thorough-bass and harmonization of chorales' gratis to the
fourteen-year-old César Cui at Wilno. Twenty years later, when he
visited St Petersburg for the production of *Halka*, Cui—now a notable
composer and music critic of the *St Peterburgskiya vedomosti*—devoted
a substantial and warmly appreciative article, including a detailed
analysis, to the opera.[11] And two years later his obituary[12] characterizes
Moniuszko as follows:

He was of Lithuanian origin [Cui himself was Lithuanian on his mother's side] and Lithuanians, despite their long merger with the Poles, have preserved many special characteristics. . . . They lack Polish vivacity, gaiety, and susceptibility, but they feel more deeply, they are more sincere, unpretending, honest, and serious. . . . These qualities are to some extent noticeable in Moniuszko's music . . . In his compositions there is no great depth, power, or beauty of the highest order, but his music is lovable, often graceful and — above all — almost everywhere pervaded by life and movement, always revealed in tasteful and accomplished forms. Moniuszko's style is extremely lucid and always melodious; the voice occupies the first plane and sings his music admirably. . . . Moniuszko's music is shot through with Slavonic colouring and nearest of all to Polish and Ukrainian song. In some places a French Auberesque vein of rhythmic and harmonic piquancy peeps through; Italianisms of dubious quality are rare. . .

It is a very fair judgement.

NOTES

1. Reprinted in *Briefe und Schriften*, iii.
2. See p. 144.
3. *Stanisław Moniuszko* (Lvov/Poznań, 1924), p. 253.
4. Leon Schiller, in his introduction to the Polskie Wydawnictwo Muzyczne libretto (1953), gives several versions of the end.
5. Quoted in Witold Rudziński, *Stanisław Moniuszko: Studia i materiały*, i (Cracow, 1955), p. 368.
6. Given in full in Zdzisłav Jachimecki, *Stanisław Moniuszko* (Warsaw, 1921), pp. 181–4.
7. As a result of which Bolesław Szostakowicz and his wife, grandparents of the half-Russian composer, were sent to Siberia.
8. The part was taken by Adam Ziólkowski, the original Janusz of *Halka*.
9. Moniuszko borrowed the huntsmen's chorus which opens the finale from his early one-act comic operetta *Bettly* (1852), the libretto of which was a translation by Feliks Schober of the Scribe–Mélesville *Le Chålet*, first composed by Adolphe Adam (1834) and then, in an Italian version, *Betly ossia La capanna svizzera*, by Donizetti (1836). This latter, translated yet again by Leopold Matuszyński, was produced in Warsaw in 1845.
10. See Aleksander Poliński, *Stanisław Moniuszko* (Warsaw, 1913), p. 40.
11. Cui, *Izbrannïe stat'i* (Leningrad, 1952), p. 154.
12. Ibid., p. 206.

12. Czechoslovakian Song

Unlike the music of Russia, that of the lands that constitute the modern republic of Czechoslovakia has always formed part of the main stream of European music, strongly influenced by it and valuably contributing to it. Indeed, so many 'Czech' composers – among whom we commonly, if wrongly, include Moravians and Slovaks as well as true Czechs – have settled in Germany, England, France, Italy, and Russia that it is not always easy to decide whether they belong to the history of Czechoslovak music. Only if Handel's oratorios are to be classed as 'German' can we consider the songs of Reicha 'Czech'. Even the language test is not decisive, for Smetana composed German poems before he turned to Czech ones. The history of Czech music is further complicated by political events – above all, the Thirty Years War – which seriously interrupted the natural development of native art, so that the rich heritage of the Middle Ages – the songs of the wandering scholars, Hussite song, the secular songs of the early fifteenth century – was not directly handed on as the basis for a deep-rooted specifically Czech tradition.

In the eighteenth century we find Czech composers employing the favourite European vocal forms without marked individuality or national flavour: e.g. J. A. Plánický (*c.* 1691-1732) in his collection of solo motets *Opella ecclesiastica seu Ariae duodecim* (Augsburg, 1723),[1] which are stronger in the recitatives than in the arias, and J. L. Dukát (1684-1717) who wrote Italianate solo cantatas with two violins (*Cithara nova*, 1707). (The earliest known Czech piece of solo church music is the *Concertus de resurrectione* (1691) of Ferdinand Bernard Artophaeus, for soprano, two violins, two violas, and organ.) Music with Czech words is rare at this period, but there is a setting of the Czech translation of the 150th Psalm as an aria for bass and orchestra by the leading Baroque master J. D. Zelenka (1679-1745), probably composed for the Bohemian Brethren at Dresden. A younger composer, František Xaver Brixi (1732-71), a member of one of the famous

Czech musical families, composed both arias in Neapolitan style and Christmas *pastorely*. These pastorals, solos or for several voices, usually accompanied by a little orchestra and organ, were performed all over the country in the village churches and very often composed in the eighteenth century by the village *kantoři*: curious fusions of the style of Czech popular song with that of the Viennese classics. They played an important part in the evolution of the Czech national idiom and lasted into the middle of the nineteenth century.[2]

It was the simple, popular songs of the village cantors, schoolmasters, and organists, to whose musicianship in the 1770s J. F. Reichardt paid generous tribute in his *Briefe eines aufmerksamen Reisenden*, which set the pattern for the later development of the Czech solo song as surely as the *romances* of the aristocratic dilettanti did for the later development of the Russian art-song. The consequence was natural; Czech song has been generally unpretentious and—lacking the stimulus of poets of the rank of Pushkin—less sophisticated than that of Russia. Famous 'emigrants' such as Jiří (Georg) Benda and Josef Mysliveček wrote solo cantatas and numerous arias and ariettas, and Leopold Koželuh, who went no farther from home than Vienna, published sets of *Ariette italiane, XV Lieder beym Clavier zum Singen* and *XII Lieder mit Melodien beym Clavier*[3] (both Vienna, 1785), and Masonic *Lieder* (Berlin, *c*. 1800). (There was a good deal of Masonic song composition by Czechs at this period.) But Koželuh did not altogether neglect his native language; his 'Číhání' (Lying in wait) was printed posthumously in S. K. Macháček's first collection of *Zpěvy české* (Czech Songs) (Prague, 1825). Jírovec (Gyrowetz) also set Czech words occasionally.

The real founders of the Czech art-song bear names much less familiar. The most important was Koželuh's pupil, Jakub Jan Ryba (1765-1815); Despite their German titles, Ryba's *Zwölf böhmische Lieder* (1800)[4] and *Neue böhmische Lieder* (1808) are settings of Czech poems mostly by Šebestián Hněvkovský and the Nejedlýs—the music as naïve as the words. In 1808 he also published *Dar pilné mládeži* (A Gift for Industrious Youth), a book of children's songs, a field in which he had been preceded by Mozart's friend F. X. Dušek. Ryba was also the composer of the earliest ballad in Czech, a setting of Vojtěch Nejedlý's 'Lenka', modelled on Zumsteeg (1808), and the earliest Czech romance, 'Průvod od dobré Bětolinky', on the same poet's translation of some verses attributed to Hölty. Jan Doležálek's *Ceské písně v hudbu uvedené* (Czech Songs set to music)[5] came out in Vienna in 1812.

It was perhaps the success of these publications which induced the

greatest Czech composer of the day, Václav Tomášek (1774-1850), to
turn to his native language. From 1800 onward Tomášek had been a
fairly prolific composer of *Lieder* by Hölty, Voss, Tiedge, and others:
sets of songs Opp. 2, 6, 33, 34, 37, and 44, Bürger's 'Lenore', Op. 12,
Schiller's 'Leichenphantasie', Op. 25, to say nothing of four Italian
canzonets, Op. 28. Then in 1813, 'lest I should quite forget my mother-
tongue' (as he says in his autobiography), he composed *Šestero písní*
(Six Songs) to Czech words, which he published in Prague, four of
them to poems by Václav Hanka: they are very naïve but not without
charm; the set is prefaced by a 'Word to Patriots' concerning the special
suitability of the Czech language for musical treatment. Tomášek did
not abandon German; indeed he composed a great many more *Lieder*,
including a series of seven Goethe sets, Opp. 53-59, and four Schiller
sets, Opp. 85-88. But he returned in Opp. 50 and 71[6] to Hanka, set
five German poems by K. E. Ebert, Op. 69, six by Heine, Opp. 77 and
78, and—most interesting of all—six *Starožitné písné* (Ancient Songs),
Op. 82 (1823), on words from the notorious Kralové Dvůr manuscript,
then generally believed to be a specimen of ancient Czech literature,
actually a forgery by Hanka and others. To Tomášek himself, and to
Hanka and his friends, it seemed that the unusual texts had opened a
new vein for him in music, and it is true that the *Starožitné písné* have
novel touches. Consider No. 5, 'Žežhulice' (The Cuckoo).

že ne - ní   vez - dy ja - ro.

'In the broad field stands an oak tree, in the oak a cuckoo;
it cuckoos and laments that it is not always spring.

Some of Tomášek's songs were published in the first volume of
Věnec ze zpěvů vlastenských uvitý a obětovaný divkám vlastenským
(A garland woven of patriotic songs and offered to patriotic young
ladies), a collection edited by the poet Josef Krasoslav Chmelenský
(not to be confused with his contemporary, the composer Jan Chmelenský). Macháček's collections of Czech songs have already been
mentioned, but Chmelenský's *Věnec* is much more important. It was an
annual publication and appeared for five years, 1835–39.[7] Despite the
title, the first volume contained a few opera songs by Mozart and other
non-Czech composers. Nor are all the Czech songs original songs with
piano; Chmelenský's co-editor František Škroup (1801–62) printed a
number of songs from his stage works—including the one which eighty
years later was adopted as the Czech national anthem, 'Kde domov
muj?' (Where is my home?) from *Fidlovačka*. All the same, *Věnec*
presents an interesting cross-section of Czech song during the period
of Smetana's youth, from Doležálek and Tomášek to such younger
composers as Josef Vorel (1801–74); many of the songs are settings
of Chmelensky's own words, obviously written 'for music'; but the
musical level is generally low.[8] A few years later Škroup tried to revive
Věnec, but only one volume appeared—in 1844.

The non-existence of a strong tradition of Czech solo song is curious,
considering the intense musicality of the Czechoslovak peoples, especially
their love of song. The explanation is perhaps to be found in two
circumstances: the country was bilingual and many patriotic Czechs,
including Smetana, felt themselves more at home in German than in
their mother-tongue, so that the better composers tended to compose
Lieder in the styles of the German masters; on the other hand, genuine
Czech song—as represented in *Věnec* and other collections—was apt to
be a weak and sentimentalized imitation of folk music, inferior to the
comparable work of Varlamov or even Gurilev in Russia. Czech song

never had a Glinka or Moniuszko to crystallize tradition, and the solo song with piano has never occupied a central or near-central place in the work of any important Czech composer.

The case of Smetana (1824–84) is typical. At sixteen he made his first—never completed—essay in song-writing: a setting of Schiller's 'Der Pilgrim'. And all but one of his handful of earlier songs are to German texts: 'Liebchens Blick' and 'Lebe wohl' (which are headed 'Gesangkomposition 1. Lied. – 2. Das durchkomponierte Lied', i.e. they are composition exercises), the Wieland 'Schmerz der Trennung' and Jacobi 'Einladung' (all four written in 1846), and the much finer 'Liebesfrühling' ('Dieses Saitenspiel der Brust' from Rückert's famous cycle) of 1853, which might be a rejected number from Schumann's Op. 37. The one early Czech song is a setting of Kollár's 'Píseň svobody' (Song of Freedom)[9] written during the patriotic excitement of 1848. Then a quarter of a century passed before Smetana returned to solo song. But for his 'jubilee concert' in Prague on 4 January 1880 he composed five of Vítězslav Hálek's *Večerní písně* (Evening Songs), a collection of rather feebly romantic lyrics which had already attracted Dvořák and Fibich. The *Večerní písně* are Smetana's best songs, but by no means his best music. The choice of words was obviously meant very personally: e.g. the first two, 'Kdo v zlaté struny zahrat zná' (Give honour to him who knows how to sound the golden strings) and 'Ne kamenujte proróky' (Do not stone prophets. For singers are like birds, for ever fleeing him who throws a stone at them.) But the music hardly suits the theme and both these songs seem pianistic in origin, the words to which have been fitted later.

Ex. 2

The third song—'Mně zdálo se' (It seemed to me that pain had already grown old)—is declamatory, the fourth a polka (with a twist), while the fifth and best and most extended—'Z svých písní' (Out of my songs I'll build a throne for you)—returns to the exultant mood and the pulsing triplet accompanying chords of 'Liebesfrühling'.

The songs of Dvořák (1841-1904) are a different matter. He was hardly one of the world's great song-writers, but, like Tchaikovsky, he was a great composer who wrote songs throughout his creative life—some of them very fine indeed. His earliest essay in this field was the cycle of eighteen *Cypřiše* (Cypresses) to poems by Gustav Pfleger-Moravský, composed in July 1865 under the immediate influence of his passion for the actress Josefina Čermáková, whose sister he afterwards married. *Cypřiše* in their original form are naive and awkward compositions and were never published, but they were always peculiarly dear to Dvořák and he used their material in operas and piano pieces; as late as 1887 he turned twelve of them into movements for string quartet. But twelve also appeared later in revised forms as songs: Nos. 1, 5, 11, and 13 were published in 1882 as Op. 2;[10] Nos. 8, 3, 9, 6, 17, 14, 2, and 4 were revised the following year and published as *Písně milostné* (Love Songs), Op. 83, in 1888. The extreme simplicity of Op. 2 has suggested to some critics that in this case revision was slight. This is not true; on the contrary, the simplicity of (for instance) No. 4 represents a great improvement on the fussy original.

Ex. 3

(a) Cypřiše, No. 13

Allegro

Na ho-rách ti - cho, a v ú - do-lí ti - cho

(b) Op. 2, No. 4

Allegretto

Na ho-rách ti - cho, v ú - do-lí ti - cho,

'Quiet on the hills, quiet in the valley.'

And four and a half 4/4 bars of piano introduction have been reduced
to two of 3/8. The workmanship of Op. 83 is finer but even here
Dvořák sometimes left the original voice-part unchanged, as in No. 8,
'O, duše drahá, jedinká' (Thou only dear one); the song was put up a
semitone, the clumsy accompaniment totally rewritten, but the original
voice-part remains except for the final cadence and a magic modification
in bars 10-11 (and 12-13).

'Oh, would I were a singing swan.'

Even in their revised forms, most of these songs of Op. 2 and Op. 83
are essentially *Lieder* in the vein of Schubert, Schumann, or (once or
twice) Mendelssohn, though with many individual touches. And some
of them—'Mé srdce často' (My heart often in sadness), Op. 2 No. 3,
'O, naší lásce nekvěte' (Our love will never blossom), Op. 83 No. 1, 'Já
vím, že v sladké naději' (I know that in sweet hope), Op. 83 No. 4, and
—a special favourite of the composer's—'Zde v lese u potoka' (Here in
the forest by the stream), Op. 83 No. 6—are things that no one but
Dvořák could have created.

During 1871-2, stirred by Ludevít Procházka's public appeal for the
creation of a Czech national music, Dvořák composed a whole group of
songs: four poems from a book by Smetana's friend and librettist

Eliška Krásnohorská, the ballad 'Sirotek' (The Orphan) by K. J. Erben, four translations of Serbian folk-songs, and six poems from the Kralové Dvůr manuscript—the same six that Tomášek had set as his Op. 82 half a century earlier. The Kralové Dvůr songs were published complete in 1873 as Op. 17; in 1879 Simrock published the first four, with *German* texts, as Op. 7. Simrock also issued Nos. 2 and 4 of the Krásnohorská songs with German texts as Op. 9 Nos. 1 and 2 in 1879, and the Serbian songs with German texts as Op. 6 the following year. 'Sirotek' belatedly found a Czech publisher in 1883 and appeared with its original words as Op. 5. The Kralové Dvůr songs are the best of this group; the Serbian songs are feeble and the Schubertian ballad, 'Sirotek', is a failure. One of the Krásnohorská songs, 'Proto' (Because), Op. 9 No. 1, is specially characteristic of a type of song with which Dvořák experimented at this period presumably in an attempt to break away from German models; the melody is broad and hymn-like but flows in asymmetrical phrases. However, 'Proto' is earthbound by its dull chordal accompaniment. A similar style is employed more successfully in No. 5 of the Kralové Dvůr songs, 'Opuščená' (The Deserted Girl), but the two most original songs of this set are 'Róže' (The Rose) and 'Žežhulice' (The Cuckoo); neither is wholly successful yet Dvořák must have been pleased with the opening of 'Žežhulice' for he used it again ten years later in the first movement of the great F minor Trio. Some of the other songs of Op. 17 are charming in a vein that suggests folk-song or, rather, Schubert at his most *volksliedartig*.

Next, in 1876, came twelve settings of Hálek's *Večerní písně*, from which Dvořák had set two (never published) as early as 1865. Instead of being published together, two appeared in 1880 (with German texts only) as Op. 9 Nos. 3 and 4, four came out in 1881 as Op. 3,[11] five were revised in 1882 and published the following year as Op. 31, and one—condemned on the autograph copy as 'weak'—never appeared at all. For the German versions of the *Večerní písně* Dvořák used an existing translation of Hálek's poems, altering his vocal line to fit it: an apparently sensible idea which, as we shall see in connexion with the *Biblické písně*, sometimes had unfortunate results. Op. 3, No. 1 ('Ty hvězdičky tam na nebi', Thou art like the little stars), with its asymmetrical phrases and its simple chordal accompaniment, is a more successful essay in the style of 'Proto', and the mature fruit of this line of experiment appears in Op. 31 No. 4, 'Vy všichini, kdož jste stísněi' (All ye that labour) with its free and original declamation in five-bar phrases. But Op. 31 contains all the best of the *Večerní písně*: the sweeping and powerful 'Když jsem se díval do nebe' (When I looked up to the heavens), the delightful 'Jsem jako lípa košatá' (I am like a spreading lime-tree), and two charming, light-handed songs in the lighter *Lied* style.

Of the *Tři novořecké básně*, Op. 50[12] (Three Modern Greek Poems, i.e. Czech translations of Greek folk-poems), the best is the third — originally the second — 'Žalozpěv Pargy' (Lament for Parga), another piece of free declamation. All three are dramatic ballads and were originally composed with orchestral accompaniment for the baritone Josef Lev to sing at the concert of Dvořák's works at Prague on 17 November 1878. But full mastery appears, though even then not always, in the songs of the 1880s: the *Zigeunermelodien* Op. 55, of 1880, the settings of folk-poems (1885–6), and the *Vier Lieder*, Op. 82 (1887). The pressure on Dvořák to produce songs with German texts is revealed here, above all in the fact that although Adolf Heyduk's poems which inspired the *Zigeunermelodien* are Czech, the music was actually written to German versions prepared by the poet himself. Again, the two songs without opus-number composed at Sydenham in May 1885 — of which the first, 'Schlaf' mein Kind in Ruh' ', is quite enchanting — are settings of Geman translations of Czech folk poems. The *Zigeuner-melodien* are too well known for their real merit to be properly appreciated; the first and last, 'Mein Lied ertönt' and 'Darf des Falken Schwinge', are full-blooded masterpieces — as in its different way is the hopelessly hackneyed 'Als die alte Mutter' — while the three dance-songs and the deeply felt, if slightly Brahmsian, 'Rings ist der Wald' are worthy foils. The whole cycle, except No. 3, is completely Dvořákian and completely Czech. The same may be said of the four songs *Ve slohu prostonárodním* (In Folk-Style), Op. 73, settings of three Slovak folk poems and one Czech; the first, 'Dobrú noc' (Good night) is a masterpiece of an unusual kind, a *passionate* serenade, and at least the second and third are hardly inferior. Op. 73 was provided with German translations by Otilie Malybrok-Stieler and in gratitude to this undistinguished poetess Dvořák composed four of her poems as Op. 82, though he had them translated into Czech and 'made the music to both texts at the same time, only hoping that the declamation is good'.[13] (Declamation was never his strongest point.) The best is No.3, 'Frühling', but the others contain some very beautiful passages.

The problem of Czech and German texts is raised in its most acute form in Dvořák's last cycle, the ten *Biblické písně* (Biblical Songs) Op. 99, written in New York in 1894.[14] He originally set these excerpts from the Psalms in the seventeenth-century Czech version of the so-called 'Kralice Bible', but realizing the impossibility of fitting a tolerable German translation to his music, he completely rewrote the voice-parts and, in doing so, destroyed much of their rhythmic life. (The familiar English text is wretchedly cobbled on to the German vocal line.) Again and again characteristic triplets and syncopations are obliterated. Yet even in their true forms, the *Biblické písně* are very unequal and often disappointing. As in other of Dvořák's works of the 'American' period, the workmanship is apt to be facile and slipshod. The exquisite simplicity of No. 4, 'Hospodin jest můj pastýř' (The Lord is my shepherd), is one thing, the embarrassing naïveté of some of its companions quite another. One would be sorry to lose 'Při řekách babylonských' (By the waters of Babylon), but several of the songs remind one too effectively that the composer enjoyed playing the organ in the village church at Spillville, Iowa.

The composer whom Czech critics tend to bracket with, if a little below, Smetana and Dvořák is Zdeněk Fibich (1850-1900). Fibich was a very fine miniaturist and a copious song composer, though the greater part of his output in this field remains unpublished. He leans toward Schumann and Franz, and appears to have composed more German than Czech poems; Heine attracted him above all and one of his very earliest songs, 'Dämmernd liegt der Sommerabend', Op. 3 No. 2, written at sixteen, supplied him years later with the chief theme of the wood-spirit in his symphonic poem *Toman*. His Op. 5, composed in 1871, consists of five of Hálek's *Večerní písně* but of the four ballads that constitute Op. 7 (1872-3), the best are the two Heine pieces, 'Loreley' and 'Tragödie', the latter a real masterpiece. Nearly all Fibich's best songs date from the 1870s: the cycles *Jarní paprsky* (Gleams of Spring), Op. 36, and *Šestero písní* (Half-a-dozen Songs), Op. 12, and a number of separate songs, including 'Kytice' and 'Žežhulice', from the Kralové Dvůr manuscript. The late opus-number of *Jarní paprsky* is due to the fact that it was withheld from publication until No. 1, Vrchlický's 'Předtucha jara' (Presentiment of Spring), was added in 1891 – a song which epitomizes Fibich's double allegiance, for the first nine bars are pure Schumann while what follows is unmistakably Czech. Among his last works are five delightful children's songs, 'Poupata' (Buds), Op. 45.

Another composer of this period who was attracted by the Kralové Dvůr poems was the rather older Karel Bendl (1838-97); like his friend Dvořák, Bendl also set a cycle of Heyduk's *Cigánské melodie* (Gypsy Melodies) (1881) and some of Pfleger-Moravský's *Cypřiše* (1882).

As in Russia at the same period, a host of talented epigones came to the fore during the late nineteenth and early twentieth centuries, most of them pupils or disciples of Dvořák or Fibich. Among those who distinguished themselves as song-writers are J. B. Foerster (1859-1951) – particularly in the two Falke cycles *Noční violy* (Night Violets), Op. 43, and *Láska* (Love), Op. 46 (1899-1900) – Rudolf Karel (1880-1945), and Vitĕzslav Novák (1870-1949). Novák was one of the few Czechoslovak composers who have written a considerable corpus of solo song (including a number of pieces, mostly to words by Jan Neruda, for voice with orchestra). In his nonage he was content to follow more or less closely in the footsteps of his master Dvořák, even venturing to rival him by setting some of Heyduk's *Cigánské melodie* (Op. 14) (1897). A slightly earlier cycle *Pohádka srdce*, Op. 8 (A Fable of the Heart), was one of the first compositions with which Novák attracted attention and during the pre-1918 period he produced several other notable cycles – *Melancholie*, Op. 25, *Údolí nového království* (The Valley of the New Kingdom), Op. 31, *Melancholické písně o lásce* (Melancholy Songs concerning Love) with orchestra, Op. 38, *Notturna*, Op. 39, and *Erotikon*, Op. 46 (the last two to German words originally) – in which he revealed a highly passionate nature and employed a more modern harmonic volcabulary. Then, except for *Jaro* (Spring), Op. 52, two sets of children's songs – one to be sung *to* children, the other *by* children – came a hiatus in his song-writing which lasted until 1944 when he took up an old idea. At the end of the last century he had published three sets of *Písničky na slova lidové poesie moravské* (Little Songs on Moravian Folk-Poems), Opp. 16, 17, and 21; now he produced two more, Opp. 74 and 75, which are comparable with similar things by Bartók and contain some of Novák's most delightful music. The cowherd's song, 'Pasu krávy, pasu', Op. 74 No. 1, for instance, is quite enchanting. A few other songs date from this last period.

The Moravian Leoš Janáček (1854-1928), though older than Novák or even Foerster, emerged from relative obscurity much later than they – in fact, only during the First World War. He is a far more original figure but he owes his place in the history of the Czech art-song to only one work: the famous *Zápisník zmizéleho* (Diary of One who Vanished), a setting of a sequence of short poems that had been found by the police in an exercise-book belonging to a young Moravian peasant of good character whose mysterious disappearance they were investigating. The poems, which were evidently autobiographical – outlining the story of the young man's seduction by a gypsy woman, his shame, and his resolve to leave home and parents and run away with her – were published in a Brno newspaper and deeply interested Janáček. During 1916-19 he made a novel semi-dramatic setting in which the tenor takes the part of the hero, Janik, singing on a half-darkened stage; in the ninth, tenth, and eleventh numbers a contralto, representing Zefka the gypsy, comes on unobtrusively and a trio of female voices comments off-stage; No. 13 is for piano solo. If the general idea is novel, the music is equally so, as far as Czech music is concerned. Whereas most Czech composers have tended to think instrumentally, or at any rate to put pure melodic line before word-setting, Janáček's ear for verbal intonation was exceptionally acute; not only does his voice-part carry the words very subtly and sensitively; his verbally inspired motives sometimes provide the thematic germs of instrumental texture – as they do in the piano-part of *Zápisník zmizelého*.

Two other Moravians, both pupils of Janáček – Vilem Petrželka (1889-1967) and Jaroslav Kvapil (1892-1959) – have been far more prolific song-composers than their teacher but far less gifted. Of Novák's older disciples, among whom also Petrželka must be reckoned, Vycpálek (1882-1969), Křička (1882-1969), Axman (1887-1949), and Jirák (1891-1972) have been the most notable song-composers, of his younger ones Alexander Moyzes (b. 1906), Eugen Suchoň (b. 1908) and Ján Cikker (b. 1911), all three Slovaks. A much more individual composer who also studied with Novák for a time (as well as with Křička and Foerster) was Alois Hába (1893-1973), protagonist of quarter-tone and sixth-tone composition; he wrote two sets of songs in the quarter-tone system – *Dětské nálady* (Children's Moods), Op. 51, and *Poesie života* (Poetry of Life), Op. 53 – as well as others in the more normal one, using the guitar as accompanying instrument in both Op. 51 and Op. 53. A more moderate, eclectic modernist was the expatriate Bohuslav Martinů (1890-1959); he too wrote songs, including settings of Czech folk poems (his *New 'Špaliček'* of 1943), but as with so many Czech composers his solo songs with piano were only relatively unimportant footnotes to his *oeuvre* in general.

NOTES

1. One specimen reprinted in Jaroslav Pohanka, *Dějiny české hudby v příkladech* (Prague, 1958), No. 112. See also the study by Camillo Schoenbaum in *Acta Musicologica*, xxv (1953), p. 39.
2. A solo *pastorela*, dated 1859, by Jan Michalička is printed in *Musica antiqua bohemica*, No. 23.

3. No. 11 of the *XII Lieder, Liebeserklärung eines Mädchens*, is reprinted in *Studien zur Musikwissenschaft*, v (Leipzig and Vienna, 1918), p. 141.
4. Example in Pohanka, op. cit., No. 155.
5. Ibid., No. 160.
6. Op. 71, No. 2, in ibid., No. 158.
7. Complete list of contents in Zdeněk Nejedlý, *Bedřich Smetana* ii (Prague, 1925), pp. 438–41.
8. Examples by Vorel and J. N. Škroup (1811–92), František's brother, in Pohanka, op. cit., Nos. 165 and 166.
9. In Pohanka, op. cit., No. 175.
10. Opp. 2, 5, 17, and 31 were published complete, but with English and German words only, as *Sixteen Songs* by Novello. Most of Dvořák's other songs were published by Simrock. They are all given in Vols. VI and VII of the Collected Edition of his works.
11. Dvořák scored the accompaniments of Op. 3, Nos. 2 and 3 for small orchestra a little later.
12. An edition with English words is published by Hinrichsen.
13. Covering letter to Simrock, 21 January 1888.
14. Nos. 1–5 orchestrated by the composer the following year.

Index

Adam, Adolphe (1803–56) 171*n*
Agostini, Paolo (*c.* 1583–1629) 104
Akhmatova, Anna 34
Albertini, Gioacchino (1751–1811)
  127, 139*n*
Alexander I of Russia 101
Allegri, Gregorio (1582–1652) 103
Alt, Heinrich 100
Alyabyev, Aleksandr Aleksandrovich
  (1787–1851) 5, 6–10 (Ex. 4),
  11, 13, 18 38*n*
Andersen, Hans Christian 33
Andreae, Volkmar (1879–1962) 56
Anerio, Giovanni Francesco (*c.* 1567–
  1630) 104
Antokolsky, Mark Matveevich 100,
  106, 110
Apelt, E.F. 100
Apukhtin, Aleksey Nikolayevich 27
Arcadelt, Jakob (*c.* 1504–after 1567)
  104
Arensky, Antony Stepanovich
  (1861–1906) 29, 30
Artophaeus, Ferdinand Bernard (d.
  1721) 172
Asafyev, Boris 36, 54
Asnyk, Adam 150
Auber, Daniel (1782–1871) 62, 171
Augustus II 124
Augustus III 125
Averkiev, D.V. 44
Axman, Emil (1887–1949) 183

Bach, J.C. (1735–82) 117
Bach, J.S. (1685–1750) 102, 103,
  111*n*, 116, 139*n*
Badini, Carlo Francesco 125
Bakunin, Alexey 41
Bakunin, Praskovya Mikhaylovna 41
Balakirev, Mily Alekseyevich

(1837–1910) 17–20 *passim*, 21–2,
  23, 28, 35, 39*n*, 40, 42–3, 45, 50,
  55*n*, 56, 60, 64, 65–6, 68, 71, 79,
  93, 106, 107, 109, 110, 111, 112*n*
Bałucki, Michał 150
Barré, Pierre 128
Bartók, Béla (1881–1945) 153, 182
Baudelaire, Charles Pierre 31
Beethoven, Ludwig van (1770–1827)
  98, 103, 104, 105, 111*n*, 146
Belinsky, Vissarion Grigorevich 102,
  109
Belsky, Vladimir Ivanovich 89–92
Bely, Andrey 31
Benda, Jiří (Georg) (1722–95) 173
Bendl, Karel (1838–97) 181
Benevoli, Orazio (1605–72) 104
Béranger, Pierre Jean de 8, 16, 38*n*,
  146
Berlioz, Hector (1803–69) 5, 90,
  102, 105, 107
Bernabei, Ercole (*c.* 1621–87) 104
Bessel, Vasily Vasil'yevich 17, 45, 69,
  71, 72
Bestuzhev (Marlinsky), A.A. 8
Bethge, Hans 151
Bianchi, Valentina 44
Bilibin, Ivan 88
Birnbaum, O.J. 151
Bizet, Georges (1838–75) 47
Blok, Aleksandr (1880–1921) 31, 32,
  34–6 *passim*
Bodenstedt, Friedrich von 151
Bogusławski, Stanisław 160
Bogusławski, Wojciech 126–8 *passim*,
  130–3 *passim*, 138, 139*n*
Bohdanowicz, Bazyli (1740–1817)
  114–15, 116, 120
Bohomolec, Franciszek 126–7
Bohte, Maria 150

Boieldieu, Adrien (1757–1834) 5, 6, 137
Bonoldi, Józef 159
Borodin, Aleksandr Porfiryevich (1833–87) 12, 17, 18, 20, 21, 27, 38n, 47, 50, 56, 65, 68, 93–8, 100, 107
Bortnyansky, Dmitry Stepanovich (1751–1825) 5
Brahms, Johannes (1833–97) 180
Brixi, František Xaver (1732–71) 172
Brodziński, Kazimierz 135, 142
Bruckner, Anton (1824–96) 81
Brunerio, Michelangelo 124
Bryullov, K.P. 102, 111n
Bryusov, Valery 30
Bulich, S.K. 1, 6
Bull, Ole (1810–80) 101
Bülow, Hans von (1830–94) 156–7
Bulwer-Lytton, first Lord Lytton 99
Bunin, Ivan Alekseyevich 30
Bürger, Gottfried August 174
Butler, Alfred 99
Byron, George Gordon 8, 22, 24, 38n, 62, 107, 155n

Caccini, Francesca (1587–c. 1640) 122
Cadéac, Pierre (fl. 1538) 104
Calvocoressi, M.D. 92n
Carissimi, Giacomo (1605–74) 104
Carpentras (Elzéar Genet) (c. 1470–1548) 104
Catherine II of Russia 1, 2
Cavos, Catterino (1776–1840) 137
Cecilia Renata of Austria 123
Čermáková, Josefina 177
Certon, Pierre (d. 1572) 104
Chaliapin, see Shalyapin
Charlemagne 133
Chaykovsky, see Tchaikovsky
Chęciński, Jan 162–3, 165, 166, 170
Chękhov, Anton Pavlovich 109
Cherepnin, N.N. (1873–1945) 29, 30, 39n
Chernïshevsky, N.G. 109
Chernov, Konstantin 66
Chmelenský, Jan (1778–1864) 175
Chmelenský, Josef Krasoslav 175
Chopin, Fryderyk (1810–49) 101, 120, 127, 131, 139n, 142–4, 145–8 passim, 150, 162

Christianowitsch, A. 93, 94, 96–8
Cikker, Ján (b. 1911) 183
Cimarosa, Domenico (1749–1801) 2
Clari, Giovanni Carlo Maria (1677–1754) 104
Cooper, James Fenimore 99
Cornwall, Barry 12
Cui, César Antonovich (1835–1918), 1, 17–21, 23–4, 35, 52, 56–66, 67n, 154n, 170–1
Czeczot, Jan 145, 147, 148

Dąbrowski, Florian 119, 128
Damian (d. 1729) 141, 154n
Dankowski, Wojciech (c. 1762–c. 1820) 113, 114, 120
Dargomïzhsky, Aleksandr Sergeyevich (1813–69) 8, 10, 14–17 (Exx. 6–7), 18, 19, 21, 23, 26–9 passim, 35, 38n, 40, 44, 47, 50 55n, 60–1, 64, 65, 93, 94, 96, 112n, 155n
Debussy, Claude (1862–1918) 33
Dehmel, Richard 151
Dehn, Siegfried 11
Delavigne, Casimir 162–3
Delvig, Anton 5, 7, 11, 14, 15, 34, 38n
Demidov, Prince A.N. 102, 103, 105
Derzhavin, Gavrila Romanovich 4, 5
Deszczyński, Józef (1781–1844) 135
Dianin, S.A. 97–8
Dickens, Charles 99
Disraeli, Benjamin 99
Dmitriev, I.I. 4, 5
Dmuszewski, Ludwik 132, 133, 135
Dobrolyubov, Nikolay 109
Döhler, Theodor (von) (1814–56) 103
Doležálek, Jan 173, 175
Donizetti, Gaetano (1797–1848) 171n
Dopper, Cornelius (1870–1939) 56
Dubyansky, Fedor Mikhaylovich (1760–96) 3 (Ex. 2), 4, 37n
Dukát, J.L. (1684–1717) 172
Duni, Egidio-Romoaldo (1709–75) 126, 133
Durante, Francesco (1684–1755) 104
Dušek, František Xaver (1731–99) 173
Dvořák, Antonin (1841–1904) 176,

177-81 (Exx. 3-4), 182, 184*n*
Dyagilev, Sergey (1872-1929) 40,
72, 83, 109
Dzerzhinsky, Ivan (1909-78) 35

Ebert, K.E. 174
Elert, Piotr (d. 1653) 123
Elsner, Joseph (Józef) Xaver
(1769-1854) 114, 120 (Ex. 8),
131-4 (Ex. 4), 137-8, 139*n*,
140*n*, 141-2 (Ex. 1)
Erben, K.J. 179
Ertini 128, 139*n*
Esaulov, Andrey Petrovich (*c.* 1800-*c.*
1850) 5, 9, 38*n*
Essenin 36

Falke, Gustav 182
Favart, Charles-Simon 125, 127, 133
Feicht, Hieronim 113
Fet, Afanasy Afanas'yevich 22, 30, 32
Fétis, François Joseph (1784-1871)
95-6, 105
Févin, Antoine de (*c.* 1470-*c.* 1512)
104
Fibich, Zdeněk (1850-1900) 176,
181, 182
Findeisen, Nikolay 1
Flaxland 155*n*
Foerster, J.B. (1859-1951) 182, 183
Fontana, Jualian 144, 154*n*
Franz, Robert (1815-92) 180
Friedrich August, King of Saxony and
Duke of Warsaw 133

Gaetani (Kajetani) (d. *c.* 1792) 127,
128, 130, 139*n*
Gagliano, Marco da (*c.* 1575-1642)
122, 123
Gall, Jan (1856-1912) 149
Galuppi, Baldassare (1706-85) 126
Gassmann, Florian Leopold (1729-74)
126
Gebethner & Wolff 155*n*, 159
Gerke, Anton 101
Giacometti, Paolo 42
Giustiniani, Ivan Antonovich 42
Glazunov, Aleksandr Konstantinovich
(1865-1936) 29, 30
Glebov, Igor, *see* Asafyev, Boris
Glier (Glière), Reinhold (1875-1956)
34, 39*n*
Glinka, Mikhail Ivanovich (1804-57)

1, 2, 5, 7, 8, 10-14 (Ex. 5), 16-19
passim, 25-7 *passim*, 36, 38*n*, 39*n*,
44, 47, 51, 57, 61, 65, 70, 71, 102,
104, 106, 111*n*, 112*n*, 154*n*,
156, 176
Gliński, Augustyn 132
Gluck, Christoph Willibald (1714-87)
105, 126
Goethe, Johann Wolfgang von 30-2
passim, 110, 145-7 *passim*, 174
Gogol, Nikolay Vasilyevich 41, 45,
46, 102, 109
Gołąbek, Jakub (*c.* 1739-89) 113,
114, 116-17 (Ex. 3), 118, 119,
121*n*
Goldschmidt, Hugo 122
Golenishchev-Kutuzov, Arseny 26
Golitsïn, S.G. 11
Gorodetsky, Sergey 32
Goudimel, Claude (*c.* 1514-72) 104
Gounod, Charles (1818-93) 55*n*, 61
Grajnert, Józef 147
Grechaninov, Aleksandr (1864-1956)
29-31 *passim*
Grekov, N.P. 28
Grétry, André-Ernest-Modeste
(1741-1813) 63, 126
Grimm, Jakob and Wilhelm 84
Grote, George 99
Grzymałowski, W. 146
Gurilev, Aleksandr Lvovich (1802-56)
6, 7, 9-10, 142, 175
Gussakovsky, A.S. (1841-75) 111
Gyrowetz, *see* Jírovec

Hába, Alois (1893-1973) 183
Haczewski, A. 113, 114-15 (Ex. 1),
120
Hafiz 30, 151
Hálek, Vítezslav 176, 179, 181
Halévy, Fromental (1799-1862)
47
Handel, George Frideric (1685-1759)
104, 105, 139*n*, 172
Hanka, Václav 174
Harasowska, Jadwiga 156
Hartmann, Viktor 109
Hasse, Johann Adolph (1699-1783)
125
Haydn, Franz Joseph (1732-1809)
3, 103, 116, 118, 119, 126
Hegel, George Wilhelm Friedrich
101, 108

Heine, Heinrich 19-21 *passim*, 27, 28, 31, 38*n*, 56-66, 102, 149, 174, 181
Henselt, Adolf (1814-89) 100, 101
Herder, Johann Gottfried von 63
Heyduk, Adolf 180-2 *passim*
Hiller, Johann Adam (1728-1804) 126
Hippius, Zinaida 30, 31, 34, 39*n*
Hněvkovský, Šebestián 173
Hoffman, François 132
Hoffmann, E.T.A. 132, 140*n*
Holland, Johann David (1746-*c.* 1825) 127
Hölty, Ludwig 173, 174
Homer 111*n*
Hugo, Victor-Marie 14, 23
Hummel, Johann Nepomuk (1778-1837) 101

Ibsen, Henrik 153
Ippolitov-Ivanov, Mikhail (1859-1935) 34
Irving, Washington 84-7, 89, 90
Isouard, Nicolò (1775-1818) 5
Ivanov, Vyacheslav 31, 34

Jachimecki, Zdzisław 122, 124, 144, 146, 148, 149
Jacobi, Johann Georg 176
Jadwiga, Queen of Poland 136-7
Jagodyński, Stanisław Serafin 122
Janáček, Leoš (1854-1928) 182-3
Jarzębski, Adam (d. 1648) 124
Jirák, K.B. (1891-1972) 183
Jírovec (Gyrowetz), Adalbert (1763-1850) 114, 173
Jommelli, Niccolò (1714-74) 104
Joyce, James 152-3

Kabalevsky, Dmitry (b. 1904) 35
Kalashnikov, P.I. 46
Kamieśti, Maciej (1734-1821) 126 (Ex. 1), 127 (Ex. 2), 128, 132, 141
Kant, Immanuel 108
Kapníst, V. 5
Karatigin, V.G. 55*n*
Karel, Rudolf (1880-1945) 182
Karłowicz, Mieczysław (1876-1909) 149
Karmalina, Lyubov 16
Kashin, Daniil Nikitich (1769-1841) 4, 5, 37*n*

Kasprowicz, J. 151
Kaszczewski (late seventeenth c.) 141
Kaszewski, J.N. (early 19th c.) 142
Kazimierz, Jan 124
Khachaturyan, Aram (1903-78) 35
Khomyakov, Aleksey Stepanovich 21, 27
Khrennikov, Tikhon (b. 1913) 35
Kitowicz, J. 114
Kochanowski, Jan 137
Kolberg, Oskar 134, 150
Kollár, J.J. 176
Koltsov, A.V. 9, 15, 19, 24, 25, 38*n*
Komorowski, Ignacy (1824-57) 148
Korff, Baron 105
Körner, Christian Gottfried 100
Kościuszko, Tadeusz 130, 131
Kotzebue, August Friedrich Ferdinand von 132, 135
Koval, Marian Viktorovich (1907-71) 35
Koželuh (Kozeluch), Leopold (1747-1818) 173
Kozlov, Ivan Ivanovich 7-8, 11, 24, 38*n*
Kozłowski, Józef (1757-1831) 4, 37*n*
Kozlyaninov, A.S. (1777-1831) 4
Kraevsky, A.A. 102
Kramskoy, I.N. 100, 106
Krasiński, J.W. 136
Krásnohorská, Eliška 179
Kratzer, Kazimierz (1844-90) 148
Krein, Alexander (1883-1951) 34
Krenz, Jan 113
Krestovsky, Vsevolod 68
Křička, Jaroslav (1882-1969) 183
Krïlov, Ivan Andreyevich 27, 31, 67*n*
Krïlov, Viktor Aleksandrovich 57
Krzyżanowski, Ignacy (1826-1905) 148
Kukolnik, Nestor 13, 14
Kurochkin, V.S. 14, 16
Kurpiński, Karol (1784-1857) 132, 133, 135-7 (Exx. 5-8), 138, 140*n*, 142
Kvapil, Jaroslav (1892-1959) 183

Laboureur, Jan le 123
Lafont, Charles Philippe (1781-1839) 6
La Fontaine, Jean de 39*n*

La Grua, Emmy 42
Lampugnoni, Giovanni Battista 124
Landi, Stefano (c. 1590–c. 1655) 123
Laroche, Herman 43, 61, 67n
Lassus, Orlandus (c. 1532–94) 104
Lazhechnikov, I.I. 41
Lejeune, Claude (c. 1530–1600) 104
Lemercier, Népomucène 37n
Lenartowicz, Teofil 146
Lensky, Dmitry 8
Leo, Leonardo (1694–1744) 104
Leonova, Darya Mikhaylovna 44, 60, 97, 98
Lermontov, Mikhail Yurevich 8–10 passim, 15, 19, 20, 23, 30, 34, 36, 102
Leroux, Xavier (1863–1919) 56
Lessel, Franciszek (c. 1780–1838) 135, 142
Lev, Josef 180
Lipiński, Karol (1790–1861) 101, 135
Liszt, Franz (1811–86) 5, 7, 18, 100, 101, 102, 105, 110
Lodïzhensky, Nikolay Nikolaevich (1843–1916) 17, 18–19 (Ex. 8)
Loewe, Carl (1796–1869) 38n, 143, 145
Lomakin, Gavrïl Yakimovich 104
Louis Ferdinand, Prince 131
Lubieńska, Tekla 133
Lyadov, Anatoly (1855–1914) 29–31 passim

Macháček, S.K. 173, 175
Maklakiewicz, Jan Adam (1899–1954) 154
Marcello, Benedetto (1686–1739) 103, 104
Marenzio, Luca (1553–99) 104
Marinelli, Karl 114
Martinů, Bohuslav (1890–1959) 183
Mascagni, Pietro (1863–1945) 56
Matuszyński, Leopold 171n
Maude, Aylmer] 100
Maykov, A.N. 20, 22, 23, 29, 42
Meck, Nadezhda von 43
Melnikov, Ivan 60
Mendelssohn-Bartholdy, Felix (1809–47) 27, 149, 178
Merezhkovsky, Dmitry Sergeyevich 30, 109
Merzlyakov, A.F. 5

Metner, Nikolay (1880–1951) 29, 30, 31–2 (Ex. 9), 33, 35
Mey, Lev Aleksandrovich 20, 21, 25, 27–9 passim, 68, 70, 71, 75, 82n
Meyerbeer, Giacomo (1791–1864) 47, 64
Miča, František Adam (1694–1744) 113
Michalička, Jan (c. 1791–1867) 183n
Michelangelo 103
Mickiewicz, Adam Bernard 23, 143–6 passim, 149
Mielczewski, Marcin (d. 1651) 124, 140, 154n
Mikhaylov, M.L. 20
Milton, John 137
Milwid, Antoni (fl. late 18th c.) 113, 114, 119
Mombert, Alfred 151
Moniuszko, Stanisław (1819–72) 16, 23, 132, 142, 144–8 (Exx. 2–3), 149–51 passim, 153, 155n, 156–71, 176
Monn, Mathias Georg (1717–50) 116
Monsigny, Pierre-Alexandre (1729–1816) 126
Moore, Thomas 7, 147
Morlacchi, Francesco (1784–1841) 137
Mosolov, Aleksandr (1900–3) 34
Moyzes, Alexander (b. 1906) 183
Mozart, Wolfgang Amadeus (1756–91) 104, 105, 111n, 116, 118, 128, 137, 139n, 173, 175
Muchenberg, Bohdan 116, 121n
Musorgsky, Modest Petrovich (1839–81) 8, 12, 15–18 passim, 21–2, 24–7, 28, 29, 33, 39n, 40, 42–4, 47, 48–50, 52, 55n, 56, 57, 64, 66, 67n, 68, 72, 80, 82n, 100, 101, 107, 109, 145, 152, 153
Musset, Alfred Louis Charles de 23
Myaskovsky, Nikolay (1881–1950) 29, 31, 34, 35, 36 (Ex. 11)
Mysliveček, Josef (1737–81) 141, 173

Namieyski (fl. 2nd half 18th c.) 114, 115–16, 117–18 (Ex. 4)
Napoleon I 130, 131, 133
Nápravník, Eduard 60
Nechayev (1895–1956) 36
Nejedlý, Vojtěch 173
Nekrasov, Nikolay Alexeyevich 21, 24, 35, 97

Neledinsky-Meletsky 4, 5
Nelvi, Giuseppe Maria (1698–1756)
    125
Neruda, Jan 182
Newmarch, Rosa 55n, 109
Nicholas I of Russia 5, 101, 105
Niebuhr, Barthold Georg 100
Niemcewicz, J.U. 137
Nietzsche, Friedrich Wilhelm 31, 153
Niewiadomski, Stanisław (1857–1936)
    149–50 (Ex. 4)
Noskowski, Zygmunt (1846–1909)
    148–9, 153
Novák, Vitěslav (1870–1949) 182,
    183
Nowakowski, Jósef (1800–65) 142,
    148
Nowak-Romanowicz, Alina 133
Nowowiejski, Feliks (1877–1946) 153

Ogarev, N.P. (1731–98) 8
Ogiński, Michal Kleofas (1765–1833)
    131, 142
Opieński, Henryk 113, 120, 149, 159
Orłowski, Antoni (1811–61) 114
Osiński, Ludwik 133
Ostrovsky, Aleksandr 45–6, 47

Paër, Ferdinand (1771–1839) 5, 137
Paganini, Nicolà (1782–1840) 134
Paisiello, Giovanni (1740–1816) 2
Palestrina, Giovanni Pierluigi da
    (c. 1524–94) 104
Pankiewicz, Eugeniusz (1857–98)
    149, 150–1
Panufnik, Andrzej (b. 1914) 154
Pasta, Giuditta 101
Paszczyński (late 18th c.) 114, 115
Pawłowski, Jakub (late 18th c.) 114
Pedrell, Felipe (1841–1922) 56
Pękalski, W. 135
Pekelis, M.S. 9
Perov, V.G. 109
Peter the Great 106
Petrov, Osip 44, 46
Petržełka, Vilem (1889–1967) 183
Pfleger-Moravský, Gustav 177, 181
Philidor, François-André (1726–95)
    126
Piccinni, Niccolà (1728–1800) 126
Pietrowski, Karol (late 18th c.) 114,
    115, 116, 118–19 (Exx. 6, 7)
Pils, A. de 128

Pitoni, Giuseppe Ottavio (1657–1743)
    104
Pizzi, Emilio (1862–1940) 56
Plánický, Josef A. (c. 1691–1732)
    172
Plato 108
Platonova, Y.F. 60
Plescheyev, A.A. 5, 10, 29, 57–8
Pollarolo, Carlo Francesco (c. 1653–
    1722) 125
Polonsky, Y.P. 22, 30, 46–7
Prach, Ivan (Johann Gottfried Pratsch/
    Prač) (d. 1818) 3
Prokofiev, Sergey (1891–1953) 32–3
    (Ex. 10) 34
Prosnak, Jan 128
Puccitelli, Virgilio 123, 124
Pugnani, Gaetano, N.P. (1731–98)
    125
Purcell, Henry (1659–95) 105, 111n
Pushkin, Aleksandr 5, 7, 8, 10–12
    passim, 14, 15, 17, 18, 20–5 passim,
    30, 32–5 passim, 38n, 43, 57,
    83, 84–5, 87, 89, 90, 146, 173

Quattrini, Giovanni 158, 159

Rachel (Élisa Félix) (1821–58) 103
Radziwiłł, Prince Antoni (1775–1833)
    126, 127, 131, |139n
Rakhmaninov, Sergey (1873–1943)
    29–33 passim
Raphael 99
Rathaus, Daniel M. 28
Ravel, Maurice (1875–1937) 153
Razumovsky, Kirill 1
Rebikov, Vladimir (1866–1920)
    29–31 passim
Reger, Max (1873–1916) 151
Reicha, Anton (1770–1836) 172
Reichardt, Johann Friedrich (1752–
    1814) 142, 173
Repin, I.E. 100, 106, 107, 109, 110
Richault 93
Richepin, Jean 23
Rileyev, K.F. 43.
Rimsky-Korsakov, A.N. 40, 47, 49
Rimsky-Korsakov, Nikolay (1844–
    1908) 17, 18, 20–3, 24, 27–9
    passim, 33, 35, 38n, 39n, 44, 51,
    56, 60, 61, 64–5, 66, 67n, 68–81,
    83–92, 93–8, 107, 109, 111,
    112n, 154n

Ristori, Adelaide 42
Rivoli, Pauline 159, 161
Rolland, Romain 34
Romani, Felice 11
Rossini, Gioacchino (1792–1868) 107, 135, 137
Rousseau, Jean-Jacques (1712–78) 135
Różycki, Ludomir (1884–1953) 149, 153–4
Rubinstein, Anton (1829–94) 27, 40, 41, 56
Rückert, Friedrich 176
Rungenhagen, K.F. 144, 157
Ryba, Jakub Jan (1765–1815) 173

Sacchini, Antonio (1730–86) 126
Salieri, Antonio (1750–1825) 126
Salvador-Daniel, Francesco (1831–71) 93–6
Sammartini, Giovanni Battista (1698–1775) 116
Santini, Abbé 104, 105
Sappho 34
Saracinelli, Ferdinando 122
Sariotti, M.I. 44, 46
Sarri, Domenico (1679–1744) 125
Sarti, Giuseppe (1729–1802) 2, 4
Scacchi, Marco (b. *c.* 1602) 123
Scarlatti, Alessandro (1660–1725) 104
Schiller, Johann Christoph Friedrich von 42, 62, 100, 103, 142, 174, 176
Schmidt, Johann Christoph (1664–1728) 125
Schober, Feliks 171*n*
Schoenberg, Arnold (1874–1951) 151
Schubert, Franz (1797–1828) 7, 12, 38*n*, 146, 147, 178, 179
Schumann, Robert (1810–56) 5, 18, 20, 22, 27, 29, 61–2, 81, 101, 102, 109, 138*n*, 146, 176, 178, 181
Ścigalski, Franciszek (1782–1846) 116
Scott, Sir Walter 62, 111*n*
Scriabin, *see* Skryabin
Scribe, Augustin Eugène 160, 171*n*
Sermisy, Claudin de (*c.* 1495–1562) 104
Serov, Aleksandr Nikolayevich (1820–71) 13, 40–55, 61, 67*n*, 101, 106–7, 110

Shakespeare, William 107, 111
Shalyapin, Fyodor Ivanovich 40, 71, 72
Shaporin, Yury (1887–1966) 35–6
Shaposhnikov, Adrian Grigor'yevich (1888 or 1887–1967) 4, 37*n*
Shaw, George Bernard 99
Schipachev, Stepan 34
Shebalin, Vissarion (1902–63) 35
Shelley, Percy Bysshe 31
Sheremetyev, Count 104
Shestakova, Lyudmila 41
Shevchenko, Taras 25, 28
Shostakovich, Dmitry (1906–75) 35
Shtrupp, N.M. 112*n*
Sikorski, Józef 158
Şimrock, F.A. 179, 184*n*
Škroup, František (1801–62) 175
Škroup, J.N. (1811–92) 184*n*
Skryabin, Aleksandr (1872–1915) 31, 32, 34, 109, 151, 152
Smetana, Bedřich (1824–84) 134, 156, 172, 175, 176–7 (Ex. 2), 178, 181
Sobieski, Jan 124
Sollogub, Fyodor 30
Solovyev, N.F. (1846–1916) 46, 47
Sołtys, Adam (b. 1890) 153
Sperontes (1705–50) 1
Spiess, Stefan 155*n*
Spohr, Louis (1784–1859) 17, 137
Spontini, Gasparo (1774–1851) 47, 137
Stanisław II August Poniatowski 125, 138
Stasov, Dmitry 21, 40, 41, 65, 66, 68, 82*n*, 96, 102, 103
Stasov, Vasily Petrovich 100
Stasov, Vladimir Vasilevich 43, 99–112
Stefani, Jan (1748 or 1746–1829) 128–30 (Ex. 3), 133, 139*n*, 141, 142
Steffani, Agostino (1654–1728) 104
Strauss, Johann, junior (1825–99) 43
Strauss, Richard (1864–1949) 151
Stravinsky, Igor (1882–1971) 32–3, 34, 151
Strumiłło, Tadeusz 118
Suchoň, Eugen (b. 1908) 183
Sumarokov, Aleksandr Petrovich 1, 3, 5
Surikov, I.Z. 28

Syrokomla, Władysław, I.Z. 29, 146
Szarzyński, Stanisław Sylwester (d.
  c. 1700) 141, 154n
Szczurowski, Jacek (1718–after 1773)
  121n
Szeligowski, Tadeusz (1896–1963)
  154
Szopski, Felicjan (1865–1939) 149
Szostakowicz, Bolesław 171n
Szweykowski, Zygmunt M. 113
Szymanowski, Karol (1882–1937)
  149, 151–3 (Ex. 5)
Szymanowski, Wacław 163
Szymański, Stanisław 127

Tagore, Rabindranath 152
Taneyev, Sergey (1856–1915) 29–31
  passim
Tchaikovsky, Pyotr Ilyich (1840–93)
  6, 10, 20, 22, 27–30, 31, 35, 39n,
  40, 43, 47, 52, 59, 61, 68, 100,
  107, 146, 177
Tcherepnin, see Cherepnin
Teplov, Grigory Nikolaevich (1711–
  79) 1, 2 (Ex. 1), 6
Temajer, Kazimierz 151, 153
Thalberg, Sigismond (1812–71) 101
Tiedge, Christoph August 174
Titov, Mikhail (1804–53) 5–7 passim
Titov, Nikolay Alekseyevich (1800–75)
  5, 6 (Ex. 3), 7
Titov, Nikolay Sergeyevich (1798–
  1843) 5–7 passim, 13, 38n
Titz, Ferdinand (c. 1742–1810) 37n
Tolstoy, Aleksey Konstantinovich
  21, 22, 26, 28, 30
Tolstoy, L.N. 100, 107, 109
Tolstoy, T.M. 43
Tomášek, Václav (1774–1850) 174–5
  (Ex. 1), 179
Trutovsky, V.F. 3
Tsïganov 9
Turgenev, Ivan 100
Tyutchev, Fyodor 22, 30, 32, 34

Uhland, Johann Ludwig 10
Ulybyshev, Alexander Dmitryevich
  (1794–1858) 105

Vaňhal, Jan (Johann Wanhall)
  (1739–1813) 114
Varlamov, Aleksandr (1801–48) 6,
  7, 9–10, 18, 38n, 142, 175

Vasilenko, Sergey Nikiforovich
  (1872–1956) 29
Vavrinecz, Mór (1858–1913) 56
Velimirovič, Miloš 93
Vereshchagin, V.V. 99, 100
Verlaine, Paul 32
Verstovsky, Aleksey Nikolayevich
  (1799–1863) 10, 38n, 41
Vielgorsky, Mikhail (1788–1856) 5
Villebois, K.P. (1817–82) 55n
Viviani, Augustino 124
Volkonsky, Prince M.A. 106
Vorel, Josef (1801–74) 175, 184n
Voss, Johann Heinrich 174
Vrchlický, Jaroslav 181
Vycpálek, Ladislav (1882–1969)
  183

Wagner, Richard (1813–83) 40, 41,
  47, 60, 72, 166
Walicki, Aleksander 160
Wański, Jan (1762–after 1800) 113,
  114, 119–20
Weber, Carl Maria von (1786–1826)
  47, 62, 137
Węcowski, Jan 113, 116
Weigl, Joseph (1766–1846) 137
Weinberg, Peter 38n
Weinert, Antoni (1751–1850) 127
Wieland, Christoph Martin 176
Winckelmann, Johann Joachim 102
Witkowski, G. 127
Witwicki, Stefan 143
Władysław I of Poland 134
Władysław II Jagiełło, Prince of
  Lithuania 137
Władysław IV of Poland 122, 123,
  124, 125
Wójcicki, Kazimierz W. 157, 166
Wolski, Wlodzimierz 157, 159, 161,
  162, 166

Yakovlev, Mikhail Lokyanovich
  (1798–1868) 5, 38n
Yastrebtsev, V.V. 65, 66, 71, 95, 96

Zablocki, Franciszek 127
Zaleski, Bohdan 143
Zalewski, Andrzej 128
Zedlitz, Joseph Christian von 10
Zelenka, J.D. (1679–1745) 172
Żeleński, Władysław (1837–1921)
  148–9

Zelter, Carl Friedrich (1758–1832) 144, 157
Zeno, Apostolo 125
Zhilin, Aleksey Dmitrievich (*c.* 1767–*c.* 1848) 4, 37*n*
Zhokhov, A.F. 46
Zhukovsky, Vasily Andreyevich 5, 10–12 *passim*, 16, 42

Zieleński, Mikolaj (*fl.* 1611) 141
Ziólkowski, Adam 171*n*
Zola, Émile 99
Żólkowski, A. 135
Zumsteeg, Johann Rudolf (1760–1802) 4, 142, 173
Zvantsov, K.I. 42, 45